PROTECT
AND
ENHANCE
YOUR
ESTATE
THIRD EDITION

DEFINITIVE STRATEGIES FOR
ESTATE AND WEALTH PLANNING

ROBERT A. ESPERTI
RENNO L. PETERSON
DAVID K. CAHOONE

New York   Chicago   San Francisco   Lisbon   London
Madrid   Mexico City   Milan   New Delhi   San Juan
Seoul   Singapore   Sydney   Toronto

1 2 3 4 5 6 7 8 9 0   DOC/DOC   1 8 7 6 5 4 3 2

ISBN: 978-0-07-178789-5
MHID: 0-07-178789-5

e-ISBN: 978-0-07-178790-1
e-MHID: 0-07-178790-9

This publication is designed to provide accurate and authoritative information in regard to the subject matter covered. It is sold with the understanding that neither the author nor the publisher is engaged in rendering legal, accounting, or other professional service. If legal advice or other expert assistance is required, the services of a competent professional person should be sought.

—From a Declaration of Principles Jointly Adopted by a Committee of the American Bar Association and a Committee of Publishers and Associations

McGraw-Hill books are available at special quantity discounts to use as premiums and sales promotions, or for use in corporate training programs. To contact a representative, please e-mail us at bulksales@mcgraw-hill.com.

This book is printed on acid-free paper.

For Liz, Karen, and Donna

Contents

Acknowledgments

We have been blessed with long careers in which we have met many colleagues in the legal, accountant, financial, banking, life insurance, medical, and numerous other fields. Although we have had the privilege of teaching and mentoring many of these colleagues, we are convinced that we received the better end of the experience by learning from each and every one of them. For every experience we shared or piece of knowledge we passed on, we received the gift of reciprocity from them. There is no way we could name all of these professionals. They know who they are. We thank each and every one of them for their kindness, support, and generosity in sharing their lives with ours.

Introduction

When this book was first released in 1982, it was called *The Handbook of Estate Planning*. As young tax attorneys in Denver, we were ecstatic that a book that we wrote for our clients was accepted by an elite publisher in an elite series of books. The Economic Recovery Tax Act of 1981 had just been passed. Its impact on planning was massive. In response, we literally shut down our law firm and retooled almost everything we were doing.

The Handbook of Estate Planning was revised once in response to changes in the law. The title of the book was changed in 1993 to *Protect Your Estate*. It was revised three times. This second title reflected the changing nature of estate planning. Why the change? The planning landscape was totally new.

We are as ecstatic about this third edition of *Protect Your Estate* as we were with *The Handbook of Estate Planning*, though you will notice that we once again changed the title. It is now called *Protect and Enhance Your Estate*, and we have added our colleague of many years, David K. Cahoone, as a coauthor.

Originally, our objective in writing *Protect and Enhance Your Estate* was to familiarize the American public with the estate planning process, impart a good understanding of that process, and offer a level of comfort and security to motivate people from all walks of life to accomplish their planning objectives. That objective remains, and at no time in our careers has it been more important.

We asked McGraw-Hill to add the word "enhance" in the title because in this time of political, social, and economic uncertainty, there is not only a mandate to plan, but to plan in such a way as to reduce risk to loved ones by using life insurance and other financial products to fund estate planning.

With collectively over 95 years in the practice of estate planning law, writing 27 books, consulting with some of the largest financial institutions in America, and teaching thousands of lawyers, accountants, financial advisors, and life insurance professionals, we have learned a fundamental rule: the greatest estate planning in the world is not worth the paper it is printed on without having sufficient resources to make it work. We have come to the inevitable conclusion that proper planning must include properly purchased and owned life insurance that is constantly reviewed and revised to meet the changing needs of individuals and families.

We were some of the earliest attorney advocates of fully funded revocable living trusts. We are proud to have led the effort to change America from a will-planning-based society to one that is trust-based. In fact, we have been challenged by bar associations and colleagues for our relentless view that wills, probate, joint tenancy, and other ways to plan do not compare to planning with a fully funded revocable living trust. That was true in 1982 and it is true today, except that not only should the living trust be funded with a person's assets, but also with adequate life insurance.

Another area where good estate planning is being assailed is in the use of software, Internet-based planning, and forms. We do not believe that you should attempt to plan your estate by yourself; estate planning loners generally do not achieve good planning results. A little bit of knowledge can be very dangerous with regard to the estate planning process—dangerous if it is viewed as complete or ultimate knowledge. On the other hand, a little bit of knowledge can go a long way if it initiates the selection and monitoring of good professionals to assist you in accomplishing your objectives.

How-to-do-it books may be fun to read, Internet Web sites might be attractive and convincing, but using fill-in-the-blank estate planning or canned software can be worse than doing no planning at all. Good planning necessitates a motivated and knowledgeable client who interacts with professional advisors to bring out the very best in them with respect to their knowledge.

Some people are unfamiliar with the kinds of professionals they should look for to assist them in planning their estates; others know what professionals they need but do not know how to go about selecting them.

We believe that estate planning should be a collaborative effort consisting of the following professional players:

- An estate planning attorney
- An accountant who is well-versed in tax law and knows your affairs
- A professional life insurance agent who knows the estate planning process and the general techniques used within it
- A financial advisor, if you have one

In addition, if you choose to name a corporate trustee to help administer your plan, getting a trust officer involved in the early stages is a wise idea. Trust companies and trust departments have tremendous resources to help in the planning process.

Today, attorneys are called upon to deal with an enormous volume of law created by an ever-growing and complicated society. In truth, most attorneys get very good at dealing with selected areas of the law. They tend to specialize because of their ability to acquire extraordinary skills in specific legal areas.

In searching for an attorney to plan your estate, always look for a specialist: an attorney who practices in the area of estate planning to the exclusion of most other legal areas. Tax attorneys readily fall into this category.

Some tax attorneys specialize only in the area of income tax planning, but most spend a significant amount of time in estate planning as well. There are also nontax attorneys who, because of their desire and experience and their clients' needs, are excellent estate planners. They know a lot about taxes too.

The problem most people have is that they don't know where to find that specialist, because many attorneys do not advertise. People in this predicament should ask other advisors for a referral or recommendation. Accountants, life insurance professionals, and financial advisors have usually had significant dealings with attorneys (both good and bad), and based on their knowledge and experience, most will be delighted to make a recommendation or two. If you do not have other advisors, discuss the matter with the officials of your local bank's trust department. Trust officers are generally knowledgeable about local estate planning attorneys.

Our advice on the selection of an attorney applies as well to selecting an accountant, a life insurance professional, and other financial advisors. Always select knowledgeable specialists with the assistance of your other advisors. The fact that one of your current advisors is a friend or relative or someone you trust does not make him or her an estate planning expert. Do not be afraid to expand your planning team.

Professional advisors should be selected for the knowledge they possess within their disciplines. All your advisors should participate in the estate planning process and should work well not only with you but also with each other. In our opinion, there is no room for the professional loner, regardless of expertise.

Encourage all your advisors to work together harmoniously for your benefit. The estate planning team should identify the best ideas of each of the professional players and coordinate them into one overall plan that satisfactorily meets your objectives.

Now, more than ever, knowledge is king. Please treat this book as a survey of what can be. After reading it, you will be prepared to work within your own planning collaborative team. You do not have to be an expert, but you should understand some of the tools with which your advisors will work. With your newfound knowledge and the expertise of the professionals you hire, you can enhance the quality of your life, knowing that you have preserved, protected, and enhanced your estate.

Robert A. Esperti
Renno L. Peterson
David K. Cahoone

1

What Is Estate Planning?

It's More Than Money

Estate planning is people: spouses, children, grandchildren, favorite family members, charities, and close friends; their security and prosperity without you. It is state and federal taxes: income, death, and gift. It is lawyers, accountants, insurance people, banks, and financial planners. It is society's rules along with the red tape and courts of law that accompany those rules. It is a world of advisors busily accomplishing things that most people do not understand. It is time and money. It is protecting and enhancing your estate from an uncertain future.

Estate planning takes time: a little now or a lot later; time to identify and accomplish goals that are personally important; or time to react to a host of external forces that may have their own interests rather than those of your loved ones.

Estate planning involves money, business, and finance. It involves dollars, lots of dollars, to create and maintain a lifestyle for you and your family while you are alive, and for your loved ones after your death. It involves the sacrifice of dollars to purchase life insurance or to invest in a portfolio, in lieu of personal indulgences, with the sincere belief that you are creating security for you and the people and causes that matter to you.

Estate planning is human ambition and the fulfillment of that ambition by acquiring and holding property. It is a life statement of commitment to others, while maintaining a lifestyle that is comfortable for you.

Estate planning is living planning. It is your attempt to use your resources to create an environment for yourself and others that will be sufficient for you and extend beyond your life. It is the ability to share and control your success during life and after death.

We always ask our clients, "What do you want done with your property and life insurance after you're gone?" The responses have been different, but they all contained thoughts that could be summarized as follows:

> I would like to give my property to whom I want, in precisely the way I want. Further, I wish my beneficiaries to receive my property when I wish them to receive it.
>
> But, and this is very important to me, I want to save every last tax dollar, both state and federal, in accomplishing my objectives. Oh yes, I also want to avoid, or at the least reduce, attorneys' fees and court costs.
>
> Finally, I don't want myself or my family involved in a lot of red tape that prevents my objectives from being accomplished quickly.

You probably know what you want to do with your property both during life and on death. You are sensitive to the red tape imposed by society's rules. You need professional help in accomplishing your planning objectives.

You are unique; therefore, planning for your estate must be unique. Planning, to be good, must fit you; it must be comfortable, like a favorite pair of shoes. You must understand the estate planning process, for without understanding there can be no comfort. Planning without understanding results more often than not in uncertainty and anxiety.

Our main objective is to assist you in understanding the rules, take the voodoo out of planning, and replace it with knowledge and comfort. In short, we hope to expand your planning horizons.

Your understanding is our mandate. With the comfort of knowledge, you should be able to confidently seek out the professional advisors and products and services you need. You should have the ability to communicate your goals and objectives to your advisors. On completing this book you should have a good grasp of the estate planning process and the techniques it utilizes. You should be able to discern between the knowledgeable professional and the not-so-knowledgeable professional. We hope to give you enough understanding of the estate planning process to enable you to participate in a meaningful dialogue with your advisors in accomplishing *your* estate planning objectives.

We have heard the question many times: "Why do today what I can put off until tomorrow?" In estate planning, tomorrow may instantly become today. None of us can predict the timing of our own deaths with certainty. Death sneaks up on most of us and respects no time parameter. Statistically, there may be a tomorrow, but don't plan on it! Planning *now* is mandatory.

Estate planning is a process that begins within your life and can continue far after death. It is not unique or indigenous to any economic class. Its audience is America, and its players are Americans. How often we have heard, "Estate planning for me? Heavens, I don't need an estate plan! I have so little." Really? No loved ones, no disposition toward a favorite family member, close friend, or institution (charitable or otherwise)? No property, no insurance or pension plan? No personal possessions, mementos, family heirlooms that require a loving pass on? No debts?

Estate planning is virtually for everyone, and it is getting more complex every day. When this book was first written in 1981, the Economic Recovery Tax Act of 1981, which was given the acronym ERTA, had just been passed. It revolutionized federal gift and estate tax laws. Since the passage of ERTA, there have been well over 150 tax laws passed, culminating with the Tax Relief, Unemployment Insurance Reauthorization, and Job Creation Act of 2010. Each time a new act passed, the new laws were intended to reform, simplify, or reduce taxation. Each time, the laws became more complicated and more people were affected.

The good news is that these laws have led to the ability to reduce gift, income, and estate taxes. The bad news is that "death taxes" have become a political football kicked around so many times that there is far less certainty in estate planning now than there has been over the last 65 years. The Act of 2010 has a life of two years, one year of which is gone. *There is absolutely no certainty what the federal estate, gift, and generation-skipping laws will be in 2013.* The Tax Relief, Unemployment Insurance Reauthorization, and Job Creation Act of 2010 was passed on December 17, 2010, because the estate, gift, and generation-skipping tax laws were to revert to the laws of early 2001, allegedly ending the uncertainty introduced by that law.

Our greatest fear is that you will be lulled into a sense of false security, believing you and your family do not have enough assets to be subject to these taxes on the very wealthy. Congress can change the definition of who is wealthy at any time. Under our new tax law, in 2013 the federal death tax laws could revert to those in existence at the beginning of 2001. That means that if your estate is over $1 million, it will be subject to federal estate tax!

We want you to understand why you should plan now and protect your estate from the vagaries of Congress and an economy that is as uncertain as the tax laws. Estate and wealth planning today is far more about risk management than about anything else. No one knows what the economy will be like and what taxes will be imposed when you die. Taxes could be low and the economy could be booming, in which case your family will likely do well if you have planned properly. But what if when you die the economy is not so good and taxes are high? Will your planning result in taking care of your loved ones or charities the way you wanted to? Planning is not assuming that things will work out for the best. That is wishful thinking. Our mantra has always been, "Plan for the worst, and you will never be unpleasantly surprised."

On the bright side, our federal gift and estate taxes are in many ways voluntary. Those with the knowledge of and access to expert professionals can escape most of these taxes. Creative lawyers, accountants, and other planners have developed very effective strategies for estate planning in light of both new and long-existing laws. In fact, the planning landscape has changed so radically that we and our colleagues now refer to estate planning as wealth strategies planning. Why? Because estate planning encompasses so many different disciplines and so many different techniques.

This book includes discussions of important planning techniques and how they can work for you and your family. It is designed to get you thinking about the incredible opportunities for planning: planning to make your life more enjoyable, planning to escape some of the economic problems of disability, and planning to reduce or eliminate federal estate and gift taxes. It is our hope that this book will motivate you to plan the right way, and right away. More important, we hope this book will make you understand that wealth planning encompasses huge doses of risk management, and that while you and those you care about hope for the best, you'll institute risk management planning to protect your estate from the worst, and enhance it as well.

2

Title

How Do You Own It?

"I don't know how I own it" is an answer we frequently hear from our clients when we ask in whose names their various assets are held. One of the major problems confronting estate planners is that people frequently buy and sell assets without the foggiest idea of how those assets should properly be held.

Not understanding how property should be owned makes estate planning a frustrating and impossible exercise. You cannot plan for property that you do not own; and if for some reason you do attempt to do planning with what you do not own (and this does happen), your attempt will be to no avail.

There are three often-used methods by which an adult takes ownership of property: *fee simple, tenancy in common,* and *joint tenancy with right of survivorship.* We will explain each method.

The concept of fee simple ownership is easy. It means to completely own something by yourself. The fee simple owner is a sole and absolute owner.

To own property in tenancy in common is to own it with one or more other people. As a tenant in common, you cannot be a fee simple owner of the entire asset. An example of this form of ownership is if you and a friend own a 100-page book. You own the book as tenants in common. Each of you owns 50 percent of the book; that is, each of you owns 50 pages. Each of you would be able to leave half, 50 pages, on death to anyone. Each of you while alive could give your 50 pages away to anyone. Each of you owns absolutely 50 percent of that book. Each of you is a tenant in common with the other.

There is no limit to the number of tenants who can own something with others in a tenancy in common; 100 people could be tenants in common in the ownership of a 100-page book. Each would then own one hundredth, or one page, of the book.

The only real issue occasioned by tenancy in common is if one of the tenants wants to sell his or her interest and the buyer wants to know what he or she is purchasing, the selling tenant in common does not know which of the 100 pages is owned. All the seller knows is that he or she owns one hundredth of the book.

Of course, we very seldom see 100 tenants in common. Generally, we see two, three, or four people who have bought something together, with each owning a half, third, or quarter of the property. Should a proposed sale by one of the tenants pose a problem as to what pages that tenant actually owns, the local court will have to become involved. The court's solution is called *partition*. The court takes the asset and makes an actual, physical division based on each tenant's percentage of ownership.

That technique does not always work well. Does one tenant get every other page of the book? The front half? The rear half? Generally, it is better for the quarreling tenants to sell the book to a third person and divide the cash according to their percentage of ownership.

All in all, tenancy in common is a frequently used method of owning property. The important thing to understand is that if you are a tenant in common, you absolutely own your percentage share in the property. Your percentage share can be sold or given away during your lifetime and can be left to your chosen beneficiaries at your death.

A potential drawback of this form of ownership is that the other tenants may not particularly like the person to whom the deceased tenant has left the percentage share in the property. We commonly refer to this problem as the "breaks of the game." If an individual chooses this form of ownership, that person's co-owners and beneficiaries may face co-owners they do not like.

The third form of ownership commonly used in the marketplace is joint tenancy with right of survivorship. In our experience, this method of taking title is greatly misunderstood by the public. In fact, it is an extremely confusing form of ownership.

Joint tenancy with right of survivorship is a great deal like tenancy in common, yet totally different in its results. For example, we again have two people, each of whom owns 50 percent of that 100-page book; now, however, they own it as joint tenants with right of survivorship. Unlike tenancy in common, this method of ownership does not mean that each of them owns 50 percent of the book, or 50 pages. If they own the book in joint tenancy with right of survivorship, they each own *100 percent* of the book for purposes of title holding. Both of them own the whole thing? Yes, that is correct.

Joint ownership—or joint property, as it is commonly called—is a *fictional* form of ownership created by English common law heritage. It is fictional in that two or more people can own the whole thing. What occurs to breathe realism into this fictional method of owning property is the added survivorship feature. Remember the proper name of this method of ownership: joint tenancy with right of survivorship. The survivorship feature means that as each individual joint tenant dies, that person simply falls off the ownership charts. Upon death, title is in the hands of the surviving joint tenants. Each of the survivors now owns a greater percentage of the property. Specifically, if there were three tenants and one died, the remaining two would own the asset. It is almost as if the deceased tenant never owned the property in the first place.

"My word," you say, "do you mean to tell me that if I own a mountain cabin with my brother in joint tenancy with right of survivorship, upon my death my spouse and children have absolutely no right to that cabin? That it all belongs to my brother? That once I die, I am removed from ownership, and since my brother survived, it is all his? That my family has absolutely no rights to that cabin?" Yes, that is exactly what we mean. Surprised? Many of our clients certainly have been.

Joint tenancy with right of survivorship is an automatic method of planning for property because taking title functions as a mini estate plan. It automatically passes ownership by law to the surviving tenants. In this case, there is no reason to plan your jointly held interest in your will or trust. As long as there is a joint tenant who survives you, the passage of the asset is already planned. So, if you have the opportunity to buy into a 100-page book as a joint tenant with 99 other people for the price of $1,000, and the total value of that book is $100,000, it might not be a good bargain. On the other hand, if the 99 other people are all 80 years of age or older and you are only 21, that might suggest a good deal. As each joint owner passes away, the remaining joint owners then own the book as 99 joint tenants with right of survivorship; 98 joint owners with right of survivorship; 97, and so on, right down to the last one to survive, which, in this example, might be you. What a deal. What a crazy form of ownership!

On the other hand, from a living point of view, let us assume that you are a joint tenant who wishes to sell your interest to someone else. You certainly could, and in most states you would not have to receive permission from the other joint owners; but what if you, as a joint tenant, wanted to carve out your interest for your sole and personal use? You would have to go to the local courthouse and ask the judge to apply that old legal remedy of partition. You would have to ask the judge to divide the property; or you could hire a lawyer to come up with a complicated and technical solution. Amazingly enough, jointly held assets, when viewed from a living point of view (without the survivorship feature), function just like assets held in tenancy in common. It is the survivorship feature that distinguishes the two.

There is another offshoot to joint ownership, a special kind of joint ownership called *tenancy by the entirety*. It is used in some states by a husband and wife to hold real estate. For most practical reasons, it works the same as joint tenancy. The major difference is that generally, under tenancy by the entirety there is no right to split the property during marriage unless both spouses consent. For our purposes, think of tenancy by the entirety as joint tenancy, except it is only available for spouses. As we will see in Chapter 34, "Protecting Your Assets," tenancy by the entirety is a method that can be used for asset protection. If you do own assets in tenancy by the entirety, consult your attorney, because your state's laws are probably unique.

Often a client will ask, "What if I just put my name and someone else's name on a piece of property and don't specify whether it is owned in tenancy in common or joint tenancy; which method have I elected, if any?" In our jurisdiction, that property would be held in tenancy in common. In others, it would be held in joint tenancy with right of survivorship. The answer, therefore, depends on the law of your state. Each state has its own laws. Do not assume anything; find out the correct answer from your advisors.

Always know how you wish to take title to assets and properly communicate that intent to others. Is it fee simple, tenancy in common, or join tenancy with right of survivorship? Know what you are doing in this area, because taking proper title to property is a very serious business, as you will see throughout this book.

Summary of Types of Title

Fee Simple

You own *all* of it. You can:

Give it away.

Sell it.

Leave it on death.

Tenancy in Common

You own *part* of it. You can:

Give your part away.

Sell your part.

Leave your part on death.

Joint Tenancy

You own *all* of it with someone else. But you can:

Give your interest away.

Sell your interest.

You *cannot* leave your interest on death.

3

Jointly Held Property

Common but Complicated

For years professionals have been taking potshots at *joint tenancy* as an ownership technique. Even *Reader's Digest* has vigorously attacked it as a trap or pitfall to avoid.

Joint ownership has some apparently good attributes. It's a convenient form of ownership, one that has been encouraged in the marketplace by financial institutions, merchants, and, to some extent, by professional advisors.

Joint ownership appears to be psychologically pleasing to people, particularly to married couples. Its very name implies "the two of us," a partnership, a marriage of title as well as of love. On the surface, at least, it has appeared as the right way to take title to property between people who care for each other.

Because of its survivorship feature, joint ownership creates an instant mini estate plan for joint owners. We saw in Chapter 2, "Title," that if two people own a book jointly and one of them dies, the other continues to own the entire book. There is no need to pass title. By law, title simply remains with the survivor.

Jointly held property requires no will, trust, or other estate planning device. It does not go through probate court on the death of the first joint tenant. In fact, this has been one of its main selling points: "If there is no probate, owning property jointly has got to be good."

Jointly held property has been most attractive among close family members. What the heck, easy to do, natural and loving in name (jointly), a mini estate plan, and no probate court. What an estate plan!

However, there are significant problems with this form of property ownership.

Jointly held property can pass property to the wrong folks, to the other joint tenant rather than to chosen beneficiaries. On the death of a joint tenant there is absolutely no question as to where that property interest is going. It is going to the surviving owner by operation of law. On death, a joint owner cannot control the way the property passes nor the time of its passage.

Death has its own timing. Who will outlive whom is an unknown. So are the results of owning property jointly. As we see it, it is one big roll of the dice. Consider the following situation:

> A widow with three adult children meets and marries a widower with one adult child. They combine their assets and title them jointly. One day later the widow dies.

What is the result of joint ownership in this situation? That's easy. The widower receives *everything*, the widow's children receive *nothing*.

Joint ownership only works if there is a surviving joint tenant. What happens if the joint owners die at the same time? All states have adopted a version of the Uniform Simultaneous Death Act. Under this law, joint property generally is distributed in proportion to the number of joint tenants, although the unique nature of Louisiana's laws makes its law a little more complex.

Simultaneous death and joint ownership do not mix well. Remember the survivorship feature? If one owner outlives the other by one second, the property goes to the heirs of the one who survived by one second. Because of the survivorship problem, critics allege that jointly owned property may go to unintended heirs.

Jointly owned property is generally beneficial to creditors of the owners. Property taken in both names can generally be seized on the default or misdeed of either owner. Either or each joint owner could lose ownership in the property, which is not good estate or creditor planning.

There is another hurdle to get over with jointly held property: the federal estate and gift tax.

Historically, federal gift tax laws attempted to tax property that was put into joint tenancy with right of survivorship. For married couples, the gift occurred when the property was titled in the names of both spouses. For nonspousal relationships, the same was true. The joint tenant who put up money to buy property was taxed when he or she added the name of someone else to the property's title if that other person did not put up money to pay for his or her share.

The federal estate tax laws attempted to tax all the jointly held property, even property held by spouses, in the estate of the first owner to die. When the remaining tenant died, it was taxed all over again. Joint property was generally taxed twice—in other words, 200 percent taxable! There were some exceptions, but in our experience they seldom seemed to apply to the situation at hand. Federal estate tax and joint property simply did not mix very well.

Today, spouses who are citizens of the United States can acquire property jointly without incurring a federal gift tax. The law is absolutely clear on this point, and there are no limits to the amounts involved. Regardless of which spouse's funds are used, no federal gift tax will result from U.S. citizen spouses taking property jointly.

The law states that unlimited tax-free gifts are allowed between U.S. citizen spouses. This unlimited gifts rule is referred to as an unlimited lifetime marital deduction.

If the spouse receiving the gift is not a U.S. citizen, however, there is no unlimited lifetime marital deduction. There is instead an exclusion from the gift tax that started as $100,000 in the value of gifts to the noncitizen spouse. It has been adjusted yearly for inflation so that in 2012 it is $139,000. This limited exception for noncitizen spouses is discussed further in Chapter 11, "The Gift Tax."

Interspousal property transfers, when made to a U.S. citizen spouse, are no longer of federal gift tax consequence. Do not, however, make the mistake of neglecting to check your state's gift tax laws, as they may apply to jointly held assets.

Some states do have gift taxes and tax jointly held property much like the federal government once did. States sometimes follow the example of the federal tax laws. Keep in mind, though, that there have been, and probably will continue to be, states that elect to go their own way in spite of what the federal laws say.

The law has not materially changed with respect to owning property jointly with people other than your spouse. For most types of assets, when the person who owns property adds another person to the title, and that person has not paid his or her fair share, a gift has been made. A common example of this type of gift occurs between a parent and a child. If Mom owns a home in her name and decides to put her daughter's name on the deed as a joint tenant, Mom has made a potentially taxable gift of one-half of the value of the home to her daughter. While there may have been no intention to make a gift, lack of intent is immaterial.

For some types of assets, such as bank accounts, just putting another's name on the account is generally not a gift. However, if the other person takes money out of the account, a gift occurs immediately. This gift may well create a gift tax liability.

Unfortunately, transactions in which inadvertent gifts are made are common. We see them in our practice regularly. Sometimes, the effects of the gifts are difficult to rectify. Some people try to change the title back to its original form. Not a good idea! When the transaction is reversed, it is a gift back to the original owner. In this case, two wrongs make a catastrophe. If you are in this situation you need to see your professional advisor so that together you can work out a solution. We will tell you ahead of time that it is not easy to cure this tax problem.

For federal estate tax purposes, there is a presumption that the full value of the property is included in the estate of the first joint tenant to die. The estate must then overcome this presumption by proving that the other joint tenant or tenants contributed to the property and therefore owned part of it. To the extent the others owned a portion of the property, the estate of the first joint tenant to die is reduced. Because of the adverse tax and practical effects of joint tenancy with right of survivorship between people who are not spouses, most knowledgeable advisors do not recommend its use.

As to spouses, the estate of the first spouse to die will include only *half* the value of the jointly held property. When the second spouse dies, the estate will be taxed on the value of the *entire* asset. Why? Because of the survivorship feature, jointly held property automatically belongs to the surviving tenant. If it all belongs to the survivor, it will all be taxed in the survivor's estate.

If, however, the surviving spouse is not a U.S. citizen, the estate of the first spouse to die will include the entire value of the property, unless the spouses acquired the property by gift or inheritance, or the surviving spouse supplied some or all of the funds to purchase the property. The estate of the first spouse to die will include only *half* the value of the jointly held property if the noncitizen surviving spouse becomes a U.S. citizen before the date on which the estate tax return is filed, and if the surviving spouse meets certain residency requirements.

Spouses can leave everything they own, including property held jointly with spouses, to their spouses free of federal estate tax. (We get into this in more detail in Chapter 12, "The Marital Deduction.") Remember: there is no federal estate tax on property held jointly with a spouse when the first spouse dies.

Great care and caution must be used in creating joint ownership with nonspouses. Don't forget that the jointly owned property will always belong to the surviving owners. Your estate might have to pay tax on the value of your interest in the property even though the property is going to a non-family member on your death. Remember that cabin owned jointly with your friend? He or she will get the cabin if you die first, and your estate may pay the federal estate tax on half its value.

There is another problem with property held jointly between spouses. It has to do with after-death income tax planning and the *step-up in basis* rules. These rules state (except for a short interlude in 2010) that upon the death of a taxpayer, property in the estate gets a new cost basis for income tax purposes. Here is an example of this concept:

> Eileen owns but one asset at her death: one share of stock. She paid $1 for it. If she sold it for $10 while alive, she would have a $9 income taxable gain. At Eileen's death the share of stock was valued at $10 for

federal estate tax purposes. If her heirs sold it after her death for $10, there would be no income tax. If Eileen sold the stock one day before her death, however, $9 would be subject to income tax. You see, her cost basis in the stock would be increased (stepped up) on her death, by operation of law, from $1 to $10, its date-of-death value. Professionals refer to this concept as step-up in basis.

In our example, if Eileen owned the stock jointly with her spouse and died, only half the stock would get a step-up in basis. If Eileen's spouse sold the stock after her death for $10, he would have a $4.50 income taxable gain. His starting cost was $0.50 (half the $1 paid). His half of the gain would be $5 ($10 price divided by 2). By subtracting his cost of $0.50 from the $5, we have a $4.50 gain. He has no gain on Eileen's half because her half got a step-up in basis to $5.

Contrast the tax problem of Eileen's spouse with this situation:

Eileen owns the stock in her name (not in joint names). She dies and leaves it to her spouse. There would be no federal estate tax. (Remember that spouses can leave everything tax-free to surviving spouses.) The entire value of the stock gets a step-up in basis to $10. Eileen's spouse sells the stock the day after her death for $10. There is no income taxable gain to Eileen's spouse.

Joint property does not get a 100 percent step-up in basis for income tax purposes, but rather only a 50 percent step-up because only 50 percent is included in the estate of the first spouse to die. When the planning is for spouses, jointly owned property becomes unattractive in many cases. Untutored planning with jointly held property can create income tax pitfalls even when this planning appears proper.

For example, if the surviving spouse is not a U.S. citizen or if the property is not held between spouses, the step-up in basis generally will depend upon the amount each joint tenant contributed to obtain the property.

Jointly held property, at least between spouses where the surviving spouse is a U.S. citizen, is now treated much more realistically; however, many of the drawbacks of this form of ownership persist even today.

Knowledgeable individuals will continue to be sensitive to potential federal and state gift tax traps when putting property in joint names. We do not recommend the use of joint ownership to our clients to any great extent in planning their estates. In spite of the many changes in our federal estate, gift, and income tax laws, our advice remains the same: joint ownership is a potential planning pitfall that should be avoided in most instances; but, as between spouses (at least if they are both citizens), the results it creates can easily be corrected.

Summary of Joint Ownership

Good Features

Easy and convenient

Psychologically pleasing

Mini estate plan

Not complicated on surface

No gift tax to U.S. citizen spouse

No death tax on the death of the first spouse, if surviving spouse is or becomes a U.S. citizen

Bad Features

Passes property to unintended heirs

Affords no planning opportunities

No control

Excellent for creditors

Gift taxes to nonspousal owners or noncitizen spouses

Possible loss of complete step-up basis

4

Disability

Living Longer Offers New Planning Challenges

Estate planning without effective disability planning is no planning at all. Most of us have a much greater chance of becoming disabled in any one year than we do of dying. Yet disability planning is, in our experience, not given the thought and attention it deserves.

There are many types of disabilities, but not all of them require special planning. Loss of a limb, a severe illness, or even a severe injury does not usually prevent a person from being able to take care of him- or herself. However, senility, Alzheimer's disease, psychological problems, drug dependence, incarceration, disappearance, or other factors may make it impossible for an individual to function at a personal or financial level.

The law has long had a method for dealing with those persons who cannot take care of themselves or their financial affairs. Courts—generally the same courts that have jurisdiction over death probate—can declare a person incompetent in a proceeding that we call a *living probate*.

In a living probate, the court appoints two types of agents to care for the incompetent person. The first type, called a *personal guardian*, acts as the "parent" of the incompetent person. As a surrogate parent, the guardian is charged with taking care of the day-to-day personal needs of an incompetent person. This includes making sure he or she is properly fed and housed, that his or her health needs are met, and that he or she is supervised much like a child. The second type of agent the court appoints is a *financial guardian*, sometimes called a *conservator*. A conservator, which may be a bank, a trust company, or an individual, is in charge of an incompetent person's financial affairs. The conservator handles all financial transactions normally handled by the individual. In fact, it is this financial guardian who gives the personal guardian the funds needed to care for the incompetent person. In some cases the personal guardian and the financial guardian can be the same person; ultimately, it is up to the judge to decide who fills these positions.

The personal and financial guardians are appointed and supervised by the court. The personal guardian must give the court periodic reports on the person's physical and mental condition, and the financial guardian must give periodic reports about the condition of the person's financial affairs.

The costs of a living probate can be quite high. Attorney fees, court costs, and the costs of retaining a personal and financial guardian are all paid out of the incompetent person's assets. Of course, if for some reason the competency of an individual is in dispute, which happens more than most people realize, these costs can skyrocket. In addition, even without controversy, the costs incurred do not go away; the guardians are paid for as long as a person is incompetent, and attorneys must be paid each time a transaction requires work with the court. Even in cases where a spouse or relative is appointed as a guardian and there are no guardian fees charged, significant legal and court fees can be generated.

It has long been recognized that this court-supervised system for disabled persons is cumbersome, expensive, subject to abuse, and, above all, humiliating for the disabled person. The process is public, as are most court proceedings. Because an incompetency hearing can be brought by almost anyone who has any connection with an allegedly disabled person, unhappy relatives or even creditors can begin such a hearing. While most of these hearings are not controversial, others can be quite messy, lurid affairs.

Over the years, there has been abuse reported in the incompetency system. There have been judges who appointed friends to act as financial guardians, excessive fee taking, and, unfortunately, physical and mental abuse of the disabled persons. Supervision of the supervisors has not been adequate.

Obviously, it makes a great deal of sense to take all action necessary to avoid an incompetency hearing. While there is no effective method for absolutely preventing someone from bringing such a hearing, there are ways to minimize the incentive for doing so. One of the functions of estate planning is to reduce the likelihood of court involvement when a person is incompetent. In recent decades great strides have been made in every state to make it much easier to plan for disabled persons in ways that reduce the chance of court intervention or supervision.

There are four documents that help avoid court intervention when someone becomes disabled:

- Durable power of attorney
- Revocable living trust
- Health care power of attorney
- Living will

Durable Powers of Attorney

Every state in the United States has passed legislation allowing the use of durable powers of attorney. These devices are extremely important in the scheme of estate planning, but are often misunderstood by clients.

Durable powers of attorney are special documents that allow a person who is alive and well today to appoint an agent, called an *attorney-in-fact,* to handle his or her financial affairs. A durable power of attorney is typically a general power of attorney that does not end if the person granting the power of attorney becomes disabled.

To understand the impact of this planning concept, a little history is necessary.

Powers of attorney have long been part of the law in the United States. In a *general power of attorney,* a person, called a *principal,* grants to another person or institution (a bank or trust company, for example) the power to act in his or her place. As such, a general power of attorney states, in essence, that the attorney-in-fact can do everything the principal can do. Thus, the attorney-in-fact can sign checks, borrow money, make investments, and generally have complete and absolute authority over the principal's finances without his or her consent. A general power of attorney is the ultimate granting of power to another.

General powers of attorney are subject to abuse. In the past, the attorney-in-fact was not held to a particularly high standard of conduct. The result was that some persons holding general powers of attorney were able to squander assets with which they were entrusted, but not be held liable for their errors. A person who grants another person a general power of attorney is placing a great deal of trust in that person, and is relying on that person to be honest, trustworthy, and careful. But reliance is not enough. Now, many states impose higher standards on attorneys-in-fact to reduce abuse, making it easier to sue the person who lost or took all the money from a trusting principal. Obviously, this is not a very effective remedy if that person squandered all the funds.

A general power of attorney terminates when a person is adjudicated as mentally incompetent. Of course, this is the time when a power of attorney is most needed.

To make planning easier, every state now has a statute that allows a power of attorney to continue even if the principal is disabled; this is called a *durable power of attorney.* Granting it eliminates, at least in theory, the need to have a person adjudicated by a court as mentally incompetent, because the power of attorney stays in effect upon the incompetency of the principal. No further action by a court or the attorney-in-fact is necessary.

There are some drawbacks in using durable powers of attorney. First, of course, the general power is so broad that care must be taken in choosing whom to name as the attorney-in-fact. Remember that durable powers of attorney are in effect when signed, not upon disability. The minute you sign one, the attorney-in-fact can exercise broad powers.

Some attorneys draft "springing" durable powers of attorney. This means that when the principal becomes disabled, as defined in the power of attorney, it becomes effective. These types of durable powers of attorney may not be effective in all states. Even if they are, third parties are reluctant to accept them without a great deal of proof that the principal is indeed disabled. This sometimes defeats the purpose of having a durable power of attorney in the first place. It may take a court hearing to determine whether the power of attorney is actually in effect!

Another drawback to durable powers of attorney is that they are not universally accepted. Banks, brokerage firms, and other institutions are sometimes wary about accepting them. They are concerned that the power of attorney may not be in effect because the principal revoked it or that it will be disputed. They often ask for further documentation, or refuse the power of attorney altogether. Some states require, by law, the acceptance of durable powers of attorney, but it is not uncommon for large institutions to ignore the law. They do not believe that an attorney-in-fact would initiate a lawsuit over the refusal to honor the power, and these large institutions often feel that refusal causes them less liability than complying might. That being said, durable powers of attorney are becoming much more acceptable because their use is now so prevalent.

Finally, a durable power of attorney almost always does not contain any instructions as to how the attorney-in-fact is supposed to use the principal's funds. If the attorney-in-fact has no guidance, then he or she must exercise a great deal of discretion. For example, does the attorney-in-fact have the power to make gifts to family members or charity, just as the principal has done in the past? Can the attorney-in-fact amend the principal's will or trust? Can the attorney-in-fact take a fee for services rendered? These are only a few of the issues that may arise. The holder of the power either has to decide, based on his or her best judgment, how to act, or, to avoid liability, must refuse to act at all. And if a power is not specifically set forth in the power of attorney, the holder may not be able to act in any way, in spite of the principal's intent.

We have seen some durable powers of attorney that include instructions. They are long, complex documents. While adding instructions may be a good idea, it is not practical. It can be hard enough to get someone to accept a durable power of attorney. It is exponentially more difficult when the power of attorney is long and difficult to read. Most persons or institutions refer the document to their lawyer, and it could be weeks or months before any action is taken to allow or disallow the power of attorney.

We recommend that a special durable power of attorney be used in conjunction with a fully funded revocable living trust. We refer to this type of power of attorney as a *special durable power of attorney*. It restricts the attorney-in-fact to funding the principal's living trust and some administrative functions that do not affect the principal's property. These include working with Social Security to claim benefits, acting as an agent for purposes of dealing with income tax returns, or making decisions regarding the principal's retirement plan administration and investments. Being limited in scope, a special durable power of attorney is far more effective and safe than a general power of attorney. A good living trust will contain effective instructions as to how the trustee is to act on behalf of the trust maker. Also, the laws governing living trusts and their universal acceptance make using them far easier than relying solely on any type of power of attorney.

How a special durable power of attorney is commonly used can be demonstrated in a short example:

> Harry Howard had a special durable power of attorney naming his wife, Sara, as the attorney-in-fact, and he had a living trust that he thought was fully funded. Harry suffered a severe stroke, making him unable to properly manage his financial affairs. His wife found that Harry had forgotten to title his 1957 Thunderbird car in the name of his trust. She used her authority in the durable power of attorney to transfer the car into his trust. Upon Harry's death, the car will now avoid probate and pass under the terms of his trust.

Fully Funded Revocable Living Trusts

Using a special durable power of attorney in concert with a living trust has a number of advantages. A living trust has instructions about how its assets are to be used for the benefit of the trust's maker and his or her family. The law is very clear in most respects as to what the trustee can and cannot do. Under a well-drafted trust, the trustee can handle funds in the manner the maker wishes with far less administrative hassle. Almost all financial institutions will accept a trustee's authority with little more than proof of the trust's valid existence and proof that the trustee has the power to act. A short affidavit or certification signed by the trustee and some excerpts from the trust are sufficient for its acceptance in most cases.

Courts do not as a rule have jurisdiction over the assets in a revocable living trust. Thus, even if the maker is judged to be incompetent, the court cannot control the assets held in the living trust. Because of this feature, there is less incentive for relatives or "friends" to ask a court to declare someone incompetent; there is no money or power in it if that person's assets are held in trust, free from court intervention under an incompetency hearing.

In our experience and that of the well over 1,000 lawyers with whom we have worked, using a fully funded living trust is far more effective than using a durable power of attorney and a will for disability planning.

A durable power of attorney can be used or necessary if the living trust is fully funded. However, a special durable power of attorney should be an element of every estate plan as a fail-safe device, in case the maker has not fully funded his or her trust.

Health Care Powers of Attorney

A durable power of attorney addresses the financial situation of a disabled person. It does not address the personal side, which may include health care decisions, decisions about long-term care, and other caregiving decisions. Health care powers of attorney allow you to address these very sensitive issues.

If you are comatose or otherwise unable to make an informed decision as to a certain medical procedure or treatment, your attorney-in-fact under your health care power of attorney is authorized to make that decision. Or, if you need to be institutionalized in a hospital or nursing home and you are not competent to make decisions about your care, your attorney-in-fact will make that decision consistent with your instructions in a health care power of attorney.

It is possible to add instructions to your health care power of attorney. If you prefer a particular nursing home, if you want to be taken care of at home for as long as possible, or if you prefer one hospital over another, these requests can, depending on your state's laws, be added to your health care power.

State law governs health care powers. You should fully explore with your attorney and other advisors the extent to which you want instructions included in your health care power of attorney so you feel comfortable with those you choose to make the decisions and with the guidelines you include in the power.

Most important, when you decide who to name as your *agent* under your health care power of attorney, you should share your ideas, thoughts, and feelings about how you would like to be cared for if you cannot make the decisions. The more you discuss how you want to be treated, the better the decisions of your agent. It is imperative that you take the time to do this, especially if you do not have a spouse or close relative that you would like to name.

One very important aspect of your health care power of attorney is an *HIPAA Authorization.* As part of the Health Insurance Portability and Accountability Act of 1996 (HIPAA), the U.S. Department of Health and Human Services issued strict guidelines regulating disclosure of patient information. These regulations prevent your health care professionals from releasing information about your health to *anyone* without your written permission. The regulations permit doctors to discuss a patient's situation with the patient's "personal representative," that is, someone authorized by the patient or by state law to make health care decisions for the patient. Thus, if the patient has not signed a HIPAA authorization document, which often may be included within a health care power of attorney, health care providers will likely refuse to share medical information with anyone except a court-appointed guardian.

Make sure that when your attorney drafts your health care power of attorney, there is a HIPAA Authorization and that you point it out to your physician.

Living Wills

Living wills, which are often part of health care powers but can be separate documents, address the situation in which you are terminally ill or in a permanent vegetative state and there is no likelihood you will recover. The living will is only in effect if you physically or mentally cannot make your desires concerning your treatment known.

Generally, a living will states that the maker does not want any procedures that will artificially prolong life, including intravenous feeding, hydration, or medication other than pain relievers. Sometimes, however, a living will states the opposite: that the maker wants his or her physician to take all measures to prolong life.

No matter what your feelings are in this area, a living will is a planning necessity. Not only are your wishes then known by your family, friends, and doctor, but the document also takes the pressure off the ones you love. It is a traumatic experience for a spouse, children, or even friends to be faced with making a decision as to what should be done if you are terminally ill or in a permanent vegetative state. Drafting a living will is a gesture of love that helps alleviate some of the emotional trauma when someone is dying.

Perhaps the most famous example of having no living will or health care power of attorney planning is the case of Terri Schiavo, who went into cardiac arrest at the age of 26 in 1990, for reasons that are still not completely understood. Her brain was deprived of oxygen for a sustained period of time, resulting in brain damage. Within a year she received a diagnosis of "permanently vegetative state," which means the brain damage was so severe that she would never recover.

In 1998, Terri's husband, Michael, petitioned the local court to allow him to have her feeding tube removed. Terri's parents did not agree with the decision. This court petition, part of the living probate process, resulted in 14 appeals, numerous hearings and motions, intervention by pro-life groups, the Florida legislature, the United States Congress, and the President. The litigation resulted in five lawsuits in federal district court, and appeals to the Supreme Court of Florida and the Supreme Court of the United States. A congressional committee even attempted to qualify Terri for the witness protection program.

The newspapers all over the world had a heyday, hounding Michael and Terri's parents. Finally, Terri was disconnected from her feeding tube and she died on March 31, 2005. All of this happened because Terri did not have a living will or any other planning that would have helped her if she became incapacitated. The financial and emotional costs were enormous.

Insurance

Everyone should look into the possibility of purchasing health insurance, disability income insurance, and long-term care insurance. Each of these may have a place in your planning. With the constantly rising costs of health care and the uncertainties of our new health care laws, it is often prudent to purchase insurance to help pay the costs and preserve more of your estate for other purposes.

Health insurance, of course, is extremely important and can be purchased through an employer or directly from a carrier through one of its agents. Disability income insurance, which is often overlooked, is especially important when there is a sole breadwinner in a family. It can be devastating to a family when the primary income earner is sick or injured and cannot provide income.

Finally, long-term care insurance may be a very important part of estate planning and should be looked into, especially if you are over 50 years of age. There are numerous policy types and companies offering these policies. You should always include a top notch insurance professional in your planning team so you can make an informed and wise decision as to whether you need long-term care insurance and what kind best fits your needs.

Long-term care policies have made significant advances in coverage options and the types of policies available. There are policies with inflation riders, policies that last a lifetime or for a set number of years, and even policies that allow you or your family to get your premiums back if you do not use any of the benefits of the long-term care policy.

Of course, price is always a major consideration when deciding if long-term care insurance is right for you and your family. When balanced against the real risk of losing all of your hard-earned assets because of the extremely high cost of long-term care, it may be a wise investment.

An important aspect when choosing a long-term care policy is to pick an insurance company highly rated by companies that constantly review the financial stability of insurance companies. Your insurance advisor will be able to furnish your with the top companies.

Finally, make sure you are working with a top-notch insurance professional. Do not work with an insurance advisor you have not thoroughly researched or who cannot provide you with references that you can actually follow up on. There are many scam artists working the insurance markets. Do not fall for a good sales pitch; know who you're dealing with.

With people living longer and the costs of care soaring, disability and long-term planning are more important than ever. One of the fastest growing age groups in the United States is those who are over 100 years of age! As we live longer, we are not necessarily living better. We need more care, not less. That is one of the main reasons why disability and long-term care planning is so vitally important to the overall estate planning process, and why each member of the estate planning team must be intimately involved in such planning.

It is imperative that an estate plan, no matter how modest, address disability and long-term care. Without disability planning, you are left purely to a legal system that, try as it might, cannot replace instructions left by you to be implemented by the people or institutions of your choosing.

To summarize to address disability, at a minimum, your basic estate plan should include:

- Special durable power of attorney
- Fully funded revocable living trust
- Power of attorney for health care that includes HIPPA Authorization
- A living will
- As much disability and long-term care insurance as you can afford

5

No Estate Plan?

Big Brother Has One for You

Many people die without having an estate plan. They die without leaving a will, or without a legally valid will, or without accomplishing complete will substitute planning. Many people simply do not take the time to plan or are intimidated by the planning process itself. Others would like to plan but do not know how to go about it. Many folks just do not get around to it. The same is true of disability planning. Some people do not plan for disability, mostly for the same reasons they do not plan for death: they just do not get around to it.

If you do not plan your estate, either for your death or disability, your state law will plan it for you. As we meet hardened nonplanners, we are tempted to say: "Worry not, plan not, if that is your choice, for Big Brother has a plan already made to dispose of your property."

Each of the fifty states has laws that prescribe in great detail what happens to a citizen's property if there is no will or will substitute. These laws are generally referred to as Statutes of Descent and Distribution or as Statutes of Intestate Succession. These Big Brother laws will distribute the property of nonplanners to the state-sanctioned heirs. The result can, at times, be most discomforting.

In order to illustrate how these laws work, let us examine the statutes of a typical state and apply them to the following family situation.

The deceased-to-be and his spouse are in their middle forties. They have one teenager and two small children. A paternal grandmother is part of the family. She has lived happily in their home, from everyone's perspective, for seven years and derives her support mainly from the deceased-to-be.

Now the unexpected happens. The deceased-to-be is deceased. A tragedy has occurred. There is no will, no plan. Wait; yes, there is. Here is Big Brother's plan [with bracketed explanations and remarks], reproduced with some fun and a little artistic license, and only a touch of exaggeration.

Big Brother's Will

Being of sound mind and disposing memory, we, the State, hereby direct the passage of the property of the departed as follows:

Paragraph 1

The surviving spouse shall receive $25,000. She will receive one-half of the balance of the property.

The last half of the property will be held for the decedent's children by the probate court of the county in which the decedent resided.

Paragraph 2

The surviving spouse *may* be named personal representative [administrator] of the deceased spouse's estate. If she is named [and the court may name anyone it wishes], she will be responsible for administering and managing the estate during the probate process. All her actions will be subject to the scrutiny and approval of the court and its officials [civil servants].

Paragraph 3

The surviving spouse *will probably* be named guardian of the children by the court. If named, she will be allowed to manage the children's property as its conservator for their benefit under the scrutiny of the court and its officials [civil servants].

Paragraph 4

The court may insist, of course, that a bond [they are not inexpensive] be posted to guarantee that if the mother exercises poor judgment in the handling of the estate property and loses it, an insurance company *may* replace it.

Paragraph 5

The surviving spouse will be required to render periodic accountings to the probate court about most of her actions. The court shall have the right to ask questions about what she has done, and the court's determination with regard to the answers will be final.

Paragraph 6

The paternal grandmother is of no concern to the state and has no rights under this will.

Paragraph 7

When the children reach the age of majority [18 in our State], they shall be entitled to a complete accounting from their mother as to her handling of their property [every last dime]. Should the children be displeased with that accounting, they shall have the right to sue their mother thereon.

Paragraph 8

Each child, regardless of his or her need, may receive only one-third of the property that did not go to the mother. Each child, upon attaining age 18, shall receive the balance of the property, if any, and will be on his or her own thereafter.

Paragraph 9

Should the deceased's spouse remarry, the new spouse may be entitled to all funds previously given by us to the deceased's spouse. The new spouse shall have no obligation to use any of said funds for the benefit of the deceased's children.

Paragraph 10

Should the spouse of the deceased also rely on Big Brother's will, upon her death the local probate court shall decide who will raise the children.

Paragraph 11

The State, through the probate court and a newly appointed personal representative [administrator], shall be in total control of administering funds. All decisions may be questioned by our loyal civil servants.

Paragraph 12

All property shall be subject to the control and resulting costs of the probate court. All costs shall be paid by the children's funds.

Paragraph 13

Significant sums may be paid to our Federal Brother as estate taxes. No attempt shall be made to reduce said taxes.

Signed,

—Your Munificent Legislature

Keep in mind that the often ridiculous results of each state's legislative wills can be avoided with a little planning, if only we could convince the hardened nonplanner to take a few hours to plan.

It is a mistake to believe that a state's will gives your property directly to the state. The state ends up with property only when there are no blood relatives alive to receive it. When this occurs, the property passes (escheats) to the state.

Another problem with legislative wills is determining which state's law is going to control the assets of the deceased nonplanner. Each of our states has the right to control real property within its borders. Land and buildings are called *real property*. If our hardened nonplanner owns a cabin in another state, that other state's law and courts will control the disposition of the cabin. Attorneys call this *in rem jurisdiction*, a simple concept. States are jealous as to soil within their borders; their laws, taxation, and other matters that apply to that soil.

Yet another issue our hardened nonplanner faces is determining which state's law will control his or her personal property. The state in which the nonplanner lived determines where the personal property will pass, but where did the nonplanner really live? Attorneys would ask, "Where was the person's domicile?" Domicile is the chief, number one, absolute, real residence of a citizen. There can be only one domicile, and it is sometimes hard to establish. States fight over whose laws apply if domicile is not clear. The state that wins collects death tax on that personal property. Take the estate of Howard Hughes. It seemed that any state Howard Hughes ever lived in wanted to tax the whole estate. By the way, there is precedent indicating that more than one state may share in the tax feast if domicile is not absolutely clear.

If you become disabled—meaning you cannot take care of your personal or your financial affairs because of mental or other problems—the state also has a remedy for you. You see, when you are this disabled, you cannot make personal decisions about your health or physical well-being. In addition, you cannot manage your financial affairs; it is likely you cannot sign checks, or even buy and sell assets. Someone must do that for you.

As we discussed in Chapter 4, that person will be appointed by the local court. You will need a personal guardian and a financial guardian. The state, through its courts, will then supervise your care and your finances under its rules rather than your desires. Of course, it's assumed that the people or institutions the court appoints will be looking out for your best interests; but the system is cumbersome, crowded, and not necessarily geared to compassion and support. Just like dying without a will or other planning, experiencing an unplanned disability can result in a great deal of sadness, misunderstanding, and expense.

The point of this chapter is that a state's will and court system are always a poor substitute for your own planning and desires. These state-sponsored planning substitutes are not very personal but, when activated, they do work.

Perhaps state legislatures, in their zeal to assist their nonplanning citizens, have given false security to too many people. Maybe each state's will should say: "If you don't plan it, Big Brother will take it and put it in the general fund." With this alternative facing people, maybe they would plan.

6
Wills

What Are They?

Generally, a *will* is a set of written instructions drawn under legal formalities that directs how a person's property will be disposed of on death. "Last will and testament" is the legal label for a will. It is an old phrase meaning, "I dispose of my personal property and real estate."

Wills do not have to be written. In some states, under certain circumstances, they can be verbal; however, for purposes of this book, wills do have to be written—carefully written.

Many clients want to know if they can write their own wills. The answer is: sure, as long as you know what you are doing and follow all the formalities required by your state's laws; that is, if you want your will to work.

Wills are a special creation of society. The law of wills is fraught with technicalities and very formal procedures. Do-it-yourselfers, as a result, should leave the drafting to professionals. Very few of the Internet or software wills we have seen actually work or accomplish what the maker intended.

Most of the law of wills that we use today is very old and steeped in tradition. For many years common folks were unable to leave all their property to their loved ones. On their deaths much of their property passed (escheated) to royalty. In 1540 the English Parliament passed truly progressive legislation: the Statute of Wills. Essentially, the Statute of Wills allowed common folks the right, under a body of rules, to pass all their property to others on death.

The legislation was revolutionary and vast. The rules adopted were complex. The lawsuits that followed, as a result of society's getting comfortable with the concept, made the law bigger and even more complex. Does this ring a familiar bell in terms of today's government, its rules, regulations, and growth?

A will can only control property belonging to its maker. There is, however, a noteworthy exception. If someone else left property for you to use during your lifetime and specifically gave you the right to dispose of it on your subsequent death, you have a power of appointment; you have the right to say in your will who gets that property.

A will controls the passage of property to others on its maker's death. A very small percentage of wills, in our experience, pass property left by another through a power of appointment.

Wills do not control property that goes to others by other planning devices or by operation of law. Jointly held property, for example, is not controlled by a will. Jointly held property automatically belongs to the other joint owners on death. The same is true of property owned in tenancy by the entirety. Life insurance proceeds are not controlled by a will if the owner names a beneficiary other than his or her estate. These other techniques are will substitutes and are discussed at length in other chapters.

If you would like to expand your vocabulary, try these terms:

Holographic will. A will in one's own handwriting

Nuncupative will. An oral will

Joint will. A will with two makers to dispose of their property on the death of the second maker

Mystic will. A name one author has given to filling in a form will (generated by software and Internet questionnaire, or even a preprinted form), and then signing it

Codicil. An amendment to a will

As we have stated, do-it-yourself wills usually do not work or, at best, do not work very well. There is much more to creating an effective will than answering a computer-generated set of questions that do not take into account you or your family's needs. Oral (nuncupative) wills hardly ever work.

Joint wills can create planning nightmares, especially in the area of taxation. In our opinion, they should be avoided. Mystic wills may be hard to resist. Buy your software or get on the Internet, answer some questions that may or may not be relevant, enter your credit card information, receive your form will, and sign it. "We'll get around those scoundrel lawyers." Need we say more than, "Good luck"?

A codicil is just an amendment to a will. If the desire is to alter one's will without doing the whole thing over again, one has a codicil prepared; but—and this is a big—*but*—codicils must be signed with all, and not less than all, of the formalities of a regular will.

Wills are public documents. Generally, a will's contents are not made public while the maker is alive. On the death of the maker, a will *must* be filed with the local court and its contents made part of the public record; everyone and anyone can read it if they want to. Private business becomes public business. Not only is the will made public, but all assets and debts as well as the proceedings disposing of them are made public.

We do not think that taking one's family public is a very good idea. Anyone, with good intentions or bad, can know a family's intimate financial affairs. It does not seem to be a sound practice to us, but you be the judge.

Wills are not effective until the maker is dead. Most people would like a little current benefit from planning, especially in view of the energy required to plan in the first place. Wills provide no current benefits, other than peace of mind, of course.

Wills simply cannot provide for the care of their makers. What if you get sick or for a period of time lose your ability to reason or conduct your affairs? Your will cannot help you. It only controls property you own after you die. While you are alive it has no effect whatsoever.

A will valid in the state in which it was made is valid in other states. The only problem is determining whether other states will follow their laws or the law of the state under which the will was drawn. Unfortunately, the former is often the choice.

Assume John draws a will in Florida, where he resides. Further assume that John and his family move to Montana. John does not have his will rewritten. John dies a resident (domiciliary) of Montana. Montana's law, not Florida's law, may control. The result can be disastrous at times.

We do not believe that wills are viable interstate planning tools. Clients move around. Twenty-first-century Americans are mobile; they seek opportunities and are too frequently relocated by their employers. Even deeply rooted, self-employed folks retire and are known to relocate to find that "better climate."

There is a need for interstate flexibility in estate planning. Wills do not provide it. The living trust does, but more on that later.

Wills must go through the probate process. In discussions with clients we have found that most clients have the notion that to prepare a will is to avoid the probate court. This is definitely not the case. The property that passes under your will must go through probate court.

Probate is the process of passing title from the will maker to others. With a will, the probate process will pass title the will maker's way. Without a will or will-substitute planning, the probate court will pass title to property the legislature's way. Either way, with or without a will, your property will go through probate. We discuss this in Chapter 8, "Probate." For now we'll just say that probate can be a needlessly expensive and time-consuming process and that it *can* be avoided.

In our experience, clients have one universal question with regard to wills: "Now that I've got it, what do I do with it?"

First, sign only one original will. If you sign duplicates and one duplicate original is destroyed, it may, by operation of your state's law, destroy all. It is a good practice to sign only one original will.

Second, store your will in a safe place. Store your will where it can be easily found by others. Tell your family, both verbally and in writing, where that safe, easily found place is.

Many attorneys recommend that clients leave their original wills with them. We do not believe this is a good practice. A law office is not safe from vandalism, theft, or a well-intended, but fatal, housekeeping. A misplaced will among thousands of files may just be misplaced, but it is lost until found. Your will is of critical importance to you and your family, but only one will among many in your attorney's office.

Storing your will in a safe-deposit box may be prudent or not, depending upon the state in which you live. If your state has a death tax and follows the practice of sealing safe-deposit boxes until the tax examiner is present to inspect the contents, valuable time can be lost when matters must be completed under the will but there is no will available because your civil servant has not gotten there yet.

We could write a volume or more just on wills, but others have already done that; besides, we are not all that keen on wills anyway. They are all right and they do work, they have been around for hundreds of years, but they have several features that we view as unattractive.

To summarize, wills

- Are only effective on death.
- May *not* control all property.
- Involve complex legal rules.
- Are public.
- Are not viable interstate planning tools.
- Must go through probate.
- Should be stored properly.

7

More on Wills

They're Not All They're Cracked Up to Be

In our experience, many clients and some professional advisors who do not specialize in estate planning still equate the estate planning process with the drafting of a last will and testament. They believe that estate planning is will planning, even though this is an outdated view of planning.

In the past, in countless situations when we have asked the question, "Do you have an existing estate plan?" the response has been, "Yes, I have a will, but it's out of date," or, "No, I've never had a will."

The belief that estate planning and will drafting are synonymous is unfortunate and, in most instances, not correct.

A will is but one method of disposing of property upon death. In our experience, people generally give little or no thought to other methods as they relate to the estate planning process. These methods have crept into the economic marketplace as practical and quick solutions to passing property at death.

In order to illustrate the impact of alternative methods of will planning, let us conjure up a meeting between a typical client and his advisor.

Attorney, accountant, insurance professional, financial advisor, or trust banker: CATHERINE

Client: JOHN

CATHERINE: Well, John, before we can recommend an estate plan for you and your family, we need to know what you own and how you own it.

JOHN: What do I own? Well, Liz and I own our home. The deed is in both our names as joint owners. I hope that's okay because that's the way the realtor said would be best. Let's see, there're the savings accounts—four of them. One is in *both our names*, you know, jointly held, I guess. One's just in my name, a few dollars, that's all. The other two are with the kids, one in my name with our son, Robbie; the other is in our son Jamie's name, but Liz and I are both on it as well. The person at the bank said it would be better this way; something about our being custodians or something; but I think we're all on with the kids as joint owners.

CATHERINE: Are you sure exactly how the accounts read, John?

JOHN: [*With some irritation*] Not really, but there's not much there. We can check, I guess.Then, we have the life insurance. There's my group plan at the office. That goes to Liz and then to the kids if she dies before I do. I've also got my G.I. insurance. That goes the same way. Oh, yes, and I also have two other policies. One's not too large, but it's permanent insurance, and the other's in six figures. It's term. They go the same way.

CATHERINE: [*Patiently, but eager to get on with it*] What else do you have?

JOHN: Our checking accounts; one's joint; one's in Liz's name. I've got my pension and profit sharing plan at the company. I signed a card at the personnel office. I think the proceeds go to Liz and the kids.

CATHERINE: [Sensing that the client is starting to move a little faster] What else do you own, John?

JOHN: We have the cabin. That's in our names with my brother and his wife; jointly, I guess. Some stocks, some in Liz's and my name; some we put in the kids' names; one's with my sister and both names are on it. That's about it.

CATHERINE: Do you have any personal possessions, John?

JOHN: Oh, do we ever. Two cars in both names; furniture; furnishings, you know; my stamp collection, been collecting since I was a kid; clothing, you know, the usual stuff. I'll tell you, though, I don't know who owns it. I guess we both do.

CATHERINE: Thank you, John.

Now, let us backtrack. Let us go through John's assets to see how they are titled and whether or not John's new will can control them on John's death or whether they will go directly to others because John used an alternative method of planning.

Summary of John's Assets

Residence:	Joint with spouse
Savings accounts:	
No. 1	Joint with spouse
No. 2	John's name
No. 3	Joint with son
No. 4	Joint with spouse and son
Life insurance:	Named beneficiaries: spouse and children
Checking accounts:	
No. 1	Joint with spouse
No. 2	Spouse's name
Pension and profit sharing accounts at company:	Beneficiaries: spouse and children
Cabin:	Jointly between families
Personal possessions:	
Cars:	Joint with spouse
Other:	Who knows?

As we review the summary of John's estate, we can quickly get to the bottom line. Those items that John owns solely in his name will be controlled by and pass under the terms of his will. The balance will automatically pass by contract or by operation of law:

- All joint property will automatically pass to the surviving joint tenants. Those assets will be the exclusive property of the new owners.

- All life insurance will go to the named beneficiaries under the terms of the policy and the beneficiary designations.

- The pension and profit sharing proceeds will also transfer pursuant to the beneficiary cards John signed.

- Checking account No. 2 is in John's spouse's name and, as such, cannot be controlled by John's will.

Our obvious point is that the only property John's will can control is one savings account and the personal property deemed to be owned by John at his death. Wills may not control the disposition of your property as much as you think (or would like to think) they do.

We discuss the whats and hows of joint ownership or beneficiary designations in other chapters. For now, the important point to remember is this: a will is but one tool available to the client and the estate planner to dispose of property on death. *Will* planning is will planning and is only a part of estate planning. *Estate* planning envisions how those other assets will pass; how they will generate or avoid tax; to whom they will pass and how they will pass. These "other" planning techniques (we'll refer to them as *will substitute* techniques) are of critical importance.

A will is just one golf club in the estate planning golf bag, a club that should be used only in the appropriate situations to pull off the right shot.

Probate

Red Tape That Can Be Avoided

Probate is the legal process of passing ownership of property from a deceased person to others. Probate courts have been a part of our legal heritage for centuries.

Generally speaking, every county in every state in the United States has its own probate court. These courts are not always called probate courts; sometimes they are called surrogate or common courts. Regardless of their names, these courts all have the same purpose: passing ownership of property to the heirs of people who died with a will plan or with no plan at all.

In 1965, Norman F. Dacey, a nonlawyer, authored a national best-selling book titled *How to Avoid Probate.* The book was 349 pages long, including 50 pages of text and approximately 300 pages of tear-out "how to do it" estate planning forms. Mr. Dacey's thesis was that probate should and could be avoided. The book generated a new crisis in the relationship between attorneys and clients. It rocked the estate planning community by savagely attacking—fairly and unfairly, in our opinion—probate lawyers.

Following publication of Mr. Dacey's book, a bar-sponsored attempt to respond to his valid allegations was launched under the direction of a noted attorney and law school professor, Richard V. Wellman. Professor Wellman then authored a Uniform Probate Code that could be used in all states.

The Uniform Probate Code addressed many of the deficiencies pointed out in the Dacey book. According to the Uniform Law Commission, 17 states have adopted that code, in one form or another: Alaska, Arizona, Colorado, Hawaii, Idaho, Maine, Massachusetts, Michigan, Minnesota, Montana, Nebraska, New Jersey, New Mexico, North Dakota, South Carolina, South Dakota, and Utah. The U.S. Virgin Islands has also enacted a version of the Uniform Probate Code.

Professor Wellman did a great service for the probate bar and the public; unfortunately, much of the probate bar rejected his work, as have 33 states. However, many states have embraced at least some of the concepts included in the Uniform Probate Code because of public and professional pressure to make probate easier, faster, and less costly.

Please understand that if you die with a will (testate), the property your will controls goes through probate. If you die without a will (intestate) and without alternative will substitute planning, your property will go through probate.

Getting the dead citizen's property into the hands of his or her or the state's beneficiaries is but one part or function of the probate process; it is in fact only the end result of that process.

The *probate agent* is responsible for most of the work to be accomplished. He or she reports and answers to the probate judge through the estate's attorney. A probate agent is given different names in different situations and in different states, such as:

- Executor (male agent named in a will).
- Executrix (female agent named in a will).
- Administrator (male agent named by the court when there is no will).
- Administratrix (female agent named by the court when there is no will).
- Personal representative (male or female agent named in those states that passed the Uniform Probate Code).

Whatever their titles, the agents are responsible for doing the work in the probate process. They work for the court or judge. Probate is a complicated legal process; the estate or agent relies on an attorney for assistance in getting through the legal maze. At times, the attorney can and will do most if not all of the work, but in some probate proceedings the attorney does very little work.

Both the probate agent and the probate attorney are entitled to compensation for serving in their prescribed roles. Their fees are usually determined by state statute but may be reviewed and awarded by the probate judge.

Probate judges are generally nonpracticing or retired lawyers. They can be brilliant or not so brilliant. They can be industrious or lazy. They are, after all, people. Most probate judges, in our opinion, are overworked and underpaid. They preside over a red-tape system that is ancient, meticulous, and time-consuming. The probate bench attracts candidates ranging from superb attorneys who are committed and self-sacrificing individuals (they could earn a great deal more in private practice) to ne'er-do-well attorneys who have become involved in local politics. Probate judges can be appointed or elected, depending on the laws of the individual states.

Most practicing attorneys handle probate estates. This is particularly true in rural areas and among attorneys who conduct a general practice. In our experience, few attorneys turn away probate work. The nature of the work is time-consuming, and most of the time not intellectually difficult. The economic rewards can be ample or splendid, depending upon whose point of view is considered.

Attorneys who specialize in probate fall into one of two categories: (1) mature attorneys who harvest the will files they have built up over a lifetime of law practice and who comprise the bulk of the specialists, and (2) attorneys who restrict their practice to after-death planning. The latter are usually estate and tax attorneys who specialize in reducing costs and taxes and assist heirs in making after-death decisions. Generally, the tax specialists did not plan the estates they represent, but rather, probate work is referred to them because of their expertise. These individuals, although looked upon as probate lawyers, are in reality postmortem planners.

The probate process, although complicated and confusing to most people, can be reduced to the following:

- Understand the will.
- Ascertain heirs.
- Locate and value all property.
- Pay the agent and attorney.
- Ascertain and pay creditors of the estate.
- Resolve all controversies between the parties.
- File all tax returns.
- Distribute property.

Understanding the will is usually not difficult. Homemade wills and wills drawn poorly can spell trouble, however. They usually result in will fights that generate a great deal of time and dollar expenditure.

Ascertaining or finding heirs is also usually not difficult. On the other hand, when one gets into the extended family (third cousins once removed), the time involved in locating heirs can run up the costs for probate. In fact, there are companies that provide services to attorneys strictly for the purpose of locating distant heirs.

Finding and valuing a deceased person's property is generally a total nightmare. It took the deceased a lifetime to accumulate wealth, and the records with regard to it were usually kept in his or her mind. Written records of the property, if they exist at all, are in many places. Finding the property is time-consuming and often a real detective job. Even the basic task of determining what the deceased owned, much less where it may be located, is enormous in the usual estate. The challenge is even greater because of the increased use of online banking, online shopping, online storage of vital documents, and e-mail.

Valuing the property that is found is a major responsibility of the agent, probate lawyer, and court. The higher the value of the property, the greater the potential state and federal taxes. Both tax laws and estate laws require that the property be valued at its fair market value. There is no black and white in the valuation process for many assets (closely held stocks, real property, partnership interests, etc.). From the perspective of beneficiaries or heirs, property should be valued on the low side of the valuation spectrum. From the judge's perspective, it should be valued fairly. What about the attorney's perspective?

The involvement of probate attorneys in the valuation of probate and even nonprobate property has often been criticized. To whom do the attorneys owe their duty? Should they attempt to assist the probate agents in the hiring of appraisers who will come in with low valuations? Is their duty to the courts and states? Must they insist on fair market value (real value)? After all, they did take an oath to uphold the law. What about their involvement? Do attorneys have a conflict of interest? Many critics take this position: if attorneys are being paid on a fee basis and the fee is a percentage applied against the value of the estate property, there is an inherent conflict. The higher the value of the estate, the higher the fee and the higher the tax. Is there a conflict? You be the judge.

Finding, sorting out, and paying creditors of the deceased and his or her estate can be frustrating. It is important to understand that creditors get paid before beneficiaries. Problems involving creditors prevent beneficiaries from getting their money until those creditor problems are solved.

According to the laws of most states, probate agents and lawyers are generally *first-class creditors*. This means they get paid off the top. In fact, they get paid before other creditors and always before the state or federal government. All states prescribe by law how probate officials get paid. Probate agents usually get paid on a percentage of the estate's value. Some states prescribe payment on a "whatever is reasonable" basis (what is reasonable depends on the judge's determination of reasonableness).

Attorneys' compensation is prescribed by law also. Attorneys are usually compensated on a percentage of the estate's value or on a "whatever is reasonable" basis. Some jurisdictions leave attorneys' fees up to the judge. Depending on the judge and his or her relationship with the attorney, fees may be very high, reasonable, or very low. Again, this depends on whose point of view is being considered.

Controversy often arises in the probate process. Potential heirs can get into some very interesting fights. The probate agent and the probate attorney can get into a dogfight with real or fake creditors. The agent and the attorney may even fight with each other or with the judge. The judge resolves all probate disputes. The estate of the deceased pays for most if not all of the cost of these fights. The cost of probate disputes is generally not inexpensive, and it can take a long time.

Ascertaining what taxes are due and paying them within the time periods prescribed by law would seem to be a relatively easy task. But do not forget that the assets have to be valued before the taxes can be computed. Another problem usually associated with the probate process is converting assets to cash to pay the taxes. What does and does not get sold can create probate battles among all of the probate players.

In many situations, payment of death taxes to both the state and the federal government involves substantial after-death tax planning. Most probate attorneys are not tax attorneys, who as a group comprise a small percentage of all attorneys practicing law. Many critics of the probate process highlight this lack of professional expertise.

The distribution of probate property can be easy or difficult. If minor beneficiaries are involved and trusts have not been created for them, the court will stay involved until the minors are adults; adult beneficiaries who are mentally incompetent bring about the same result, and again the court may stay involved for a very long time.

The probate process is complex and full of red tape. Its weaknesses can be summarized as follows:

- Probate is public.
- Probate is time-consuming.
- Probate is expensive.
- Probate puts the real control in the hands of lawyers and the judge's chambers.

There are several ways that you may choose to avoid probate. Commonly used methods include:

- Joint tenancy with right of survivorship
- Properly designating life insurance proceeds
- Properly designating beneficiaries of employee fringe benefits
- Using payable-on-death (POD) or transfer on death (TOD) designations
- Creating and funding a living trust

Below, we briefly define and discuss each of these methods.

Joint Tenancy with Right of Survivorship

The survivorship feature unique to joint ownership automatically passes title to property upon the death of a joint owner. As a result, on the death of a joint owner, joint property does not go through probate. But remember, joint ownership has several drawbacks associated with its use that may outweigh the benefits of avoiding probate.

Properly Designating Life Insurance Proceeds

Life insurance proceeds made payable either to adult beneficiaries or to a living trust as beneficiary escape probate. If, however, you designate your estate as beneficiary, your insurance proceeds will go through probate. Do not make your estate the beneficiary of your insurance contracts.

Do not name minors as the beneficiaries of your life insurance proceeds. If this is done, the proceeds will end up in probate court. Minors need court supervision until they reach legal adulthood. Under state law this can be 18 or 21 years of age. Instead, leave your insurance proceeds to a living trust created for the benefit of your minor beneficiaries. If you do, your life insurance proceeds will avoid the probate swamp.

If your life insurance proceeds are left to a trust you created for your minor beneficiaries in your will (this is known as a testamentary trust), the probate court will become involved with the proceeds. Wills, and the trusts created in them, are always under the jurisdiction of the local probate court; this is particularly true when the trusts are created for minors.

Life insurance proceeds can easily avoid probate when they are properly designated.

Properly Designating Beneficiaries of Employee Fringe Benefits

Many Americans have significant sums due them or their beneficiaries resulting from employer-sponsored fringe benefits such as pension and profit sharing plans. To whom fringe-benefit funds are paid on the death of the employee-participant is determined by a beneficiary designation placed on a company form. Do not forget to fill in and sign the appropriate designation forms. If you do not properly fill them out and sign them, the proceeds will go wherever the retirement plan directs. This may be your estate;

if that is the case, the proceeds will go through probate. The same is true if you name your estate as beneficiary. Do not name minors as your beneficiaries because, just like life insurance proceeds, your benefits will be controlled by the probate court.

Always name adults or a living trust as your beneficiary to avoid probate. Remember to complete your company's forms properly; most companies have trained personnel to assist you.

Using POD and TOD Designations

Another method of avoiding probate may be available in most states. This technique applies to savings and checking accounts as well as certificates of deposit. The owner, in setting up the account, instructs the bank clerk to type on the account a payable-on-death designation. The owner then names the person or persons to receive the account proceeds upon death of the owner and has those names typed on the account after the letters POD. It is as simple as that. These accounts by *law* will not go through probate. The POD is merely a beneficiary designation for these assets. If you live in one of these states, however, do not use this technique to leave the accounts to minor beneficiaries.

All U.S. jurisdictions except for Louisiana, Texas, and Puerto Rico have adopted the Uniform Transfer on Death Securities Act. This newer version is called a transfer-on-death designation. A TOD applies to investments and investment accounts, which represents an expansion of POD from bank accounts to all types of investment accounts and individual securities.

You should consult with your banker, trust department, or attorney to determine if you can use one of these designations.

Creating and Funding a Living Trust

Living trusts are complete will substitutes. They have been around for hundreds of years; assets placed in a living trust have always avoided the probate process. They were created, in part, to do just that.

Using a living trust as a will substitute has certainly come of age. Traditionally, living trusts were only used by nobility. In modern times they have been used mostly by the wealthy. Today, living trusts are used, and should be used, by just about everybody.

Property placed in a living trust is instantly available for the use and benefit of the trust maker's beneficiaries. No matter how vast and diversified your holdings may be, a living trust can accommodate all of them in avoiding the probate process.

Every probate-avoidance technique other than the living trust has potential planning disadvantages. This does not mean that the other techniques cannot or should not be used. It does mean that the living trust can be used to avoid probate for all your property and that, as a technique, it has few if any disadvantages compared to the other techniques we have discussed.

We include two chapters on the living trust: Chapter 17 discusses what it is and how it works. Chapter 18 describes how property can be put into a living trust (how the trust can be funded).

Probate itself, you will recall, involves the collection of assets and the passage of title to beneficiaries under the control and supervision of the probate judge. Probate your own estate while you are alive. Organize your affairs and retitle your assets so they will not go through probate on death. Most people know what they own and can generally find the paperwork that evidences their ownership quickly. Organize your e-mail accounts, online banking and investment accounts, and passwords. Once that is done, a professional advisor can quickly recommend the right ownership techniques to get the job done.

The discussion on probate can be summarized as follows:

- Planning to avoid probate involves time, some financial housekeeping, and, regardless of the methods you use, requires the following: Collect all assets and the papers that evidence title to those assets (deeds, stock certificates, partnership agreements, etc.). This means getting your affairs organized and all the paperwork together in one place. Pay special attention to all of your online and other electronic accounts.

- Review with your advisors the way ownership has been taken to your existing assets.

- Change the way you own your assets in one of several ways we have discussed, so that upon your death your property will escape probate.

9

The Federal Estate Tax

The Final Sting

One of the most overused clichés is: "The only certain things are death and taxes." Death is still certain. Congress has added such a level of uncertainty in taxes over the last several years, especially with regard to federal estate taxes, that the old cliché itself is dying!

There has been so much change and so much controversy over the so-called federal "death tax" that planning for it has become an exercise in uncertainty. The purpose of this chapter is to familiarize you with the federal estate tax and demonstrate how it has changed. The most important point that you can take from this chapter is that *you must plan your estate based on the worst case scenario.* By failing to plan or by planning for the best, you are not planning, you are wishful thinking. We will give you a lot of ways to properly plan your estate in uncertain times, but those planning ideas will be easier to understand if you read this chapter thoroughly.

A Short History of the Federal Estate Tax

Federal death tax has been and continues to be serious business. The Economic Growth and Tax Relief Reconciliation Act of 2001 (EGTRRA), which set forth the estate tax laws from 2001 through 2010, and the Tax Relief, Unemployment Insurance Reauthorization and Job Creation Act of 2010 (TRA 2010), have made estate tax planning even more serious and certainly more complex. It's very important for you to understand the historical perspective in order to understand and appreciate the current law.

The U.S. government's death tax is properly called the federal estate tax. In existence in one form or another since the inception of our country, it has been permanently repealed several times, only to return. America's first death tax—the *Death Stamp Tax* of 1797—helped finance the Revolutionary War. In 1802 it was repealed. It came roaring back in the Civil War. The Revenue Act of 1862 helped finance the war; in 1870 it was repealed.

Another war sparked another estate tax. The War Revenue Act of 1898 imposed another death tax to finance the Spanish-American War. But it too was repealed in 1902. Gone for a short while, the federal estate tax rose again in World War I in the Revenue Act of 1916. The Revenue Acts of 1917 and 1924 increased federal estate tax rates, but they were lowered in the economic good times of 1926.

The Depression once again gave Congress the incentive to raise federal estate taxes. The 1932, 1934, and 1935 Revenue Acts raised, and raised again, death tax rates to 70 percent. In 1940, Congress added a 10 percent surtax, and in 1941 it increased the maximum rate to 77 percent.

A number of changes in the federal estate tax system were made during the 35-year period following 1941. In 1976, Congress made an attempt to initiate reform in the death tax area; the result was the Tax Reform Act of 1976 (TRA 1976). TRA 1976 did a great deal for the coffers of the U.S. government; it did not do a great deal for its citizens.

The Economic Recovery Tax Act of 1981 (ERTA 1981) raised the amount that was free from federal estate and gift tax and made planning much more flexible between spouses. Between 1981 and 1999, 126 laws were passed that affected the Internal Revenue Code, most of which had some impact on federal estate and gift taxation. That is an average of seven new laws every year. It is no wonder our laws are so complex.

In the Reagan/George H. W. Bush/Clinton administrations, nine major tax acts were passed that affected federal death and gift taxes. In the George W. Bush administration, the above-mentioned Economic Growth and Tax Relief Reconciliation Act of 2001 was passed. It generally increased exemptions, reduced rates, and repealed the federal estate and generation-skipping transfer taxes—but not gift tax—for the year 2010. Originally, EGTRRA was set to expire in 2011. Upon its expiration, the federal estate tax would have reverted to the estate tax amounts in effect before EGTRRA. This would have meant a tax-free amount of $1 million per person and graduated federal estate tax rates reaching 55 percent on very large estates.

In December 2010, Congress passed the Tax Relief, Unemployment Insurance Reauthorization and Job Creation Act of 2010 (TRA 2010). It gave new life to estate, gift, and generation-skipping taxes and prevented the federal estate tax from reverting to the 2001 levels. However, TRA 2010 is scheduled to expire on December 31, 2012, at which time federal estate taxes, without action from Congress, will revert back to pre EGTRRA levels.

From this short history of the federal estate tax (with a little bit of gift and generation-skipping tax thrown in), it is obvious there is nothing so certain as the uncertainty of the federal estate, gift, and generation-skipping taxes. Planning for this uncertainty is critical, and we are going to show you how to do it. First, however, it is important to understand how the federal estate tax works—at least for now.

How Federal Estate Tax Works

Federal estate tax has two distinct features. First, it can be described as an "everything tax." Yes, Uncle Sam taxes everything, including the proverbial kitchen sink. Second, this tax is a "top tax." Uncle Sam receives his tax before your beneficiaries receive anything.

Federal estate tax is not a tax levied against a deceased person or his or her property. It is not a people or property tax at all. It is a tax levied against the "right to transfer" property on death. We could write volumes on the various property interests that Uncle Sam taxes under the federal estate tax. Fortunately, that will not be necessary. What is important to remember is that federal estate tax is an everything tax, and that it is paid before beneficiaries receive their share of the proceeds.

Uncle Sam will tax all the property owned in your name at your death. Uncle Sam will tax all the life insurance proceeds owned by you on your life. Uncle Sam has attempted to tax the total value of all assets held in joint ownership. Uncle Sam has even taxed property that was given away during people's lifetimes if any of the income from that property was retained by the maker of the gift.

We can play the game of Uncle Sam Will Tax until your eyes close and the book slides from your hands, but that would belabor the point. It would be easier to list what Uncle Sam does not tax. Federal estate tax does not apply to:

- Money going directly to beneficiaries through an annuity purchased by your employer
- Funds passing to beneficiaries pursuant to death-benefit-only plans created by your employer
- Social Security payments to your dependents
- Insurance proceeds on your life if you did not own or have any control over those policies

There are other property interests, although not many, that are not subject to federal estate tax; these other property interests are rarely applicable, and an understanding of them is not necessary to a general understanding of Uncle Sam's estate tax.

Can you believe that Uncle Sam taxes life insurance proceeds? This does not mean that Uncle Sam taxes the premiums paid for that insurance; it means that Uncle Sam taxes all the death proceeds whether they are paid in installments or in a lump sum to your designated beneficiaries. If you paid $1,000 in premiums for a $100,000 life insurance policy, the proceeds of which go to your children upon your death, all $100,000 is subject to federal estate tax but not the federal income tax. Many people believe that life insurance proceeds are not taxed on death. Some states may not have a death tax on life insurance proceeds, but the U.S. government does.

Traditionally, federal estate tax rates have been progressive. The more a taxpayer owned, the more tax that taxpayer paid; this should be a surprise to no one. Historically, the federal estate tax has redistributed wealth; it has been a tax targeted to take from the wealthy and redistribute that wealth to the not-so wealthy. The Tax Relief, Unemployment Insurance Reauthorization and Job Creation Act of 2010 (TRA 2010) has only one tax bracket. For those who die with a high enough estate, a 35 percent federal estate tax rate is imposed.

For many years (in fact, up until 1976), the first $60,000 of estate value was not taxed. As a result of the Tax Reform Act of 1976, that amount went up in stages until it peaked at $175,625 in 1981. Congress raised the tax-free amount to $225,000 for individuals dying in 1982, and then continued to increase the tax-free amount annually until it reached $600,000 in 1987. The Taxpayer Relief Act of 1997 (TRA 1997) increased the tax-free amount for individuals dying after 1997. The increase was to be phased in over nine years. This changed with the Economic Growth and Tax Relief Reconciliation Act of 2001 (EGTRRA), which phased in higher tax-free amounts, culminating with $3.5 million in 2009. The federal estate tax rate in 2009 was 45 percent. Then, for one year, 2010, there was no federal estate tax.

The increase in the tax-free amount, which is referred to as the "applicable exclusion amount," was designed to reflect inflation and a growing dislike by Congress of the federal "death tax." In TRA 2010, the tax-free amount was raised to a whopping $5 million per person or $10 million for a married couple. For those who were taxed, the federal estate tax rate was 35 percent. Under TRA 2010 the $5 million per person tax-free amount is indexed for inflation beginning in 2012. The inflation adjustment increased the 2012 applicable exclusion amount to $5,120,000.

Marital Deduction

Congress has traditionally taken notice of the family unit and made some allowances for leaving property to spouses in the federal estate tax laws. For many years the law provided that spouses could leave one-half of their property free of federal estate tax to surviving spouses. This provision of the estate tax appeared to salve the congressional conscience. The Tax Reform Act of 1976 increased this spousal benefit to $250,000 or one-half of the estate, whichever was greater. The real change was adding a base of $250,000 that went tax-free to the surviving spouse.

The tax-saving spousal device we have been discussing is referred to as the *marital deduction*. Property accumulated by husband and wife that was left to the surviving spouse was taxed only when it exceeded $425,625 (the sum of $250,000 of marital deduction and the $175,625 exemption equivalent).

Whether this rather arbitrary marital deduction was a good deal was a matter of opinion. Former President Reagan was not of that opinion, nor was Congress. In passing ERTA, they expressed a belief that if a little was good, more would be better. Today, the marital deduction applies to all property left to a U.S. citizen spouse. Just think, a 100 percent marital deduction. A marital deduction is available to the surviving spouse, but the full amount is taxed upon the spouse's subsequent death.

The marital deduction for a noncitizen surviving spouse is different. There is no tax-free amount, while there would be for a citizen spouse. To use the tax-free amount on both deaths, the citizen spouse must create a *qualified domestic trust* for the noncitizen spouse. Called a QDOT, this special trust ensures that estate assets passing for the benefit of a noncitizen spouse are available to pay any estate taxes that may be due when the noncitizen spouse dies. We discuss the qualified domestic trust in more detail in Chapter 25, "Planning for a Spouse." Alternatively, if the noncitizen surviving spouse becomes a U.S. citizen within certain strict time limits and meets certain residency requirements, the now citizen spouse is allowed all of the benefits of the marital deduction.

Valuation of Assets

It is important to understand the rules of federal estate tax. It is equally important to understand how property is valued for purposes of applying the death tax. Understanding a tax table is not too difficult. Arriving at the value of the property prior to applying that table can be very difficult.

Uncle Sam's death tax is based on the fair market value of the property in an estate. It is not a tax on the value of the property when it was originally purchased. It is based either on the fair market value of the property at the date of the estate owner's death or the value of that property six months after the date of the owner's death. The latter date is referred to as the *alternate valuation date*.

Uncle Sam gives beneficiaries a valuation choice. They can value the property at its date of death value or its value six months later. Your postdeath agent can only use the alternate valuation date if it will both reduce the value of your estate and reduce the federal estate tax due. Generally, due to inflation, property goes up in value; but that does not always happen. Valuation should be computed on both dates to see if there is any decrease in the overall value of property that would result in a lower federal estate tax. Your postdeath agent must be careful, however. Your agent cannot pick and choose different dates for different assets. The date selected applies to all the assets.

If the value of property should go down after the six-month valuation date, the estate has no federal estate tax recourse; the law provides no relief for this contingency.

It is important to recognize that the fair market value of property can be astoundingly high. Most of us want to know who determines the fair market value of our property. Does the family determine the value? The attorney? The agent of the estate? Does the Internal Revenue Service determine its value? The fair market value of the property in an estate is ultimately determined by the courts if the postdeath agents and the Internal Revenue Service cannot agree on a value. The standard the courts use is the price that a willing buyer would pay a willing seller, both having no compulsion to buy or sell and each being aware of all the facts surrounding the sale.

Most assets have a spectrum of value. For example, a particular car that is two years old may range in value from $26,000 to $35,000, depending upon who is selling and who is buying. Its value also depends on the environment in which it is being bought and sold. This range in value is referred to as the *spectrum of value*. Generally speaking, postdeath agents representing an estate should always shoot for the low end of the value spectrum when submitting valuations on a federal estate tax return. At the same time, agents should not underestimate the Internal Revenue Service. The goal of the IRS is to collect revenue. In zealously seeking to achieve their objective, you can be assured that, in many cases, the IRS will go for the highest value possible within the value spectrum.

Often this difference in approach leads to heated arguments and some rather spirited negotiations between the representatives of the estate and the IRS. The result of these negotiations is usually a settlement. Sometimes, however, the two sides remain miles apart, and the courts are called upon to make the ultimate decision. Remember, the roles of the estate's agent and the IRS require that each lean toward a different end of the value spectrum.

Some types of property are easily valued for federal estate tax purposes. Property of this type includes:

- Stocks that are publicly traded
- Bonds
- Savings and checking accounts

- Certificates of deposit
- Money market accounts
- Treasury bills

Most property holdings are not so easily valued. Property fitting this description includes:

- Real estate
- Closely (privately) owned business interests, including corporations, partnerships, and limited liability companies
- Equipment and machinery
- Personal effects

The best way to reduce federal estate tax is to reduce the value of the property subject to the tax. The job of the estate's agent is to keep that value down. The job of the IRS is to keep it as high as possible. There used to be very effective methods for reducing the value of certain types of property by passing their future appreciation to family members on a tax-free basis. These so-called freezing techniques have been significantly curtailed. There are still some very effective techniques for reducing the value of property; we discuss them in other chapters.

Since 1976 land (real property) used in farming or ranching can be valued lower than its arguable fair market value if certain requirements are met. This exception to the general rules of fair market value resulted from intense lobbying efforts on the part of farm and ranch associations. The exceptions to the general rule apply to special interests and are covered in Chapter 40, "Special Use Valuation." In our opinion, these legal exceptions are fair.

Paying the Tax

Another important aspect of federal estate tax law is that it is not a tax that can be easily deferred to a time when payment may be convenient. With few exceptions, the Internal Revenue Code says that Uncle Sam's death tax shall be paid in cash nine months from the date of death. Cash is a method of payment that does not allow for postponement. The result of not paying federal estate tax promptly unless you have special approval from the IRS is that the property will be seized by the IRS, which will be more than happy to collect what proceeds it can by means of a tax sale. The federal estate tax is a tough, no-nonsense tax.

The federal estate tax can be summarized as follows:

- It only applies to estates valued in excess of $5 million per person and $10 million per married couple for 2011 and 2012. The 2012 amount is indexed for inflation, and that indexed amount is $5,120,000. The federal estate tax rate is 35 percent.

- Absent action from Congress, the federal estate tax reverts to the 2001 law; estates valued in excess of $1 million will be subject to federal estate tax, with graduated tax rates reaching a maximum of 55 percent.

- Spouses are able to leave property of an unlimited amount to their U.S. citizen spouses free of federal estate tax.

- Planning for the worst case scenario is critical to protect an estate.

10

The Unified System

Robbing Peter to Pay Paul

Prior to the Tax Reform Act of 1976, the federal tax law favored lifetime gifts over transfers upon death. The federal gift tax rates were actually 25 percent less than the federal estate tax rates. The 1976 Tax Reform Act unified the federal estate and gift tax systems. As a result of this unification a single exemption was given to taxpayers to use, at their choice, either for lifetime gifts or at death. This was called the *exemption equivalent*.

ERTA continued the unified system concept. Under ERTA the exemption equivalent was gradually increased to $600,000. The old exemption equivalent was replaced by the applicable exclusion amount, which started at $600,000 and was to be phased in, reaching a maximum amount of $1 million in 2006. This changed with the Economic Growth and Tax Relief Reconciliation Act of 2001, EGTRRA, which phased in higher federal estate tax-free amounts, culminating with a high of $3.5 million in 2009. However, it also ended the unified system. Instead of the gift tax exemption equaling the federal estate tax exemption, Congress capped the amount of lifetime tax-free gifts at $1 million. The clear message was that it was better to die with assets in an estate rather than making lifetime gifts.

The death of unification made planning more difficult and confusing. It led to relatively inconsistent planning results. Even in 2010, when the federal estate tax was in its one-year hiatus, the gift tax exemption remained at $1 million. Lifetime gifts over that amount were subject to a 35 percent gift tax.

TRA 2010 once again unified the federal estate and gift taxes. In 2011 and 2012 the federal gift tax rate is 35 percent, which is the same as the federal estate tax rate. The lifetime exemption for gifts is $5 million, which is the same as the applicable exclusion amount for federal estate taxes. On January 1, 2013, absent new legislation, the top gift tax rate is scheduled to revert back to 55 percent under the 2001 Tax Act sunset provision. The lifetime exemption will also revert back to $1 million, the same amount as the federal estate tax applicable exclusion amount, thereby keeping unification intact.

Here is an example of how the applicable exclusion amount works:

> Ginny Monday, not married, makes $500,000 in gifts that are subject to federal gift taxation during her lifetime. Ginny dies in 2011. Her taxable estate for federal estate tax purposes, before her remaining applicable exclusion amount is applied, is $5.8 million. Since Ginny used $500,000 of her applicable exclusion amount to make her lifetime gifts tax-free, her estate has $4.5 million of remaining applicable exclusion amount (her $5 million applicable exclusion less the $500,000 she used during her life). As a result, $1.3 million of Ginny's property ($5.8 million taxable estate less the $4.5 million of remaining applicable exclusion amount) is subject to federal estate tax. The tax is 35 percent of $1.3 million, which is $455,000.

When deciding whether it is better to use the applicable exclusion amount during your life instead of at your death, the *time value of money* must be considered. A dollar in hand today is worth much more than receiving that same dollar in the future. You can invest a dollar today at 10 percent and next year have $1.10. But if someone promises to pay you $1 in one year, you have lost that $0.10 investment. Applying this concept to the applicable exclusion amount, if you give a highly appreciating asset away, you avoid gift tax by using your applicable exclusion amount, thereby removing both the asset and its appreciation from your estate. The value of using your applicable exclusion amount for lifetime gifts is twofold: you remove the asset and its appreciation from your estate, and do it in terms of today's dollars.

There is one other advantage to making taxable gifts rather than holding onto property until death. It has to do with how federal gifts are taxed and how the federal estate tax is imposed. Estate planning practitioners refer to the federal gift tax as exclusionary and the estate tax as inclusionary. To understand why, let's take an example of an individual, Edward, who wants to either give or leave his daughter, Carlye, $1 million but wants to pay the least amount of tax. Let's further assume that Edward has used his full applicable exclusion amount and that he is in the 35 percent estate and gift tax bracket.

If Edward wants to leave Carlye $1 million at his death, he must leave her $1,538,461. With a $1,538,461 inheritance, there would be $538,461 of federal estate tax ($1,538,461 multiplied by a tax rate of 35 percent equals a tax of $538,461, leaving Carlye her $1 million). On the other hand, if Edward gave Carlye $1 million while he was still alive, the tax on the gift would be 35 percent of the value of the gift, $350,000. The reduction in

Edward's estate by making a gift would be the $1 million he gave Carlye and the $350,000 tax on the gift. The cost of leaving Carlye $1 million at his death would be the $538,461 tax plus the $1 million bequest, a total of $1,538,461, as opposed to the $1,350,000 cost of the gift. The savings in tax would be $188,461. Now, assuming Edward made the lifetime gift, he would have that extra $188,461 in his estate at his death, generating a tax of $65,961 (35 percent of $188,461). So, comparing the two, the gift saved $122,500 in tax.

There are other considerations when deciding whether giving a lifetime gift is better than leaving property at death. One is the time value of money. Giving a lifetime gift means that the federal government gets its money before you die. The government has the use of the money; you do not. If you live for a number of years, it is possible that the money you would have earned on the money paid in taxes would eventually leave your beneficiaries better off economically. Generally, this is not the case, but it is a consideration worthy of calculation. Another concern is that property you give away does not receive a step-up in cost basis, which it does get when you die. This is discussed at length in Chapter 15, "Step-Up in Basis at Death."

If you have a taxable estate and you want to give the maximum amount of property to your children or others, always consider making a lifetime gift. Consult with your tax advisors to see if you can benefit materially with a lifetime gift rather than leaving property at your death. You may be surprised at the results. In Chapter 30, "The Irrevocable Life Insurance Trust," we will show you how to leverage the $5 million applicable exclusion amount to leave large sums of money to your heirs.

Many estate planning techniques involve the use of a gift program that takes current advantage of the applicable exclusion amount. With proper professional advice, you might want to consider beginning a gift program.

11

The Gift Tax

The Manner of Giving Is Worth More Than the Gift

Like the federal estate tax, the federal gift tax is not a tax on property. It is a tax on the privilege of transferring property. How the transfer is made determines whether a gift has been made.

Definition of a Gift

A *gift* is defined as any transfer of property for which the giver receives less than the full property value in return. To the extent the transfer is for less than full value, a gift has been made. Intent or desire to make a gift is generally irrelevant for federal gift tax purposes. The mere act of delivering the property to its recipient is enough to create a gift subject to the federal gift tax laws. Professional estate planners call the person who makes a gift a *donor* and the person who receives the gift a *donee*.

It is apparent from the definition of a gift that an inadvertent gift can easily be made. For example, payment of someone else's expenses or debts is a gift, unless there is a legal obligation to do so. Forgiving a debt, putting property into joint tenancy, or purchasing something for the benefit of another can all be construed as a gift.

Back to the Unified System

In Chapter 10, "The Unified System," we explained the unified system of federal estate and gift taxation. If you make a taxable gift, the amount of the gift is offset against the $5 million (in 2011 and originally in 2012) applicable exclusion amount. The applicable exclusion amount was indexed for inflation beginning in 2012, and the 2012 applicable exclusion amount is $5,120,000. Unless you make cumulative gifts in excess of the applicable exclusion amount, whatever that is at the time you make the gift, there is no federal gift tax liability for making the taxable gift. There are some gifts that are exempt from gift taxation. These gifts are special exceptions to the general rule that all gifts are subject to federal gift tax.

Annual Exclusion

The Internal Revenue Code has, for many years, allowed a certain amount, called the *annual exclusion,* to be free of federal gift tax; that is, a giver can give certain gift amounts each year to as many individual recipients as the giver wants, all free of federal gift tax. Any amount given to a recipient in excess of the annual exclusion is subject to taxation.

Initially, the annual exclusion was $3,000 per recipient. In 1982, the annual exclusion was significantly increased, to $10,000 per recipient per year. Beginning in 1999, the annual exclusion amount was adjusted for inflation. When the cumulative inflation reaches $1,000, the annual exclusion will be bumped up by $1,000. For example, if inflation is low for several years and when applied to the current annual exclusion does not add up to $1,000, then no adjustment would be made. However, when the cumulative amount of inflation is $1,000 or more, then an adjustment will be made. The U.S. government announces the inflation adjustment, if any, each year. For 2012 the annual exclusion amount is $13,000.

The annual exclusion is eligible for gift splitting. *Gift splitting* is a method by which spouses can combine their annual exclusions and make a joint gift. For example, a mother with three children could give $39,000 with no federal gift tax to her children: $13,000 per child under the 2012 amount. However, if she decides to give an additional $39,000 to the children in the same year (a total of $26,000 per child) and her husband consents, then their combined annual exclusions can be used. Under the 2012, $13,000 annual exclusion, they have a total of $78,000 in annual exclusion amounts available for their children. Thus, all $78,000 is free of federal gift tax because of the annual exclusion and gift splitting. The gift-splitting maximum amount is subject to the same inflation adjustment as is the annual exclusion.

It is important to remember two things about gift splitting. The first is that each spouse must consent to the gift, which is done by filing a federal gift tax return. The second is that if a spouse consents to gift splitting, each spouse will use up part or all of his or her annual exclusion as to the recipient for whom the consent was given. Thus, if an $18,000 joint gift is made to one child in 2012, each spouse uses $9,000 of his or her annual exclusion for that child. Each spouse can only give an additional $4,000 to that child in that year and have it qualify for the annual exclusion.

The annual exclusion only applies to a gift of a present interest. The annual exclusion does not apply to a gift of a future interest. A *gift of a future interest* is defined as a gift of property that does not give the recipient immediate use and benefit of that property. An example of a gift of a future interest is a gift to a trust in which the trustee is not required to immediately distribute the property to a beneficiary. Two exceptions to this trust rule are a 2503(c) minor's trust, discussed in Chapter 16, "Trusts"; and a gift of an insurance policy or money to pay its premiums to an irrevocable life insurance trust, discussed in Chapter 30, "The Irrevocable Life Insurance Trust."

All gifts between spouses, when the spouse who receives the gift is a U.S. citizen, are free of federal gift tax. If the spouse who receives the gift is a noncitizen, the gifts are subject to an annual exclusion of up to $100,000, which has been adjusted each year for inflation. In 2012 the annual exclusion amount for gifts to a noncitizen spouse is $139,000.

Educational and Medical Gifts

Some medical and educational expenses that are paid for by another person are not subject to federal gift tax. Payments of tuition to qualifying domestic and foreign educational institutions are not taxable gifts. These gifts must be for tuition; no other educational costs are exempt. The tuition payments must be made directly to the institution. If they are made to the student, who then pays the tuition, then the amount paid to the student is a gift. The IRS defines what educational institutions this exclusion applies to, so be sure to check with your tax advisor before you pay tuition.

Medical expenses of all kinds that are paid on behalf of another individual are not taxable gifts. As long as medical expenses for the diagnosis, cure, mitigation, treatment, or prevention of disease are paid directly to the person or institution that provided the care, there is no taxable gift, no matter the amount. Even payments for medical insurance qualify for this exemption. Once again, make sure you make the payments directly to the provider, not the person who is getting treated. As with any type of gift, you should always speak with a tax expert prior to making these gifts just to make sure that you do not mistakenly make a taxable gift.

Step-Up in Basis
Considerations

Before you start making gifts, you should know that there are some potential drawbacks associated with them. To explain these drawbacks, we must review the rules of step-up in basis. All assets of a deceased person are valued at their fair market value upon the owner's death. The assets then receive a step-up in basis to fair market value. (Please note that there are exceptions to the step-up in basis rules for a person who died in 2010. We explain those in Chapter 15, "Step-Up in Basis at Death.") For example, if an individual purchased a painting for $1,000 (cost basis) and its fair market value at death was $10,000, the painting receives a new or stepped-up basis of $10,000. If the painting was sold by the estate for $11,000, only $1,000 would be subject to federal income tax.

A lifetime gift does not get a step-up in basis. Had that same individual given the painting to a spouse prior to death, the surviving spouse would receive the deceased spouse's cost basis of $1,000. If the surviving spouse sold the painting for $11,000, then $10,000 would be subject to federal income tax. Thus, assets that have a low cost basis are not the kinds of assets you should be giving, at least from a federal income tax perspective. As to gifts to a spouse, remember that all assets that go to a U.S. citizen surviving spouse at death pass free of federal estate tax and receive a step-up in basis.

Other Considerations Before
You Make a Gift

There are many other considerations that you should examine when making gifts. One major consideration involves the removal of highly appreciating assets from your estate. The trick is, of course, picking assets that will actually appreciate in value. However, if a highly appreciating asset is given to your spouse and you die first, the asset with all its appreciation will not be subject to federal estate tax on your death; the asset and its appreciated value will be subject to estate tax on your spouse's death. If you give highly appreciating property to someone other than your spouse, you will remove both the asset and *all* its future appreciation from your estate and your spouse's estate. If you give highly appreciating property to someone other than your spouse, you may pay federal gift tax on its value, as of the date of the gift, but neither you nor your spouse nor your respective estates will ever pay federal gift or estate tax on the appreciation of the property.

Another consideration in making lifetime gifts involves reducing federal income tax. If you own property that generates taxable income, you may wish to give the property to one or more family members who are or will be in lower federal income tax brackets. The current income tax rates have made this reason for making gifts less attractive, however. Because tax brackets are lower, reducing income tax has become less important.

If you have a child who is under the age of 18 and for 2012 has more than $1,900 in taxable income in a year, his or her income could be taxed in the same income tax bracket as you are. This could also be true if you are supporting a full-time student who is under 24 years of age. Check with your tax advisor before attempting to use gifts to shift income to family members.

Connecticut and Tennessee have their own gift tax laws. Each of these state's gift tax laws are unique, and a discussion of these laws is outside the scope of this book. When making gifts, be sure to consider whether your state has a gift tax.

How you give something away may be as important as *what* you give away. The making of gifts can be critical to the estate planning process, and like all other major estate planning tools, should be discussed with your professional estate planning team.

Gifts for tax purposes can be summarized as follows:

- Can be made inadvertently.
- May not be taxable because of the annual exclusion or other exceptions.
- Can be split with a spouse.
- Are tax-free when made to a U.S. citizen spouse, but are limited for a noncitizen spouse.
- Do *not* qualify for step-up in basis.

12

The Marital Deduction

Federal Recognition of a Spouse's Efforts

The marital deduction is a tax concept that describes a tax-savings benefit given to spouses for purposes of federal gift and estate taxes. It is also used by many states for purposes of their death and gift tax laws. An understanding of the marital deduction is critical when planning for a spouse.

The federal estate and gift tax marital deduction is a direct result of community property ownership, which is discussed in Chapter 13, "Community Property."

The federal government had to recognize the right of each of the community property states to create its own unusual form of ownership between spouses, because of the Tenth Amendment to the U.S. Constitution. As a result, the federal government structured its estate and gift tax laws so they would apply fairly both to citizens of the "normal" states and citizens of the maverick, or community, states.

Because each spouse in the community property states owned half of the marital assets, the federal government could only tax half of the marital property on the death of either partner. This created an inadvertent marital deduction in community property states. In order to maintain fairness, Congress was eventually persuaded in 1948 to create the marital deduction for spouses who did not reside in community property states. Allowing spouses to leave half of their property tax-free to their surviving spouses appeared to equalize the federal estate tax treatment of marital property in all the states.

Citizens of community property states did not get the federal estate tax marital deduction except with respect to separate property; they did not need it because community property laws already gave them the same benefit. This was true of the federal gift tax marital deduction as well, except for separate property.

The federal government also gave citizens of the other 41 states at the time the right to exclude from federal gift tax the value of one-half the gifts made between spouses. This was also fair, because property acquired by community partners was acquired 50 percent by each of them without a gift tax.

Marital Deduction and Federal Gift Tax

Since 1948 there have been several different types of marital deduction laws. Prior to 1982 the Internal Revenue Code restricted the amount of tax-free gifts one spouse could give to the other. In that year, Congress passed what is now known as the *100 percent marital deduction*. Any gift, regardless of its value, made to a U.S. citizen spouse is tax-free for federal gift tax purposes.

The unlimited marital deduction provisions of the federal gift tax law apply to married taxpayers living in all states, including the community property states (Alaska, Arizona, California, Idaho, Louisiana, Nevada, New Mexico, Texas, Washington, and Wisconsin).

Gifts from a citizen spouse to a noncitizen spouse are treated differently. If the spouse who receives the gift is a noncitizen, the gifts are subject to an annual exclusion of up to $100,000, which has been adjusted each year for inflation. In 2012 the annual exclusion amount is $139,000. Annual gifts to a noncitizen spouse that exceed the annual exclusion amount for the year are considered taxable gifts, which require the filing of a federal gift tax return. Taxable gifts result in the reduction in the donor spouse's lifetime applicable exemption amount. If the taxable gift exceeds the lifetime applicable exemption amount, it will result in immediate gift taxation. You need to work closely with your advisors when considering transfers to a noncitizen spouse.

Marital Deduction and Federal Estate Tax

Just like the federal gift tax, since 1982 there has been a 100 percent federal estate tax marital deduction when the surviving spouse is a U.S. citizen. Prior to 1982 only part of the amount a deceased spouse left to the surviving spouse was not subject to federal estate tax, as Congress continued to deal with how to equalize treatment between community and noncommunity property states.

In order to qualify for the unlimited federal estate tax marital deduction, the following minimum rules must be met:

- The surviving spouse must be a citizen of the United States.
- The property interest must be included in the value of the deceased spouse's estate.
- The surviving spouse must receive, at least annually, all the income from the marital deduction property for life.
- The surviving spouse must have the right to require that the property be invested in income-producing assets.
- No person can have the power to give any part of the marital deduction property to anyone other than the surviving spouse.

The last three requirements are called *qualified income interests.*

In order to qualify for the marital deduction, a surviving spouse only needs to receive a qualified income interest from that property. If income is not given for the surviving spouse's life, it is not a qualified income interest and *no* marital deduction will be allowed.

Estate planning professionals describe this marital deduction requirement as "qualified terminable interest property." Most of the professional literature on the subject has nicknamed a trust used to provide the surviving spouse with income as a QTIP trust: qualified terminable interest property trust. Although the term QTIP has become a popular acronym for lawyers and other professionals, we find that using it confuses our clients. We prefer to refer to a QTIP as a spouse's trust or marital trust instead. In Chapter 25, "Planning for a Spouse," we discuss the planning opportunities available under the unlimited marital deduction.

A form of the unlimited marital deduction is available to a surviving noncitizen spouse when property is left in a qualified domestic trust, or, QDOT. However, most principal distributions during the surviving spouse's lifetime as well as the full amount remaining in the QDOT at death is taxed upon the spouse's subsequent death. (For more information on QDOT planning issues for noncitizen spouses see Chapter 25, "Planning for a Spouse.")

The marital deduction discussion can be summarized as follows:

- You can give or leave all or part of your property tax-free to your U.S. citizen spouse.
- Your U.S. citizen spouse must receive, at least annually, all the income from the marital deduction property for life.

- Your U.S. citizen spouse must have the right to require that the property be invested in income-producing assets, and no person can have the power to give any part of the marital deduction property to anyone other than the surviving spouse.

- Property passing to a QDOT for the benefit of a noncitizen spouse on the death of his or her citizen spouse qualifies for estate tax deferral, but is subject to federal estate tax on most distributions of principal to the surviving spouse and when he or she dies (absent other planning).

13
Community Property
Maverick Law in Maverick States

Forty of our states base their laws of property ownership entirely on our English common-law heritage. Eight states base their laws of property ownership as to property owned between a husband and wife on a heritage of French and Spanish law. These states have community property laws with respect to the ownership of property acquired during the term of a marriage. Each of these eight states has its own brand of community property laws; but all community property laws, regardless of a state's variations, must be differentiated from the law of the 40 noncommunity property law states.

Concerning the other two of the 50 states: Wisconsin was not a community property state initially but changed its laws to a form of ownership that for most purposes is community property. Alaska also was not an original community property state, but changed its laws to allow its residents and special trusts for nonresidents to treat property as if it were community property. We consider both of these states community property states.

Thus, the community property law states are:

Alaska
Arizona
California
Idaho
Louisiana
Nevada
New Mexico
Texas
Washington
Wisconsin

In reviewing this list, you can see the historical influence of the Spanish and French tradition. The French brought the Napoleonic Code to Louisiana, and the Spanish tradition was adopted by the other states.

Community property law manifests the social and legal belief that property acquired by spouses during the marriage should be construed as one total "community" of property. Regardless of how ownership is taken in that property, it belongs to a marital partnership. Each of the spouses, as a 50–50 partner, owns 50 percent of the partnership or community property.

To facilitate understanding of community property, we will call the marriage the "community partnership." The property that a husband and wife own before they enter into their community partnership is their separate property; it was acquired outside the community partnership and remains the separate property of each. This is also true of gifts or inheritances received by either spouse during the marriage. If that separate property is sold and the proceeds commingled with other community-partnership activities and investments, it generally becomes part of the community partnership's holdings.

Income generated from the community partnership's holdings is owned 50 percent by each of the community partnership's partners. From this perspective, community property should be understandable and, in fact, logical.

One of the great advantages of community property has to do with the step-up in basis rules, which are further explained in Chapter 15, "Step-Up in Basis at Death." When a person dies, his or her assets take on a new cost basis, which is their value at the date of death. This step-up in basis is important for income tax purposes, because whoever inherits the property also inherits the new cost basis. If the assets increased in value between the time they were purchased by the deceased person and the time he or she died, the person who inherits, when selling those assets, will have less gain and therefore less tax.

If a married couple in a noncommunity property state own property in tenancy by the entirety, joint tenancy with right of survivorship, or tenants in common, only one-half of the property receives a step-up in basis when one of them dies. If the surviving spouse sells property that was held jointly with the deceased spouse, there is a full gain on the half that is considered to be owned by the surviving spouse.

This rule does not apply to community property. When one spouse dies, 100 percent of the community property receives a step-up in basis. This single characteristic of community property makes it very attractive.

For purposes of community property laws, how property is titled is irrelevant. All property acquired during the term of a marriage is property that belongs to the community partnership, and each partner has a 50 percent ownership in that property, because the spouses are 50–50 partners.

In Alaska, title to property may be relevant. Alaska's laws allow residents and special trusts holding property of nonresidents to designate their property as community property. So, unlike the other nine "pure" community property states, Alaska requires affirmative actions in order for the community property rules to apply.

Alaska's community property trust law is unique in that it allows married couples who reside in other states to convert their property to community property. By doing so, these out-of-state couples can take advantage of the step-up in basis without moving to a community property state.

An Alaska community property trust requires an Alaskan trustee. This trustee can be a person who resides in Alaska, or trust companies and banks whose principal places of business are in Alaska. There are many different ways these trusts can be drafted. They are highly technical and should only be done by experienced estate planning attorneys. For those married couples who have low cost basis assets, it is well worth the trouble. The income tax savings can be huge.

Understanding community property is important because:

- Special planning is required for community property.
- Step-up in basis rules affect community property.
- There are opportunities for those married couples who reside in non-community property states to receive the benefits of community property using an Alaska community property trust.

14

State Death Taxes

States Need Revenue Too

The current state of state death taxes is in flux. Prior to 2005 the federal government's estate tax tables allowed as a credit against federal estate tax certain dollar amounts that were paid to the individual states instead of to the federal government. In essence, the federal estate tax system provided for a little bit of revenue sharing with those states.

In 2005 the federal government phased out the credit for state death taxes paid and replaced the credit with a deduction. Beginning in 2013 this deduction is scheduled to revert back to a credit, as it was prior to 2005, unless Congress enacts new legislation before then. Prior to 2005 more than half of the states tied their death tax system to the federal credit amount. When the credit went away in 2005, so did the state death tax revenue to all of those states. Since 2005 some of these states enacted laws to collect state death taxes, but many have not and are waiting for the credit to return in 2013.

Before 2005, all states' death tax laws fell into one of three general patterns: states that collect their taxes directly from the federal government (gap tax states); states that tax the estates of their citizens much like the federal government does (estate tax states); and states that base their death taxes on the value of the property that passes to certain defined beneficiaries (inheritance tax states). After 2005 a number of states that were in the gap tax category enacted legislation creating a fourth category, often referred to as "a pickup tax state."

To help your general understanding of the current state of the state death taxes, we provide a classification of the states in terms of the four categories.

Gap Tax States

Historically, a number of states structured their death tax rates so the tax they collected was exactly the same amount the federal government forgave in the federal estate tax tables through the federal revenue sharing program. States that structured their death tax laws so they receive funds only from the federal estate tax revenue sharing program are referred to as gap tax states by estate planning professionals.

In reality, the gap tax states only received death tax revenues that would have gone to the federal government. A portion of the federal estate tax is paid to the gap tax state, instead of all the tax being paid to the federal government, allowing the states to collect the tax painlessly (for them).

Before 2005 the gap tax approach was used by more states than any other method for collecting state death tax. Today there are a number of states that still take the gap tax approach. In those states that still have a gap tax, there are no death tax revenues from 2005 through 2012. Beginning in 2013 these states will once again receive death tax revenues, if the federal state tax credit returns as scheduled.

The gap tax states are:

Alabama	Missouri
Alaska	Montana
Arizona	Nevada
Arkansas	New Hampshire
California	New Mexico
Colorado	North Dakota
Florida	Oklahoma
Georgia	South Carolina
Idaho	Texas
Illinois	Utah
Kansas	Virginia
Louisiana	West Virginia
Maine	Wisconsin
Michigan	Wyoming
Mississippi	

The federal estate tax tables spell out what the tax will be, bracket by bracket, for different-sized estates. Prior to 2005 and beginning again in 2013 under existing law, these same tables provide that a small percentage of the federal estate tax will be forgiven if that amount is paid to the state in which the deceased citizen resided, pursuant to that state's death tax laws.

Pickup Tax States

Following repeal of the federal state tax credit in 2005, a number of gap tax states enacted legislation that converted their state to a pickup tax state. This legislation specifies an estate size threshold and imposes a state death tax on those estates greater than the threshold amount.

The tax rate is taken directly from the federal state tax credit amounts that applied before the state tax credit began to be phased out. The thresholds vary by state. For example, Minnesota imposes a state death tax equal to the former federal state death tax credit on estates in excess of $1 million. Illinois imposes a state death tax equal to the former federal state death tax credit on estates in excess of $2 million. Check with your estate planning attorney to determine the threshold amount in your state.

The pickup tax states are:

Delaware	Minnesota
District of Columbia	*New Jersey*
Hawaii	New York
Illinois	North Carolina
Maine	Oregon
Maryland	Rhode Island
Massachusetts	Vermont

(Note: Maryland and New Jersey are quasi-pickup states and inheritance tax states.)

Estate Tax States

Some states tax the estates of their deceased citizens under death tax systems that are structured very much like the federal estate tax. These states apply their own unique tax rates and have their own unique sets of rules as to how their rates will be applied.

Estate tax states will also get the benefit of the federal estate tax revenue sharing program in 2013 if it returns as scheduled. Unlike gap tax states, these states not only get revenues under the federal estate tax revenue sharing program (if available), but also collect substantial additional funds as a result of their death taxes. Their death tax rates are always higher than the amount from the federal estate tax revenue sharing program.

The estate tax states are: Connecticut, Ohio (scheduled for repeal on January 1, 2013), and Washington. Puerto Rico also has an estate tax.

Inheritance Tax Only States

States that fall into this category apply their death tax rates against the value of the shares that pass to certain defined classes of beneficiaries. Because the state death tax is calculated on the share that *each* beneficiary will receive or inherit, it is called an inheritance tax.

Inheritance tax states have different tax rates that apply to different kinds or classes of beneficiaries. Generally, however, the closer the beneficiary's blood relationship is to the deceased, the lower the inheritance tax rate will be; spouses almost always pay inheritance taxes at the lowest tax rates. An example of an inheritance tax table is shown in Table 14-1.

The inheritance tax table illustrates how most state inheritance taxes are structured. Your review of this example should highlight the fact that the more distant a relative is to the deceased, the lower the exemption and the higher the tax will be.

Inheritance tax states will also receive funds from the federal estate tax revenue sharing program if it is reinstituted in 2013. Many inheritance tax states provide that if the amount of the inheritance tax due is less than the federal estate tax revenue sharing amount allowed, then the inheritance tax due will be a minimum of the federal estate tax revenue sharing amount. This assures that they will receive the largest amount of federal funds available.

The inheritance tax states are:

Indiana

Iowa

Kentucky

Nebraska (imposed at county level)

Pennsylvania

Tennessee

A few states also have their own gift taxes. Like state death tax laws, gift tax laws are unique in each state. Connecticut and Tennessee have some form of gift tax.

State death and gift tax laws change from time to time, so the lists of states in this chapter may not reflect the current law in your state. A detailed discussion of individual state death and gift tax laws is outside the scope of this book. Your state's gift and death tax laws should be discussed with your professional estate planning team. The impact of your state's death and gift tax laws is important to consider when you are planning your estate.

Table 14-1

State Inheritance Tax

	Exemption ($)	Share in Excess of Exemption ($)	Tax ($)	Rate on Next Bracket (%)
		CLASS 1 BENEFICIARIES		
a. Widow or minor child	10,000 each	0	0	2
		25,000	500	4
		50,000	1,500	6
b. Husband or adult child, grandchildren	4,000 each	100,000	4,500	8
		200,000	12,500	10
		500,000	42,500	15
		CLASS 2 BENEFICIARIES		
Sisters, brothers, nieces, nephews	1,000 each	0	0	4
		25,000	1,000	6
		50,000	2,500	8
		100,000	6,500	12
		200,000	18,500	16
		500,000	68,500	20
		CLASS 3 BENEFICIARIES		
Uncles, aunts, and their descendants	500 each	0	0	6
		25,000	1,500	9
		50,000	3,750	12
		100,000	9,750	15
		200,000	24,750	20
		500,000	84,750	25
		CLASS 4 BENEFICIARIES		
All others	0	0	0	8
		25,000	2,000	14
		50,000	5,500	20
		100,000	15,500	30

15

Step-Up in Basis at Death

It Almost Pays to Die

Basis is a word developed for federal income tax purposes. Basis—or *cost basis*, as it is sometimes known—is the amount that is generally used to compute the taxable gain for federal income tax purposes on the sale of property.

A simple example of this principle is the purchase of a family car. If you pay $5,000 for your car, $5,000 is your cost basis in the car. Upon a sale of the car for $6,000, the gain subject to federal income tax is $1,000 ($6,000 sales price less $5,000 cost basis).

For purposes of the federal estate tax, at death, or six months thereafter, the fair market value of all the assets owned by the deceased person is determined by the agent of the deceased person's estate. The fair market value of all the assets, less debts and expenses of the estate, is then subject to the federal estate tax. The end result of the federal estate tax is that all the appreciation in value of the assets in the estate can be taxed. Unlike the federal income tax, the cost basis is ignored.

Congress has generally recognized that there may be an inherent unfair federal income tax element of the federal estate tax. If all assets are subject to federal estate tax (everything tax), and after death the same assets are subject to federal income tax (sales price less cost basis), there is a great danger of double taxation. Appreciation (growth) of assets could be subject to the federal estate tax as well as the federal income tax. This inherent unfairness has been turned into a magnificent benefit for most estates.

Assets that are in the estate of a deceased person, whether the estate pays federal estate tax or not, take as their cost basis for federal income tax purposes the fair market value of those assets at date of death or six months after death, whichever valuation date is used. Sometimes the date of death fair market value of assets is less than the cost basis. In such a case there is a step-down in basis to the date of death fair market value. However, whenever there is a step-up in basis, it means that the appreciation of assets in an estate is *not* subject to federal income tax.

For example, if the family car is purchased for $5,000 (original cost basis) by the income-earner spouse, and at that spouse's death it has a fair market value of $6,000 (step-up in basis), the $1,000 in appreciation is not subject to federal income tax. If the estate sells the car for $6,000, there is *no* taxable gain.

The step-up in basis rules apply to *every asset in an estate*, and the rules apply whether or not any federal estate tax is paid. The step-up in basis rules, however, do not apply to lifetime gifts. A recipient of a gift has the same cost basis in the asset that the giver had. The federal gift tax is determined based on the fair market value of the asset given. Thus a gift tax may be paid on the lifetime gift, and when the recipient of the gift sells it, there may be federal income tax due. Double taxation is possible.

In 2010, when the federal estate tax was optional for one year, the step-up in basis rules were modified. In essence, if an estate elected not to be subject to the federal estate tax, there was a $1.3 million basis adjustment available; there was an additional $3 million basis adjustment for certain property passing to a surviving spouse. Unless you were a beneficiary of an estate of someone who died in 2010 and affirmatively opted out of the estate tax, this law will not affect you or your planning. The step-in basis rules continue to be alive and well. If you were a beneficiary of an estate of a person who died in 2010, it is likely you suffered through the choices that had to be made and are probably glad it's over!

When lifetime gifts are contemplated, not only is the federal gift tax effect important, but the federal income tax must also be considered. For example, if an elderly taxpayer owns property with a low cost basis, making lifetime gifts may not be wise. It may be better to have the individual retain the assets so their basis will be stepped up at death. On the other hand, if the elderly taxpayer has assets with a high cost basis, it may be good planning to use these assets for lifetime gifts.

Married residents of community property states have a distinct advantage over their noncommunity property counterparts when it comes to step-up in basis rules. If a community property spouse dies, *all* the community property may receive a step-up in basis, not just the interest of the deceased spouse.

There is a tax gimmick affecting step-up in basis that should be avoided because it will not work. A person with assets having a low basis could give those assets to someone who is going to die in the near future. The individual who is dying could make a will giving the property back to the original giver at death. The result was that the original giver would receive a step-up in basis on the giver's original property. This transaction will not work for any property given to the dying individual within one year of death when the property is left to the original giver.

Some types of property do not receive a step-up in basis. There is a concept in the Internal Revenue Code called Income in Respect of a Decedent (IRD). Basically, this rule states that if a person, prior to his or her death, had earned income but not paid income tax on it, that income remains subject to income taxation. The only question is, "Who is going to pay it?"

The most prominent example of IRD is an IRA or other qualified retirement plan. Because the property held in most IRAs and retirement plans have not been subject to income taxation, but were earned by the owner, whoever inherits those accounts will have to pay income tax on them. Depending on a lot of complex rules, the income tax could be payable upon the death of the owner or can be deferred for many years. When the tax will be due and who will pay it is largely a product of the beneficiary designation for the account or plan.

Other examples of IRD are:

- Uncollected payments on an installment note
- Deferred compensation benefits
- Bonuses earned but not yet paid
- Uncollected proceeds of a sale made before death
- Accrued but unpaid interest, dividends, and rent
- Unpaid fees and commissions

If you have an IRA, a qualified retirement plan, installment notes, or any other of the IRD assets, you should plan for them. *All* IRD assets are included in your estate for federal estate tax purposes. This means that your IRD assets could be subject to federal estate tax and income tax. The following short example should motivate you to plan.

Let's say you have $1 million in your IRA and your estate is large enough to be subject to the federal estate tax. Your IRA, at just a 35 percent estate tax bracket, will generate $350,000 in federal estate tax. Your beneficiary will be taxed on the income. Assuming a 30 percent federal and state income tax (a low-ball amount), your beneficiary will pay an additional $300,000 in income tax when $1 million is distributed out of the IRA to the beneficiary. That $1 million will be reduced to $350,000, which represents a 65 percent tax rate. Ouch! That is why planning for IRD is so important, especially if you believe that estate and income taxes are more likely to go up than down.

The step-up in basis rules under our federal estate tax system are of the utmost importance. Because of their far-reaching effects on estate planning, the step-up in basis rules should be discussed at great length with your professional estate planning team.

16
Trusts

The Estate Planner's Golf Clubs

A significant number of estate planning techniques are implemented in the form of a trust. Trusts can be designed to accomplish a host of planning alternatives. Most professionals use a panoply of trust documents in accomplishing the objectives of their clients. An estate planner uses trusts like a professional golfer uses clubs. In our experience, however, very few clients we initially meet understand what trusts do, what they involve, and how they are structured. The subject of trusts and how they are used is apparently seldom taught outside the professional domain.

Many people believe that trusts are on the government hit list, and this is understandable. They read in their daily papers or favorite magazines about antitrust lawsuits between government and big business. Before we explain what trusts are, how they work, and what they accomplish, let us make some sense out of this antitrust nonsense.

We start with John D. Rockefeller, Sr. Toward the end of the nineteenth century Mr. Rockefeller was engaged in the capitalist pursuit of controlling the petroleum marketplace. Regardless of your politics, he made a pretty good job of it. One of the problems he faced, however, was that different states had different laws, and these legal impediments threatened to curtail his interstate growth.

With the help of his chief legal mogul, Mr. Dodd, Mr. Rockefeller signed a document called the Standard Oil Trust. He transferred all his Standard Oil stock to his trust, and he then named trustees to run that trust. Using a bold common-law form of title holding, Mr. Rockefeller set the world of finance on its ears. Through the use of the Standard Oil Trust, he crossed state lines with impunity and an empire was established.

A monopoly resulted from the Standard Oil Trust because Mr. Rockefeller indeed controlled the petroleum marketplace. Government stepped in and passed antitrust laws. These laws were passed to curtail and regulate

Mr. Rockefeller's monopoly and other monopolies throughout the American marketplace.

These laws were antimonopoly laws, not really antitrust laws, but because Mr. Rockefeller's legal genius, Mr. Dodd, chose to use an old form of ownership to effectuate his client's industrial dominance, trust became synonymous with and a symbol of monopoly. The *World Book Encyclopedia* for years has defined trust as a "term used in economics to describe a large industrial monopoly." Even a popular twenty-first century source, Wikipedia, includes as a definition of trust "a business entity formed to create a monopoly or fix prices." Estate planners have inherited a public that, too often, equates a trust with its Rockefellerian usage.

In Appendix D we have included a short history of estate planning. It explains the ancient roots of trusts and why they survive today. This history will give you a perspective on how trusts have been adapted to our laws in the United States and other countries that are based on English common law.

In estate planning, trusts enable people to pass title to their property to others either during their lifetime or at death. When a person creates a trust and places property in a trust, the trust maker, in effect, makes a gift. Trusts enable their makers to make gifts to their beneficiaries and allow the trust maker to exercise significant control, on a prearranged basis, over the disposition of the trust property. In effect, trusts allow property to pass to others with strings attached.

All trusts have the following characteristics:

- A trust is created by a *trust maker*. Attorneys call the maker a *settlor, trustor, creator,* or *grantor.*

- The person responsible for following the maker's instructions is called the *trustee.*

- Trustees can be individuals or licensed institutions. The maker can also be his or her own trustee.

- Trusts can be created by more than one maker. Joint makers are called *joint makers* or *comakers.* Trusts can be operated by more than one trustee, called *cotrustees.*

- Trusts can be created for the benefit of the maker or for the benefit of other people. The people for whose benefit a trust is created are called *beneficiaries.*

- Trusts can accomplish just about any objective of the maker as long as it is not illegal or against public policy.

- Trusts cannot last forever unless the beneficiary is a legally recognized charity or unless state law allows them to last forever. Today more than half of the states allow properly drafted trusts to last at least 360 years, and a number of those states allow them to literally last forever.

- The beneficiaries who have the first rights to the trust property are called *primary beneficiaries*. If the primary beneficiaries die or become disqualified, and according to the instructions given to the trustee by the trust maker, then the property will go to other named beneficiaries called *contingent beneficiaries*.

- Trusts, to be effective, must be in writing. They must be signed by the maker, and if a living trust is used, it should be signed by the trustee, although the trustee's signature is not necessary to make a trust valid. If the trust document is not signed by a trustee, the trust is not void; it still exists.

- The law has always stated that "no trust shall fail for lack of a trustee." The local court having jurisdiction over trusts will name a trustee if one is not named in the trust document.

- The trust document is often referred to as an *indenture* or a *trust indenture* (historically, a deed to which two or more persons are parties).

- Trust beneficiaries do not have to sign the trust document or will containing a trust.

- Any number of separate trusts can be created in a single trust document; these are called *subtrusts*.

- When the maker puts property in a trust, the maker funds the trust.

- Trust makers can be primary or contingent beneficiaries of their own trusts.

There are several different kinds of trusts that accomplish a host of estate planning objectives (see Figure 16-1). All trusts can be categorized in one of two ways. A trust is either a *living trust* or a *death trust*. Living trusts are often referred to as *inter vivos* (Latin for living) trusts. Death trusts are called *testamentary* (from the Latin *testamentum*) trusts and are created in a person's will. They do not come into existence until the death of the will maker.

A living trust is always created during the lifetime of the trust maker. A living trust usually provides that the maker is to be his or her own primary beneficiary. Living trusts can also pass the trust property to the maker's beneficiaries on the maker's death. Because living trusts can pass property on the death of the maker, they are often referred to as *will substitutes*. We discuss the living trust in greater detail in Chapters 17 and 18.

A death, or testamentary, trust can only be created in a valid will. These trusts are never created to benefit the maker. Death trusts are created by a will maker, and although they are created or drafted during the will maker's life, they are not operative until the maker's death. Death trusts have no life until the death of the maker. A male will maker is called a *testator*. A female will maker is called a *testatrix*.

Because a will goes through the probate process, the trusts created in that will also go through the probate process. Testamentary trusts are involved in

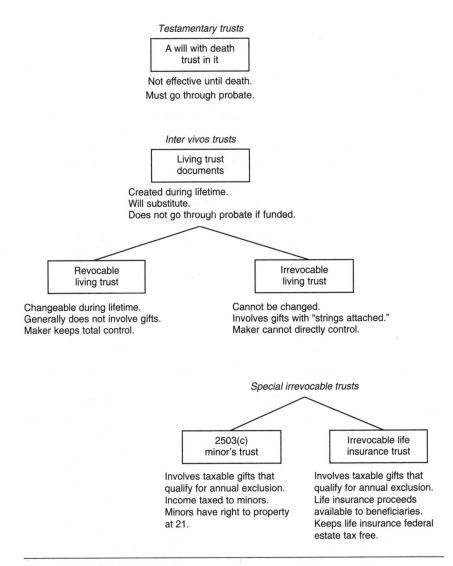

Testamentary trusts

> A will with death
> trust in it

Not effective until death.
Must go through probate.

Inter vivos trusts

> Living trust
> documents

Created during lifetime.
Will substitute.
Does not go through probate if funded.

| Revocable living trust | Irrevocable living trust |

Changeable during lifetime.   Cannot be changed.
Generally does not involve gifts.   Involves gifts with "strings attached."
Maker keeps total control.   Maker cannot directly control.

Special irrevocable trusts

| 2503(c) minor's trust | Irrevocable life insurance trust |

Involves taxable gifts that   Involves taxable gifts that
qualify for annual exclusion.   qualify for annual exclusion.
Income taxed to minors.   Life insurance proceeds
Minors have right to property   available to beneficiaries.
at 21.   Keeps life insurance federal
                                estate tax free.

Figure 16-1 Different kinds of trusts.

the probate process and are subject to the local probate court's direction and control (jurisdiction).

Both living trusts and death trusts are important tools to estate planning professionals. They allow professionals to accomplish their clients' estate planning objectives. You may recall from our discussion in Chapter 1,

"What Is Estate Planning?" that estate planning involves more than the outright passing of property from one person to another. People want to give what they have, to whom they want, in the way and at the time they want. They wish to reduce taxes, attorneys' fees, and court costs to the greatest extent possible. These objectives are almost always accomplished by using various trust formats. Remember that trusts are gifts with strings attached: instructions and conditions given to the trustee as to the who, how, and when of distribution of property.

Death trusts can always be canceled or changed by the maker, as long as the maker is competent, up until the maker's death.

Living trusts can be structured so the maker can retain the right to change or terminate the trust while alive. Living trusts that give the maker the right to change his or her mind are called *revocable* living trusts. Living trusts that cannot be changed are called *irrevocable* living trusts; trusts created under this format can be altered only by court action or by provisions in the trust that allow an independent trustee or other designated persons to make certain changes. The maker cannot alter these trusts.

When a trust maker creates a revocable living trust, a gift is not made. Because the maker has the right to change his or her mind about all the terms of the trust document, there can be no gift for federal or state gift tax purposes. If, however, property does pass to others while the maker is alive (even though the trust is revocable), there may be a gift for both federal and state gift tax purposes.

It is important to remember that whether a person gives property directly to others or gives property to others through a trust, a gift will always result. Whether that gift will be taxed depends upon the amount of the gift and the circumstances surrounding how the gift was made.

When a trust maker funds an irrevocable living trust, a gift will almost always result. By creating an irrevocable trust, a trust maker gives up all control to the trust property *and* to the terms of the trust. Once the irrevocable trust is signed, a maker cannot change his or her mind or alter the terms of the trust.

By creating an irrevocable living trust, a trust maker makes a gift with strings attached. That is usually why these trusts are used. Irrevocable living trusts allow a person to give the use of property to others on a living basis pursuant to the maker's wishes and instructions to the trustee as to its use. Without the use of such a vehicle, gifts could not be made with instructions that would guarantee and control their use. Without the use of an irrevocable trust, a gift made is a gift completed; the recipient can do anything with the property received.

Irrevocable trusts are used in many situations, including:

- To own life insurance policies on the life of the trust maker. These trusts are designed to keep the insurance proceeds federal estate tax-free on death and are discussed in Chapter 30, "The Irrevocable Life Insurance Trust."
- To hold title to property for two or more generations. These trusts are called *dynasty trusts* and in some states can last forever.
- To hold property for a period of time for the use of the trust maker, and then allow the beneficiaries to use the property.
- To hold title to property given to minors so the gift maker can exercise control over the property.

When a person wishes to make a gift to minors but wants to control the use of the property, a *minor's trust* can be created. A minor's trust is often called a 2503(c), or *accumulation,* trust. It is named after the Internal Revenue Code provision that gives the trust its existence.

When a minor's trust is created and property is given to the trustee to manage and distribute to the minor beneficiaries according to the written instructions of the trust maker, the trust must be irrevocable. The income from the trust will be taxed for income tax purposes to the minor beneficiaries. Under prior law, this was an advantage because parents could give their children income-producing property and control the property by putting it into a minor's trust. This income would be taxed in the children's lower income tax brackets.

Because shifting income to children was so effective in the past, it is more difficult currently to do it. Part of a child's investment income will be taxed at the parent's tax rate if the child's investment income was more than $1,900 in 2012 (this amount is indexed for inflation each year), and the child was under age 18 at the end of the tax year or was a full-time student under age 24 at the end of the tax year. These rules do not apply if the child's earned income exceeds one-half of the child's own support for the year. As you can see, it is difficult to shift income to minor children or children who are in school.

It should be noted that for these trusts to be effective, the trust maker should not be the trustee; the minor must have the right to the trust principal on attaining the age of 21; and the income from the trust cannot be used to discharge a support obligation the maker of the trust owes to the minor beneficiary.

Trusts created under section 2503(c) of the Internal Revenue Code are often used to pass property to children or grandchildren subject to controls provided by the maker in the trust document. A minor's trust should be drafted carefully by an estate planning professional.

Other trusts include special short-term trusts, called *grantor retained income trusts*. In Chapter 33, "Discounting the Value of Your Estate," we describe how these trusts are used to discount gifts while allowing the trust maker to retain income from the assets placed in these trusts. There are also trusts used to give personal residences and vacation homes to children or others. These *personal residence trusts*, discussed more fully in Chapter 38, "Personal Residence Trusts," are very effective in lowering the value of an estate and also allowing the giver to use the home.

There are many different kinds of trusts that professional estate planners use to accomplish the objectives of their clients. Estate-planning trusts are designed to allow people to pass title to their property to others either during lifetime or at death. In the chapters that follow, we demonstrate how some of these trusts can be utilized to meet most estate planning goals.

17

The Revocable Living Trust

The Foundation of Estate Planning

When this book was originally written in 1981, the living trust was a little known but highly controversial estate planning concept. Living trusts had been used for years by a small group of professionals who recognized the great value of trusts but were considered to be out of the mainstream because of their "avoid probate" theme. At that time, the probate process was almost a sacrosanct pillar of the estate planning bar.

Since then there has been a living trust revolution. As the public became more aware of the often unnecessary costs and time delays associated with wills and probate, many lawyers and other advisors began to realize that living trusts were in virtually every way superior to will-based planning.

We tried very hard to educate both the professions and the public about the benefits of living trusts. In 1988 we wrote *Loving Trust*, a book detailing the wonderful planning opportunities available in using living trusts for estate planning. In 1992 we wrote *The Living Trust Revolution*, which compared living trusts and will planning with probate in detail. It presented an overwhelming factual case for living trust planning and sounded the death knell for many of those practitioners who still clung to wills as superior planning vehicles. Finally, in 1996, we wrote *The Living Trust Workbook*. It is an owner's manual for living trusts that allows individuals and families to work closely with their attorneys, accountants, and financial planners to design, create, and implement proper living trust planning.

Today, living trusts are not the "new kids on the block." They have replaced wills and probate planning as the foundation for all planning. While there are still some diehard professionals who cling to the will and probate notion, they have mostly fallen by the wayside. At one time these professionals called for wills in every situation. Now they admit that living trusts are certainly viable, but are not for everyone. This is another myth that will disappear over time.

Even Congress, through the Internal Revenue Code, recognizes living trusts as a tremendous force in estate planning. For years probate estates had certain after-death income tax advantages that trusts did not. Congress has changed the laws so that now probate estates and living trusts are offered identical after-death income tax benefits. While the income tax advantages of probate estates were not significant, especially after 1986, this recognition by Congress announced the death of will planning and probate as the planning of choice.

We have always, in our professional careers, strongly believed that estate planning professionals should use the revocable living trust as the main or foundation document to accomplish most of their clients' estate planning objectives. The revocable living trust is a most attractive estate planning device. It can be used instead of a will to accomplish the bulk of your estate planning goals. Revocable living trusts have been used successfully for centuries. In our opinion and that of virtually all our colleagues, they should be used by just about everybody.

Living trusts can be revocable or irrevocable (we discussed the difference in Chapter 16, "Trusts"); this chapter focuses on the revocable trust that you can create and change at your whim while alive.

Here's a preview of the benefits that can be derived from the use of this very attractive estate planning vehicle:

- Subsequent to your death, you can give what you own to whom you want, when you want, through the use of a revocable living trust. As the trust maker, you can spell out all the distribution terms and requirements as to how your property passes after your death.

- Your revocable living trust can provide one receptacle to receive and distribute all your assets on your death.

- A revocable living trust can control, coordinate, and distribute all your property interests while you are alive, if you become disabled, and on your death. By using a revocable living trust, you can better arrange for your well-being under your terms as you advance in years or become ill or mentally incompetent.

- The use of a revocable living trust assures that your plans and affairs will remain private, rather than made public, on your death or incapacity.

- Revocable living trusts are easy to create and maintain during your lifetime.

- It is not difficult for you to change or amend your revocable living trust during your lifetime.

- There are no adverse lifetime income tax consequences that result from the use of a revocable living trust.

- Property placed in a revocable living trust during your lifetime is not subject to and does not pass through the probate process on your death; it is probate-free.

- Continuity of cash flow and investments in your portfolio is not interrupted by your death.

- All opportunities of death tax planning available through will planning are equally available through the use of a revocable living trust.

- Revocable living trusts are legal in every state. Your trust can easily be moved with you as you cross state lines.

- By using a revocable living trust, you can measure your postdeath trustees' abilities to manage your assets while you are alive.

- Revocable living trusts are more difficult to attack, and usually less successfully, by disgruntled beneficiaries than are wills.

If you choose to use a revocable living trust, you can avail yourself of all the benefits we have highlighted above. A detailed discussion of each of these benefits follows.

Property Distribution after Your Death

On and after your death, all property in your trust and the income that property generates will be distributed by the trustee according to your precise written instructions. Anything that can be accomplished through the use of a trust created by a will (testamentary trust) can be accomplished identically through the use of a revocable living trust.

Property in a revocable living trust can be left to the beneficiaries outright on your death, or it can remain in trust and be distributed over a certain period of time to your beneficiaries. Several trusts can be created within a revocable living trust, which will become operative for designated beneficiaries on your death. In fact, there is no limit to the number of separate trusts that can be created in a single revocable living trust. Each trust created within the trust document can spell out its individual terms with regard to the amounts to be distributed and the timing under which those amounts are to pass to your beneficiaries. Each of the trusts created in the trust document may have different terms and conditions as to the distribution of income and principal to your selected beneficiaries.

If you are married, you and your spouse can create a joint revocable living trust. In this single trust for the two of you, you can make all the distributions that each of you want. By creating subtrusts, there are unlimited possibilities for making after-death distributions.

One Receptacle to Receive and Distribute All Property

Through the use of a revocable living trust, you can control the distribution of all your property. This is true not only for the property you put in your trust while alive, but also for other property that flows into your trust on your death. Proceeds from life insurance can be left to your trust if you name your trust as the beneficiary; the same is true with respect to proceeds from pension and profit sharing plans. For that matter, any proceeds from third-party beneficiary contracts can be left to your trust if you simply make the trust the beneficiary of those contracts.

Property not placed in the trust during your lifetime can still be put in the trust after your death through the use of a short, well-drafted will that attorneys call a *pour-over will.* The provisions of a pour-over will simply state that any property you neglected to put in your trust will, nevertheless, pass to your trust (pour over to it) after your death. The pour-over will should always be used in conjunction with a revocable living trust. We often refer to these special wills as *fail-safe wills*; their use assures that any forgotten property will ultimately be placed in the planning pot to be controlled pursuant to your master plan.

It is important to understand, however, that property owned jointly cannot be put into a trust on your death. We have discussed this in several other chapters, but we say it again: beware of owning jointly held property; you cannot control it on your death, and it may go to unintended heirs.

Take Care of Yourself Too

A revocable living trust can be designed to provide for your care during your lifetime. In your revocable living trust, you can spell out in as much detail as you like how you wish to be taken care of with *your own* trust property in case of your incapacity, which could result from senility, accident, or illness. You can specify who your trustees will be if you become incompetent. You can also provide for the care of your loved ones should you lose control of your mental faculties.

The ability to provide for your care as well as the care of your loved ones during your lifetime is, in our opinion, one of the greatest attributes of a revocable living trust. When a living trust is properly coordinated with a living will, health care powers, and other documents now approved by all states, you and your family can be protected from some of the huge problems associated with incapacity. In Chapter 4, "Disability," we discussed these very important documents and how failure to use them can result in tragedy.

A revocable living trust can avoid all the confusion and publicity occasioned by court proceedings that would otherwise come about upon your incapacity. Our point takes on even greater significance in light of the ability of modern medicine to keep people alive under almost unbelievable circumstances.

All 50 states and the District of Columbia allow the use of a durable special power of attorney. This document allows you to give the right to someone you trust to place your property in your revocable living trust if you are unable to do so. It is durable in that, unlike general powers of attorney, its legality continues even if you are incompetent. By using a durable power of attorney as an addition to your revocable living trust, you can assure yourself that your property will be placed in your trust and used pursuant to your directions for you and your loved ones' benefit without costly court interference and publicity.

Trusts Are Private

Unlike a will, revocable living trusts are private documents. They are not made public either while you are alive, at your death, or subsequent to your death. By using a revocable living trust, you can be assured that you will not be making your affairs and your family's affairs public. We have read too many books that have exposed the affairs of great people to public scrutiny. The authors of these books had at their fingertips the probate court's records concerning all the affairs of these people, because they elected to use wills rather than revocable living trusts.

Michael Jackson is a great example of how a celebrity's advisors can use a living trust to protect privacy. Upon his tragic death, there was tremendous press coverage. Everything Michael had done, his children, his other family members, his ex-wives, the circumstances of his death, were all under scrutiny. Michael did have a will, but it was a pour-over will. It simply stated that he left all his property in a living trust that held virtually all his property already. The living trust did not have to be filed with the probate court. There was no way the press or anyone else who was not authorized could look at the terms of the trust or what was in it. Family members and others let out bits and pieces of the trust's content, but in the end most of its terms were hidden from public view.

Some professionals take the position from time to time that living trusts are not private because third parties such as banks and financial brokerage firms ask to see the full trust. The reason they want to see the trust is to make sure that the correct trustees have the authority to act and that the trust is in effect. There is usually no reason for anyone to see the full trust, especially those private provisions as to how you leave your property.

The only parts of a trust that have to be disclosed are the provisions relating to who the trustees are, the powers given to the trustees under the trust document, and evidence that the trust is in existence. Generally, all of this information can be put into a special affidavit, which have different names in different states. In states that have adopted a version of the Uniform Trust Code, this affidavit is called a *Certification of Trust.* Your advisors will be familiar with this document. When properly prepared and then signed by the trustees, this affidavit or certification gives third parties enough information to know who the trustees are, who the trust maker is, and that the trust is valid. It can contain certain provisions of the trust that show the trustees have the powers to enter into certain transactions or perform certain functions.

This is another document that should not be done by you, even with the help of the Internet or software. Before you put one of these affidavits in effect, consult your attorney to find out what you need to let others see and what you do not.

Revocable living trusts, their provisions, and the property they control remain the exclusive business of the beneficiaries for whom they were created; other than the trustee, the trusts are nobody else's business.

Trusts Are Easy to Create and Maintain

Revocable living trusts are easy to create. In our opinion, you should always seek out an attorney who knows estate planning, then convey your wishes and set a time for a future meeting to review your trust.

We absolutely think it is a huge mistake to fill in preprinted forms sold in books, to buy will and trust software, or to rely on the many Internet sites that offer to help you through the preparation of a trust. We strongly believe that you should be knowledgeable but at the same time always seek the assistance of estate planning professionals.

Time and again we have seen the aftermath of using forms or software. The cost to fix a problem is far more expensive than to do the document correctly in the first place. If something goes wrong and it is the fault of the author who sold the book, the company that provided the software, or the Web site that touted its legal expertise, your family is going to have a hard time suing for damages. These Web sites are pretty good at disclaiming all liability, even as they happily take your money.

Living trusts are easy to create and maintain if you work with professionals who know what they are doing. Trusts are complex legal instruments that have a huge impact on you, your family, and your property. An attorney, who can be held responsible for not doing a proper job of drafting or following up on a living trust, will make the process easy because he or she has the expertise to do so. Relying on a questionnaire and over-the-Internet help is subjecting you and your loved ones to unnecessary risk.

Once the attorney completes your plan, sign it if it meets your objectives. Unlike a will, in most states the formalities of signing a trust are less burdensome, but this varies by state. For example, in Florida a living trust has to be witnessed and notarized. In other states it requires only the signature of the trust maker and the trustee. Your attorney will make sure that your trust is properly signed.

Once you have your trust, it needs to be funded. That too is not terribly difficult. It is discussed at length in Chapter 18, "Funding a Revocable Living Trust."

After creating your revocable living trust, you should check back with your attorney from time to time to make sure your trust has kept current with your objectives and with new legal developments. Keeping current is important.

It is a good idea to set a schedule with your attorney and other advisors to periodically review your living trust and your estate and financial planning. In our complex world, changes seem to occur more frequently than ever. By forming a team of trusted advisors and periodically meeting with them, you can exchange ideas and make changes so your planning will maintain its relevance.

Trusts Can Be Changed Without a Great Deal of Formality

In Chapters 6 and 7 we discussed that wills have to be signed and executed, with a great deal of legal formality, and that codicils (will amendments) have the same formal requirements. This is not the case with revocable living trusts. These trusts, except in some states, need only your signature to infuse life into them. Trust amendments, regardless of their scope, require the same signature rules as a trust. Witnesses are generally not required, nor is the signature of the trustee (each state's laws are different in this area). There can be no doubt that you must know what you are signing when signing your trust or an amendment to it. Most states' laws are very clear on this subject. The point is that signing a trust amendment does not require a great deal of time or effort, and it can be accomplished with few legal formalities.

Avoid Adverse Lifetime Income
Tax Consequences

There are no adverse income tax consequences associated with the use of a revocable living trust during your life. Because the trust is revocable, the income generated by the property that is in the name of the trust is taxed to you and reported on your personal income tax returns. A revocable living trust for which you are the trustee is not required to have a separate federal identification number or file a separate tax return. This is also the case if you are married, as long as either you or your spouse is a trustee. Thus, income generated by the property in the name of the revocable living trust requires little extra effort by its maker.

Trusts Are Probate-Free

Property in a revocable living trust will not go through the probate process. Probate is a process that passes title to assets. Because the title to your property is already in your trust and the trust does not die with you, there is no passing of title required; title has already passed during your life. The probate process is not applicable to trust property.

Total avoidance of probate is an enormous benefit to you and your beneficiaries. It represents significant savings in costs, time, and court interference with respect to your affairs.

Please understand that there are still some administrative expenses for most trusts upon the death of their maker. These fees are substantially less than the standard fees charged for probate and administration. Based on our many years in the practice and our interaction with over a thousand attorneys who were part of the National Network of Estate Planning Attorneys, we estimate that trust administration fees are about one-third those charged for probate and administration.

Continuity in the Handling
of Your Affairs

Because there is no probate associated with revocable living trust property, you can be assured that a smooth and uneventful transition will occur with respect to your affairs on your death. Your beneficiaries automatically begin to receive income and principal on your death, pursuant to the terms written in your trust document. This fluidity with regard to your affairs is of major importance because it reduces cost and does not create unnecessary change or crisis for your survivors.

Death Tax Planning Opportunities

A host of techniques are used to reduce federal estate taxes by professional estate planners. In the main, these techniques have traditionally been implemented by planners through the use of trusts created by the client's will (testamentary trusts). A significant percentage of estate planning professionals have used—and some continue to use—the will as the vehicle within which they plan to reduce federal estate taxes.

Remember, every technique of federal estate tax savings that can be implemented in a will can also be implemented in a revocable living trust.

Good in Every State

Every state's laws recognize the validity of a revocable living trust. A truly beneficial feature attributed to these estate planning instruments is that they can cross state lines with their makers without any need to redraft their terms to comply with local law.

You may change your domicile; many people do. People now move around the country with increasing regularity. These moves are usually associated with career opportunities or a better place to live after retirement. With each move the question is generally asked, "Do I have to redo my estate plan?" If a revocable living trust has been used, the answer is no. The state law under which that trust was prepared will still have legal validity. Most well-written revocable living trusts provide that the law with respect to the administration of the trust will be the law in whatever state the maker and trust reside.

Revocable living trusts can cross state lines much more easily than their will counterparts. This flexibility gives you the security and knowledge that you will not have to redo your estate plan every time you are transferred or move to another state. Anytime you do move to another state, however, you should have your estate plan reviewed by an estate planner in that state, because additional planning opportunities may be available to you with regard to your new state's law. This review will probably result in the preparation of a new pour-over will, durable power of attorney, and health care documents, all of which are generally state specific. Remember, each state has its own system with respect to death taxes.

Measuring Trustees during Life

Most trust makers elect to be their own trustees during their lives. Many of our clients elect to be their own trustees and name their spouses or close family members or friends as cotrustees. The advantage of the cotrusteeship is that on the incapacity or death of the trust maker, the cotrustee can continue the operation of the trust without the need to seek court assistance.

You may elect, however, to name the persons or professional institutions who will be handling your trust after your death on a current, or living, basis. If you decide to name your death trustees on a current basis, you will be able to observe their performance and abilities as they manage the trust property for your benefit. By using a revocable living trust, you can measure the performance of your after-death trustees while you are alive.

Difficult for Disgruntled Heirs to Attack

Most of you are aware of the horror stories associated with unhappy heirs attacking the will of a maker who did not leave those unhappy folks what they thought they had coming. Attacking a will is called a *will contest* by attorneys. Will contests occur too frequently. Wills are usually contested by family members who were cut out or who received less than their antici- pated share of the maker's property.

Revocable living trusts are much more difficult for disgruntled heirs to attack than their will counterparts. Revocable living trusts are private docu- ments that are not involved in the probate process. They are not placed in a public forum that encourages debate and advocacy, like their will counter- parts. They generally are not subject to all the legal formalities associated with wills. Because there are fewer legal rules with regard to their creation, there are fewer legal opportunities to invalidate them. Our experience has driven this point home most convincingly. Our firm has prepared several thousand revocable living trusts over the years, and to the best of our knowledge, not one has ever been attacked, much less attacked successfully.

Criticisms of Revocable Living Trusts

The revocable living trust has so many attractive features unique to it that we cannot understand why it is not used universally as a will substitute by more professionals. Some professionals are suspicious of it because they do not understand it. Others are critical of it and allege the following negatives with regard to its use:

- It is difficult to establish and maintain.

- It is expensive.

- It is less effective in limiting creditors' claims after death.

Revocable living trusts are not difficult to establish. A professional estate planner can create them, at times, more easily than their will counterparts.

In our experience, they are not difficult to maintain. It is true that if you do create a revocable living trust, you will have to take time to organize your affairs and keep them organized within your trust's parameters. We believe that this is a positive feature that should encourage their use. Remember, what you do not do while alive, the probate court and your beneficiaries must do after you are gone. Reread Chapter 8, "Probate," if you doubt our conclusion.

It is true that revocable living trusts can cost more to create than their will counterparts. The increase in cost is due to an increase in work required of the planning professionals. But consider this: When an attorney draws a will, that's only a small part of the total estate planning job. The attorney will finish that job when the will is taken through the probate process.

In contrast, the attorney who utilizes a revocable living trust as an estate planning vehicle charges one fee. That fee may be for both drafting the document and funding the document so there will be no probate process. Some attorneys charge separately for funding and some work with other advisors who assume the responsibility of funding the trust.

Common sense and our experience would indicate a huge difference in cost between wills and fully funded revocable living trusts. Generally, the fee for a will coupled with the cost of probate is enormous when compared to the cost of preparing and funding a revocable living trust.

Some attorneys believe that a revocable living trust is not as effective as a will in cutting off the claims of creditors against the assets of a deceased trust maker. In some states, however, a revocable living trust is actually a better device than a will for limiting creditors' claims after a trust maker's death. In the states in which a will has an advantage in limiting creditors' claims, a living trust can be used in conjunction with a will to effectively and promptly settle the claims of creditors.

It is our belief that a revocable living trust should be used as a will substitute whenever *any* of its benefits are desired; the size of one's estate should not dictate its use.

The advantages of a revocable living trust can be summarized as follows:

- Distribute property after your death.
- Create one receptacle for all your property.
- Take care of you.
- Offer privacy.
- Are easy to create and maintain.
- Are easily changed.
- Have no adverse lifetime or after-death income tax consequences.

- Are probate-free.
- Provide continuity in your affairs.
- Provide planning for death tax.
- Are good in every state.
- Can measure trustees during your life.
- Are difficult to attack.

18

Funding a Revocable Living Trust

Placing All Your Eggs in One Basket

A revocable living trust can be unfunded, partially funded, or totally funded during the lifetime of its maker; it can also be funded on its maker's death. When estate planning professionals refer to *funding*, they mean property that has actually been placed in a living trust or, more accurately, in the name of the trustees of the trust.

The advantages that result from funding a revocable living trust during the lifetime of the maker are profound:

- Property in a revocable living trust does not go through the probate process on the death of the trust maker.

- Property in a revocable living trust can be used to care for the trust maker and loved ones in the event of the trust maker's incapacity, without the intervention and control of a court.

To understand the funded revocable living trust, it is important to contrast it with its unfunded counterpart.

Unfunded Revocable Living Trust

A living trust that has no assets in it is called an *unfunded revocable living trust*. Sometimes an unfunded revocable living trust is referred to as an *unfunded life insurance trust*. It gets this nickname because there is no property placed in the trust when it is created except the *right* of the trust to receive the death proceeds of life insurance on the life of the trust maker. The trust is funded with only the expectancy of receiving those insurance proceeds. This expectancy legally funds the revocable living trust in many states even though, in reality, nothing is in the trust at all.

In those states that require something more than a mere expectancy to establish the trust, professionals generally instruct their clients to place a nominal amount of cash in the trust, such as $10.

Either technique or both techniques used together still result in an unfunded living trust. Why is either of these techniques required? Because in some states a trust must have some type of property in it to be valid. Both of these techniques can do the job. A number of states do not require either of these techniques in order for an unfunded revocable living trust to be valid under state law. In those states, the mere creation of the trust establishes its legal validity.

Advocates of the unfunded revocable living trust make the following points in defense of its use:

- The trust can receive all life insurance proceeds as well as all other third-party beneficiary contract property. These include pension and profit sharing proceeds paid on the death of the maker.

- The revocable living trust can be funded at a later time, even if the maker is incapacitated, if the trust maker gives a durable special power of attorney to others. Durable special powers of attorney are discussed later in this chapter.

- Because relatively few deaths result from accidental causes, most trust makers can generally predict or have notice of their impending demise, and as a result, trust makers can fund their trusts at that time.

- A pour-over will can transfer property into the trust after the death of the trust maker.

There can be no doubt that an unfunded revocable living trust is far better than its will counterpart; however, when contrasted with its funded counterpart, it leaves much to be desired.

There are several problems usually associated with unfunded living trusts. If the trust maker dies accidentally or unexpectedly, his or her property will have to go through the probate process before it can ultimately end up in the trust. Thus, a pour-over will guarantees probate on the assets it passes to the unfunded trust. Because most people set up a revocable living trust to avoid probate, not funding the trust defeats one of its primary purposes.

In our experience, if a trust is not funded from the outset, it does not get funded properly later. If funding is accomplished from the outset, the maker is much more likely to continue funding the trust as new assets are acquired. This new habit assures that a great many of a maker's assets will be in the trust upon disability or death.

A problem that we see much more of is the sale of revocable living trusts at a low cost by living trust companies rather than skilled attorneys. Not only are the trusts themselves woefully inadequate, but they are not funded. Thus, a maker ends up with an inferior document that does not avoid probate. However, these trusts are sold as if they were fully funded. The maker and his or her family are misled and probate is not avoided. Consumers should avoid these types of fraudulent schemes.

Funded Revocable Living Trusts

A *funded revocable living trust,* as its name implies, has within it property owned by the maker. You may be wondering, "How can the trust have the property when the trust maker still owns it?" The answer is that the property is titled in the trust's name, but the maker owns the right to use, possess, and enjoy the property. The maker owns the trust and is its beneficiary, and therefore owns the property.

Another way to explain this legal phenomenon is to say that the trust maker owns equitable title and the trust owns bare legal title. Equitable title is greater than legal title. Regardless of the explanation used, a revocable living trust that is properly funded leaves the ownership and control of the trust property in the hands of its maker.

Funded revocable living trusts have these advantages:

- All property in the trust totally avoids the probate process on the death of its maker.

- The trust maker has full access to the property in his or her living trust.

- The trust assets are instantly available to the maker's beneficiaries pursuant to written instructions.

- Should the maker become incapacitated or be adjudicated mentally incompetent, the trust property can be used to care for the trust maker and loved ones without the delays, expenses, and publicity associated with court proceedings.

- Funded revocable living trusts take the guesswork out of probate avoidance. By funding a revocable living trust, the maker can be assured that trust assets are put to their highest and best use.

Estate planning professionals use different techniques to fund revocable living trusts, but generally there are two major approaches:

1. Retitling the trust maker's property in the name of the trust, for example, "Karen Smith as Trustee of the Karen Smith Trust."

2. Retitling the trust maker's property in the name of an entity, called a *nominee partnership*, which is a holding device for the trust.

Titling Property Directly in the Trust

In order to place property directly in the name of a trust, the property must be retitled in the name of the trustees of that trust, such as noted above: "Karen Smith as Trustee of the Karen Smith Trust." This form of trust funding certainly appears simple and, to most people, is very understandable. It does, however, create some problems.

1. If real estate is transferred directly into the name of the trust, the entire trust agreement may have to be recorded in some states. This recording requirement can abrogate the privacy feature of the trust. There are several alternatives available that avoid the necessity to record the full trust document.

2. Publicly traded stocks and bonds that are titled directly in the name of a trust sometimes present logistical problems. When the stock or bond is sold, the transfer agent may require a complete and certified copy of the trust. The privacy feature of the trust can then be lost. Generally, only certain provisions of the trust will have to be disclosed, none of which deal with how the trust assets are ultimately to be disposed of.

3. Safe-deposit boxes taken directly in the name of the trust have the same problem; a complete, certified copy of the trust may have to be kept on file in the institution where the box is located. This obstacle usually can be overcome by giving successor trustees signature authority on the box.

4. Titling property directly in the name of a trust can present some problems when the trust maker attempts to dispose of trust property. It is easy to put property directly in the name of a trust, but may be somewhat more difficult to get that property out of the trust. Some of the people with whom the trustees deal with regard to the trust property will want to assure themselves that the trustees do indeed have the right to dispose of the property.

5. People who deal with trustees may get sweaty palms because without a complete review of the trust document, they can never be sure the trustee

has the power to properly pass title to the trust property. Most trusts are written in legal jargon, and that means the wary buyer or transfer agent may want to seek the services of an attorney prior to completing any transaction involving trust property.

A common technique to reduce or eliminate problems associated with titling property directly in the trust is called an *Affidavit of Trust* or a *Trust Certification.* This is a short document signed by the trustees, sometimes signed by the attorney who prepared the trust, stating that the trust is in existence and the trustees have the power to transact business on behalf of the trust. Certain provisions of the trust document may be attached to the affidavit or certification, including who the trustees are, their powers, and the signature pages of the trust itself. Many banks and other financial institutions have their own short forms for trusts, and if they are signed by the trustees, there is no problem transacting business by the trust.

Over the years, revocable living trusts have been criticized because of the expense and time it takes to fund them. While this may have been partially true at one time, it is certainly not true now. For the most part, revocable living trusts have been accepted as the estate planning vehicle of choice by a majority of attorneys and other estate planning experts. Banks, stock brokerages, and other financial institutions are set up to expedite transfers into living trusts. Rarely will an individual run into a reputable business or financial institution unwilling and unable to help fund a living trust. In fact, many financial institutions encourage the funding of revocable living trusts by advertising their expertise in helping to fund the trusts.

Even with the acceptance of living trusts, sometimes it may be more difficult to do business with assets that are titled in the trust name than if they were titled in the name of individual owners or a business. This fact of life should not deter most people from titling property directly in the names of their trusts. More and more, dealing with trusts and trustees is becoming common in the business world. If problems are encountered, there are usually alternate methods of funding that are effective and less likely to cause problems.

Using the Nominee Partnership to Fund the Trust

This is a method we recommend to many of our clients in order to facilitate funding their trusts. It is easily accomplished and facilitates commerce as trust makers buy and sell property during their lifetimes. It protects the privacy of the trust document and results in little additional expense to the trust maker or trustees. Most corporate fiduciaries have used this technique for years in dealing with property in their various trust accounts. Its simplicity in expediting the buying and selling of trust assets both within the home state and across state lines has fostered its use.

The concept of a nominee partnership is simple: rather than put the assets directly in the trust's name, they are put in a holding vehicle created expressly for dealing with trust property. As noted above, this holding vehicle is called a nominee partnership, and it holds bare legal title to the assets for the trustees of the trust. It generally does not own any property in its own right. Its terms provide that the partners deal with the trust property to expedite the buying and selling of trust assets.

The partners of the nominee partnership are totally responsible to the trustees, and usually are the trustees. In fact, the partners of the nominee partnership and the trustees enter into a short agreement that makes it clear that the trust is the owner of the property and that the partners must abide by the trust's terms. Here is an example:

Bill, as a partner in Bill and Diana Company, can buy and sell assets without saying, "Look at us, we're trustees."

> Bill Wagner makes a trust. Bill and his wife Diana are the trustees. Bill and Diana Wagner are also partners in Bill and Diana Company, a nominee partnership. Bill funds his trust by retitling all his assets in the name of Bill and Diana Company. As partners in Bill and Diana Company, they report to Bill and Diana, as trustees of Bill's trust. As trustees of Bill's trust, they report to Bill, the maker of the trust. What a paper tiger!

In our example, the fact that Bill is buying and selling property as a partner in Bill and Diana Company, a nominee for the Bill Wagner Trust, is of major consequence. Buyers and sellers are used to doing business with partners of partnerships; they may not be used to doing business with trustees.

The benefits of a nominee partnership can be summarized as follows:

- Trust documents stay private because the only document that needs to be recorded is the *partnership agreement* or a substitute agreement called a *trade name affidavit*. It is generally short and does not divulge any private matters.

- Property can be bought and sold for the trust in the partnership name without buyers, sellers, and transfer agents getting sweaty palms.

- Subsequent to the death of the trust maker, successor trustees can become successor partners so the buying and selling of trust property continues to be commercially expedient.

- Nominee partnerships provide an excellent solution to the trust funding problem. The only thing a trust maker who uses this technique will have to learn to do is to sign his name "Bill Wagner, Partner," instead of "Bill Wagner, Owner." In the eyes of the world, Bill and Diana Company, a partnership, owns the property. In reality, Bill Wagner owns the property.

- As we discussed in Chapter 17, "The Revocable Living Trust," there are no income tax consequences with respect to the use of a revocable living trust. If the nominee partnership method of funding is used, the partnership simply files an information tax return that says, in essence, "See Bill Wagner's tax return." This practice presents no problems. In our experience, the Internal Revenue Service does not raise an eyebrow when presented with these returns. It understands them and sees them frequently.

Other Methods of Funding a Trust

In some states estate planning professionals have additional techniques available to them to fund a revocable living trust. These techniques are generally used in addition to the nominee partnership and are used on a frequent basis. The four techniques are: durable special powers of attorney, unrecorded deeds, after-death assignments, and POD or TOD designations.

Durable Special Powers of Attorney

A trust maker can give others the power to place the maker's assets into the maker's living trust. This power is given by using a durable special power of attorney. Unlike most powers of attorney, a durable special power of attorney continues even if the maker is incapacitated because of illness or injury. The durable power of attorney is "special" because it limits the power to this single function.

Unrecorded Deeds

In using this technique, the trust maker deeds real estate to the trustee or successor trustee of the trust, but the deed is not recorded until after the death of the trust maker. If the trust maker disposes of the deeded property during his or her lifetime, the unrecorded deed is reclaimed and destroyed.

If the trustee at death is a bank or nominee partnership, the existence of the trust does not have to be revealed for title to the deeded property to pass to the trust. Some states have title standards specifically creating presumptions in favor of the validity of such transfers.

The disadvantage of this form of funding is that it may be argued that no effective transfer took place when the deed was signed; however, if the trust maker's heirs and unsecured creditors are adequately provided for, it is unlikely that anyone would raise an objection. This is an excellent funding technique that can be used in the states that allow it.

After Death (Postmortem) Assignments

Most of the Uniform Probate Code and the Uniform Trust Code states provide that many property interests, with the exception of real estate, can be assigned by an owner to a revocable living trust but that the transfer will not take effect until the owner's death. This technique, where permitted, allows a property owner to retain the use and control of property during his or her lifetime and pass that property automatically to a revocable living trust on death. These assignments are not made public.

From a practical perspective, publicly traded stocks and bonds are not suited to this technique. The New York Stock Transfer Association apparently does not and will not recognize this approach under its rules. As a result, individual stock transfer agents will not transfer the stock or bond that was assigned by use of this technique. The Stock Transfer Association is, in effect, ignoring the laws of the states that allow this technique. We believe that the New York Stock Transfer Association should change its rules, but until it does, we recommend to our clients that they put their publicly traded stocks and bonds in a nominee partnership or directly in the name of their trusts.

Postmortem assignments, where allowed, are extremely effective in transferring closely held (private company) stock certificates and partnership interests into a property owner's revocable living trust.

POD and TOD Accounts

In virtually all states, owners of savings accounts, checking accounts, and certificates of deposit can create a payable-on-death (POD) designation. In creating an account, the owner simply designates a revocable living trust as the entity to receive the account proceeds on death. When the owner dies,the account proceeds pass automatically to the trust without the intervention of the probate court.

All but two states have adopted the Uniform TOD Security Registration Act. TOD stands for Transfer on Death and it is the same concept as POD. The primary difference is that TOD applies to investments and investment accounts, which represents an expansion of POD from bank accounts to all types of investment accounts and individual securities. Texas and Louisiana have not adopted this act.

A POD or TOD account solves one of the most prevalent problems in estate planning. It is very common for one family member to create a joint account with another family member who is not a spouse. This type of account ownership, as we explained in Chapter 3, "Jointly Held Property," creates an immediate gift and may very well result in the account proceeds going to the wrong heir. By naming a revocable living trust as the recipient of the account or security, the owner can be assured that her revocable living trust will control the distribution of the account or security and at the same time avoid probate.

Online Accounts

Of growing concern among estate planning lawyers is access to online accounts and other electronically stored information. A large percentage of Americans have online banking accounts, investment accounts, e-mails, or documents stored in the cloud, flash drives, and other devices. It is likely that each account has its own password. Many people have multiple e-mail addresses, some or all of which may not be known to family members.

If this information has to be gathered after a person dies, it can be a nightmare. For example, after Lance Corporal Justin Ellsworth was killed in 2004 in Iraq, his father tried to have Yahoo! provide him access to his son's e-mail account. Yahoo! refused because Justin's father did not have the password. It took a court order from a Michigan probate court to force Yahoo! to provide access to the account. Yahoo! stated that it would continue its policy of not providing this type of information.

Many of the problems with accessing online accounts are related to numerous state and federal privacy laws that are complex and confusing. Often, it is easier for a company to refuse to cooperate rather than face civil or criminal penalties. A court order takes it off the hook.

It is better to put electronic banking and investment accounts in the name of your trust. Your trustee can then access the account if you cannot. Of course, you will have to provide a method for your trustee—or someone—to have access to your passwords.

Password protection is a tricky business for most of us. It is difficult to find a place to store them so we are not subject to hackers or identity thieves.

We have a few solutions. The first is to establish a safe deposit box to store your passwords, one that allows access by a trustee or a trusted family member or friend after you have died or become disabled. You may even allow access while you are alive and well. You should also put any other information about accounts and the like in the box so that someone has a clear picture of what you own and how to find it if you become disabled or die.

You can leave this information in your lawyer's office. He or she has strict ethical and legal standards as to the safekeeping of client information. Through your living trust instructions or a durable power of attorney, you can name those people who can obtain this information in the event of death or disability.

As a final resort, you can use your own safe to store this information, and then make sure others have access to the combination.

In Appendix A we have provided a booklet entitled "Getting Organized." By filling this in, it will help you organize your online assets and electronic documents.

How Much Funding Is Enough?

As you can see, we are great believers in fully funded revocable living trusts. One question that must be asked, even if a living trust is fully funded, is: "Have you done enough?" Over the years, we have been able to draft some wonderful estate planning documents that have spelled out in great detail how a loving person or couple wants to take care of loved ones or charities or both. A lot of care and thought was put into these plans. The trust makers funded these trusts in the expectation that there was enough fuel in the living trust gas tank to get it to its ultimate destination.

In too many cases (which means there was more than none) there was not enough fuel. All those great plans had to be reduced or eliminated because the intent was not backed up by the funds.

In Chapters 27, 28, 29, and 30 we discuss the fuel your living trust vehicle needs. It is critical that you read those chapters as you contemplate the creation and funding of your revocable living trust. Do not commit the ultimate folly of proper planning and forget that you must fund your trust with enough to meet your planning objectives.

Funding a revocable living trust is an important aspect of the estate planning process. As you can see, there are many techniques available to fund your trust. Please understand that assets not in your trust at your death will be subject to the probate process. Assets that are not in the trust if you become incapacitated can be titled in the name of your trust by a durable power of attorney. However, there is no assurance this method of funding will be effective. Funding your trust when it is set up, and as you acquire new property, assures you that your trust will work as intended. Always make sure your trust has enough fuel to take it to its destination, whatever that may be.

19

Trustees

Superagents

The trust relationship necessitates three types of players: a trust maker, trust beneficiaries, and the person who runs the trust, the trustee.

A good synonym for trustee is agent, or better yet, superagent. Our law refers to superagents as fiduciaries. The word *fiduciary* is used interchangeably with *trustee*, a word meaning "a person who runs a trust." Fiduciary comes from Roman law and means a person who has the same duties and responsibilities as a trustee.

Trustees in General

When a trustee is named, that trustee is given, both by the maker and by operation of law, massive rights and powers to be exercised on behalf of the trust's beneficiaries.

Trustees can be individuals or properly licensed state and federal institutions. Individual trustees are usually family members, friends, or advisors of the trust maker. Institutional trustees are either trust companies or trust departments of commercial banks. Institutional trustees are often referred to as corporate fiduciaries.

Whether individual or institutional, trustees must act in a fiduciary capacity. When acting in that capacity, trustees have the ultimate duty imposed by law as to relationships between people. When they make mistakes and those mistakes are proven, they are liable to the beneficiaries for those mistakes. For a long time trustees' actions and liability for their actions have been measured by what attorneys refer to as the "reasonable person rule." This rule asks the question, "Would a similar, reasonably prudent person acting in the same capacity, in the same or similar circumstances, have made the same judgment?" If the answer is no, trustees will be liable for the consequences of their actions.

The trend today is to apply even tougher standards in the measurement of trustees' actions. Forty-three states have adopted the *Prudent Investor Rule,* or some version of it. Under this rule, trustees must minimize the risk at any given level of return on trust assets. Therefore, in effect, the prudent-person rule has quickly become the prudent-expert rule, at least in most states. Clearly, a prudent expert makes no mistakes—or so it would seem.

Becoming or naming a trustee is serious business. Trustees are fiduciaries, fiduciaries are superagents, and superagents are superliable for acts or failures to act that are not superbeneficial to beneficiaries.

Knowledge of the trustee's role and the consequences of poor performance should dissuade kind but ill-prepared folks from acting as trustees. One does not accommodate a family member, friend, or client by accepting a trusteeship without opening one's eyes about what a trustee is and does. If you have volunteered to be a trustee, please reexamine your decision.

The trustee's role can be a confusing one. They are totally responsible for expert performance and judgment while following the written instructions of a trust maker for the benefit of that maker's beneficiaries. Trustees are responsible, as experts, for the preservation of the maker's property (principal), its growth with respect to income and capital appreciation, and its application to the beneficiaries.

People create relationships. Each relationship involves different expectations, duties, and results. Most relationships are not fiduciary relationships; they are business or personal relationships. Laws have been created to govern these relationships, and all of them fall short of the excellence required under fiduciary law.

In terms of practicality, however, trustees have only two major responsibilities: (1) they have an absolute mandate, by operation of law, to follow precisely the written instructions of a trust maker; (2) they have absolute responsibility to read between the lines and make judgment calls when there is no clear-cut alternative. If trustees are called upon to make decisions that are too tough for them, they ask a court to assist them. This is particularly true in a controversial environment.

Most clients view the trustee's role as primarily financial. After all, trustees are financial advisors. But not all trustees' decisions are financial. People decisions may affect financial decisions; thus, our superagent needs to be supersensitive, indeed.

It is difficult to find competent and willing trustees on both a personal and an institutional basis because trustees must work superhard and are always held superaccountable for their actions.

In discussing the selection of an appropriate trustee with our clients, concerns center in the area of the trustee's knowledge of their families' affairs, investment performance, and the empathy that will potentially be accorded their beneficiaries.

A trustee's knowledge of the affairs of most trust makers is usually deficient. Our experience would suggest that people carry most of their affairs in their heads. Most spouses and children know too little about the family's economic affairs. We believe that you should fully brief your loved ones as to your financial affairs when possible and start now to communicate your affairs to your ultimate trustee.

As to investment performance, we often hear, "He's no good, he can't even handle his own money," or, "She's made a bundle for herself; she'll do all right for me." Also, "What rate of return can he get?" and, "How effective will she be in making my principal grow?" and, "What guarantees do I get?" There are no easy answers to these questions.

Trustees cannot speculate with principal or the income it generates. This does not mean that assets cannot be sold or traded, nor does it mean trustees cannot invest in assets that may go down in value, such as real estate, stocks, bonds, and so on. It does mean they must invest in proven investment areas on a conservative and cautious basis. It also means they diversify, using good judgment in all cases, or not diversify if the assets they are given are profitable on a proven basis. It also means they must exercise prudent judgment.

Trustees should not knowingly (if they are aware of their liability) attempt to achieve a return predicated on speculative investment. Trustee speculators are liable for their losses. Speculation with regard to one's own funds may be all right; if losses are incurred, they may be earned back through labor and industry. If trustees speculate and lose, that is *not* all right; if trustees cannot pay back what they have lost, it probably cannot be replaced.

The trustee's investment approach should always be cautious. It should be prudent and relatively risk-free. There is little room for speculation in the trustee's portfolio.

Conversely, trustees have been known, all too frequently, to be too conservative in their investment strategies. The investment of funds at a below-market yield, in terms of both income and capital appreciation, can result in trustees being liable for lost opportunities. Safe investment is not necessarily prudent investment.

The accountability of trustees concerning the empathy shown to beneficiaries is difficult to ascertain and measure. Regardless of whether individual or institutional trustees are selected, there are no guarantees that sound overall performance will result or that the beneficiaries will be satisfied with the trustees.

The point to remember is that trustees have awesome power, accountability, and liability, all wrapped together in their roles as superagents.

Institutional Trustees

Now that we have discussed trustees in general, let's take a closer look at the role of the institutional trustee. Often called corporate fiduciaries, institutional trustees fall into two separate categories: the full-time trust company, and the trust department or trust division of a commercial bank. A number of financial brokerage firms have formed or purchased separate trust companies. For our purposes, these are the same as full-time trust companies.

Both the full-time trust company and the trust division of a commercial bank do precisely the same thing. They function as professional trustees. To discuss one is to discuss the other. How can they be the same if one is a separate professional trust company and the other is just part of a bank? The answer is fairly simple.

Originally, banks were banks and trust companies were trust companies. Both existed side by side. Commercial banks accepted depositors' money and loaned most of that money back to the public. Trust companies, in contrast, historically managed trust assets for a fee. The two were separate entities, both serving the public in a different way. Each had its own building, ownership, and board of directors; each served the same local population.

A trend developed that resulted in the merging of the two institutions. The opportunity was taken to consolidate and reduce the overhead of the surviving institution and provide full-service banking. To a certain extent this has taken place in the major stock brokerage firms. They too have consolidated their function as financial advisors and investment managers with the option to manage money under a separate trust company.

This has been the trend for many years. Look around you. Some banks still have the title "and Trust Company" at the end of their names. At some point in time they acquired or created a trust company and brought it within the umbrella of the concept of a full-service bank.

Today, though there are still trust companies that have elected not to merge with or be acquired by a commercial bank, they and bank trust departments function the same way.

The first question every client asks when we discuss the institutional trustee is, "Does the bank lend my trust funds to bank customers?" The answer is, "Absolutely not." That is a bank function conducted with the money of the bank's commercial depositors. It does not occur with trust assets.

The trust division of the typical commercial bank is an entirely separate entity. Literally, it is the successor of the historical trust company. Within a bank's trust division, assets are managed for beneficiaries of individual trusts. The same is true for the trust company that is part of a stock brokerage firm; it is a separate entity in which assets are managed for beneficiaries of trusts.

An interesting note with regard to the dual relationship of a bank and trust company is that the commercial sector of the bank is 100 percent liable in terms of the fiduciary liability of its trust division. On the other hand, individual trusts are never liable for the acts or omissions of the bank with respect to the bank's banking function. This means that if the trust division makes a mistake, the beneficiaries can go against all the bank's assets. On the other hand, if the commercial sector of the bank makes a mistake, the bank's creditors cannot go against individual trust assets.

The institutional or corporate fiduciary is basically no different from any other trustee. It has the same duties, the same responsibilities, and the same opportunities to fail or succeed as any other trustee. As a practical consideration, however, it should be noted that the corporate fiduciary appears to have a higher duty or standard of care in administering and investing trust assets than a personal trustee. A judge or jury is more likely to measure the prudent person standard on a tougher basis against the professional fiduciary than against a personal, nonprofessional trustee.

Trust divisions or companies are basically organized into distinct and separate areas. The first we will call the *administrative* section. It contains the trust department's hand-holders, the people who work directly with the beneficiaries to accomplish their goals and objectives as well as those set forth by the maker of the trust. These men and women are usually attorneys, although there are many excellent trust officers who are not. They are people who tend to be public relations–oriented and who are extremely patient with beneficiaries.

In addition, most trust departments have an *investment* area. The people in this area assist the hand-holders in fulfilling investment objectives. They are usually trained in investing in stocks and bonds.

Many trust departments are large enough to have an additional investment function called the *real estate* area or the *special asset* section. The individuals in this section obviously specialize in the managing, purchasing, and selling of real estate and other not-so-easy-to-manage assets to meet investment objectives.

Apart from the account management and investment functions, most trust entities have a *taxation* section. The function of this area, as its name implies, is to consider all tax ramifications of investment decisions. Anytime an asset is purchased or sold, the tax implications of the transaction should be analyzed.

Depending upon the sophistication of the institution in question, additional services may be available to assist beneficiaries. Figure 19-1 illustrates a typical bank's organization.

When looking at these functions—administration, investment, and tax—one may wonder how anything gets done. The answer is that all final decisions are made by committee. Corporate fiduciaries work almost exclusively through the committee approach to problem solving. The advocates of this approach say every decision is examined and reexamined, questioned and requestioned, before it is made. This process, although lengthy, is supposed

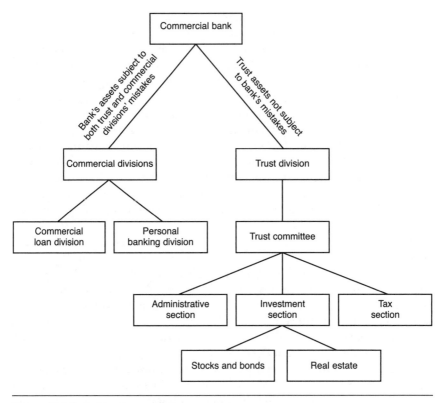

Figure 19-1 Typical bank organization.

to be in the best interests of the beneficiaries. Conceptually, it should result in little or no error.

The opponents of institutional trustees cite the committee approach as the horse-and-camel approach (referring to the committee that decided to design the horse and ended up with a camel instead). The criticism may or may not be fair, depending on the institution and the types of decisions to be made.

A sound critique of institutional trustees attacks their speed and timeliness, not necessarily their ultimate conclusions.

One of the claims made by most financial institutions offering trust services is that they provide professional advice. Opponents of institutional trustees state that this is so much baloney, that what they provide is nothing but cautious investment in stocks and bonds. Regardless of what assets are left in trust, these critics assert it will not be long before the institution will have sold the original assets and invested all the proceeds in a stock and bond portfolio. Critics also attack, with frequent justification, the investment abilities of these institutions.

These traditional claims may have some validity, but not so much today. Financial institutions offering trust services have primarily centered their investment portfolios in stocks and bonds. They have done this in one of two ways. They either purchase stocks and bonds especially suited to a particular trust's objectives and held exclusively for that account, or purchase and hold stocks and bonds through *common trust funds*. These are funds created within the trust department to meet a broad range of investment objectives. These funds may be equity funds (funds that are supposed to grow over the years by way of capital appreciation) or they can be fixed-income funds (funds invested to provide current income). Another common trust fund frequently used is a tax-free fund. This fund is invested in securities, primarily municipal bonds, which will produce tax-free income. Some trust companies also use certain mutual funds for the same purposes.

By creating common trust funds, institutional trustees have attempted to offer diversification and lower management costs for many of their trusts that have common investment objectives.

Because one trust may be able to own relatively few securities due to the size of its principal, that principal can be pooled with the principal of other trusts by using a common trust fund. Each trust owns units in a common pool or fund that owns a diversified portfolio of stocks or bonds. This, proponents of professional trustees claim, provides a benefit for individual trusts at no additional fee and provides sound diversification.

Opponents of professional trustees assert that these common trust funds, as well as directly invested accounts, are nothing more than studies in carefully planned mediocrity—that, in fact, all investments are made in the same static pool of stocks and bonds selected by the institutions. Opponents claim that trust department employees are underpaid and their collective investment decisions generally result in substandard performance. However, there are a number of excellently managed trust companies and trust departments with a proven record of above-average performance.

Without taking sides, let us examine the reasons for using a corporate fiduciary.

First and foremost, a corporate fiduciary is generally always collectible. It is backed by the entire institution's resources, so if a mistake is made, there is a good likelihood that recovery will be made. This can be very comforting. If the institutional trustee makes a mistake, you can, with some security, rest assured that if proven wrong, the institution will return what was lost as a result of its error. Most do have money. Also, keep in mind that the money being returned is not coming from other trusts, but from that institution's shareholders.

Another reason that a corporate fiduciary is often selected is that it will not die or become mentally incompetent, sick, or senile. It is there day after day, year after year. The institution generally does not change. This is an important attribute of the institutional trustee. Even in this climate of bank takeovers and mergers, there is continuity. Trust departments have been consolidated in the same manner as the banks. Like the banks, the trust departments have continued in spite of name changes and new ownership.

Opponents of corporate fiduciaries believe these fiduciaries have a high turnover rate among their personnel, and claim that as a result there is no continuity in the management of a trust account. Turnover is high, opponents say, because institutions pay too little. Indeed, institutional trustees have been accused of underpaying talented people, which, in effect, makes them training grounds for talented young professionals and havens for others less blessed.

In fact, there is more than a little truth on both sides. The important thing to keep in mind is this: a trust instrument names the institution as trustee, not its employees. It is the institution that can boast when a good job has been done, and it is the institution that will pay if it is proven in error. Collectibility is of utmost importance. In our opinion, that is the ultimate justification for naming an institutional trustee. And, there are trust companies and trust departments that can boast of longtime employees and management in spite of the turnover in other institutions.

Another factor emphasized by proponents of institutional trustees is that institutions are capable of objective, third-party decision making. Opponents, meanwhile, argue that third-party institutional objectivity does not exist. They claim that decisions are usually made by one or two employees who do not care about the beneficiaries. These critics claim that relationships are distant at best and accountability for poor results is relatively nonexistent.

Institutional vs. Individual Trustees

How do institutional trustees measure up against individual trustees? Before discussing this question, we would first like to outline the pros and cons of personal trustees.

Personal trustees are people. They have all the human strengths and weaknesses we all have. A personal trustee can be you or others with whom you are close.

Tables 19-1, "Personal Trustees," and 19-2, "Institutional Trustees," outline pros and cons attributed to different types of personal and institutional trustees. Obviously they are not all-inclusive. We are sure you can add pros and cons yourself, and we encourage you to do so. Our outlines contain the essence of what clients and professionals have communicated to us about individual trustees over the years. They contrast the pros and cons of an individual trustee with the pros and cons of an institutional trustee.

Table 19-1
Personal Trustees

Pros	Cons
FAMILY MEMBERS	
Family knowledge	Indecisive and insecure
Personal	No track record or experience
Investment	Too emotionally involved
Business	Unskilled at business
Empathetic, loving	People-prejudiced
Bright	Uncollectible as to mistakes
Good common sense	
Personally involved	
FRIENDS OR BUSINESS ASSOCIATES	
Family knowledge:	Human:
Personal	May embezzle
Investment	May speculate poorly
Business	May die
Empathetic	Not enough time; a burden
Good businessperson	May play favorites
Good investor personally	Probably not collectible
Good common sense	
Tough, honest, hardworking	
PROFESSIONAL ADVISORS (Attorney, CPA, Investment Advisor)	
Family knowledge:	Human:
Personal	May embezzle
Investment	May speculate
Business	May be too conservative
Tough, honest, hardworking	May die
Trained professional	Not enough time
	May not be collectible
	Conflicts of interest
	Limited investment knowledge

Table 19-2
The Institutional Trustee

Pros	Cons
Professional	Dispassionate
Experienced	Ignorant of family affairs
Established track record	High turnover among staff
Collectible	Hard to reach
Will always be there	Too conservative
Not emotionally involved	Slow to act
Objective	
Regulated	

Practical Advice on Your Trustees

Our advice is that rather than pick a single trustee, whether an individual or an institution, create combinations of trustees in your trust and provide a pattern for trustee succession. Planning for trustee succession involves stating which trustees you want to take over in the event previous trustees quit, die, or are fired. Providing for this succession is good business, for both personal and institutional trustees.

In your trust document, always spell out who has the authority to terminate a trustee. Those who are not doing the job to the satisfaction of the beneficiaries should be terminated. Many trusts we have reviewed do not provide for trustee termination. We believe this is a mistake. Poorly performing trustees who continue as trustees become a burden to beneficiaries. They are not easy to get rid of unless the document provides for their termination.

To remove a trustee without termination rights in the trust itself requires review and approval by a court of law, generally the probate court. In our experience, using the court as a planning alternative is poor planning. There is no guarantee the court will agree with the unhappy beneficiaries. The legal process can be slow, expensive, and its results disappointing.

The trust maker should always stipulate which beneficiaries may exercise the right to terminate trustees. For example, the termination rights may be given as follows:

> My spouse can fire the trustee at any time for any reason. After my spouse's death, a majority of the children may do so. If they are minors, then their guardian or a majority of their guardians can fire the trustee.

Another might say:

> My spouse and my sister, if they agree, can fire the trustee at any time for any reason. If either dies, then the survivor along with my attorney can fire any trustee. If everyone is deceased, then a majority of my living beneficiaries can fire the trustee.

The important point to understand is that you should communicate your list of those individuals, in succession, who are to have the power to fire the trustee at any time, and see that your instructions are placed in your trust.

Another major—and in our opinion mandatory—planning tool is for you to set forth whom you want to take over as trustee when a trustee is fired, quits, or dies. For example:

> If my sister is fired, quits, or dies, she shall be replaced by my friend, Fred. Likewise, if Fred is fired, quits, or dies, then he shall be replaced by First National Bank.

You can also provide for the appointment of trustees by giving others the right to select them. For example:

> If my spouse quits or dies, my attorney, Ellen, may select a new trustee, either personal or corporate, but my attorney is not to serve as trustee. Should Ellen not be living, a majority of my children may select a trustee to replace my spouse, as long as their choice is made among institutional trustees with a capital and surplus of not less than $5 million.

There is no limit to the personal and creative choices you can make; just make sure that you think your choices out and see to it that your estate planner accomplishes your goals in this area.

When naming trustees for your trust, a good general rule is not to name your spouse sole trustee. Give your spouse some help. If you desire, name an adult child of yours or, if you prefer, all your adult children. Perhaps you are close to another family member, business associate, or advisor. If you feel good about that person or people, name one or more as trustee with your spouse; just remember to provide for their termination and replacement.

If your planning situation dictates that there are no personal trustee candidates to assist your spouse, select an institutional trustee. There is nothing wrong with naming an institution as cotrustee with your spouse. In fact, our experience suggests that some clients prefer this approach. If you do this, always give your spouse the power to fire the institution and replace it according to your instructions.

You might want to combine the strengths of a personal trustee with the strengths of an institutional trustee. You may get the best of both worlds. You should choose your trustees based on your beliefs, inclinations, and particular situation.

Trustees' Fees

"Does a trustee get paid?"

"How much do they charge?"

Our clients commonly ask these questions. Trustees are compensated. There is no such thing as a free lunch in the trust business.

Historically, trustees—especially professional trustees—charged an annual fee calculated as a percentage of the income earned by the trust property over the course of a year. This method is rarely used today.

Today most if not all institutional trustees charge and are paid pursuant to published fee schedules. These schedules generally are a percentage of the dollar value of the assets managed by the trustee. They are published to avoid any confusion that might otherwise arise between the trustee and the beneficiaries. The value to which trustees apply their percentage is the fair market value of the trust property as determined by the trustee. Institutional trustees almost always have a minimum fee that will be charged regardless of the value of the trust property. The minimum fee is not based on a percentage of the assets; it is a fixed amount.

Each institution, although independent, closely follows the fee structure of its competitors. Competition in the marketplace dictates this.

Institutional trustees generally apply their percentage fees on a sliding scale of asset value; for example, 1 percent on the first $100,000, three-quarters of 1 percent on the next $400,000, and one-half of 1 percent on the balance. It is common in the institutional fiduciary world to reduce the fee percentage as the value of the trust assets increases in size.

The amount institutional trustees charge varies if extraordinary management services are provided. For example, managing a closely held business interest may necessitate a special or negotiated fee. Many institutional trustees do not publish special fees for managing special property in their fee schedules.

Our review of several published fee schedules of institutional trustees suggests that:

- Fee schedules are all pretty much the same. Shopping for trustees' fees may not be very productive.

- Most, if not all, have a minimum fee.

- Most use the percentage-of-value approach.

- Most have sliding scales rather than escalating schedules.

- The larger the institution, the more likely it is to charge differently for extraordinary services.

- Some have termination fees.

The last entry in our synopsis suggests that some institutions charge termination fees; that is, they have language in their fee schedules setting forth additional charges that will be levied against the trust assets if the institution is fired or quits. These additional charges can involve hourly billing, percentage billing, or flat fee billing to cover the costs of terminating the trust.

We strongly disagree with the institutional practice of charging termination fees. We do not accept the institutional arguments offered in their defense. If the trust is run properly, a great deal of time should not be required to turn over trust assets and records to another trustee. The time that is involved should be minimal and, in most cases, should have been covered by the ongoing fee.

Termination charges become a rear-end load. They might dissuade unhappy beneficiaries from terminating the trustee, but usually only result in bitter feelings, fee disputes, and arguments. These charges should be discussed with the institution from the outset and eliminated if at all possible.

On the other hand, we believe that most institutional trustees do not charge enough. Most fee schedules hover at around 1 percent. That is not significant when compared with the trustees' duties and responsibilities.

Many of our clients question the fees of institutional trustees. Clients are too shrewd to believe that in the commercial marketplace they get a lot for little cost. Low rates generate suspicion as to promised results. There are, however, some institutions that are well operated and provide sound investment results. They provide some of the great bargains still around.

Personal or individual trustees are not sophisticated in the manner in which they charge fees. Many negotiate their fees. Many provide their services on a gratuitous or quasi-gratuitous basis. Some overcharge; but most do not charge enough.

Some states set fee schedules in their laws. Many trustees' fees are set by the court having jurisdiction over trusts. These courts are generally, but not always, probate courts. Fee disputes are ultimately settled by the judge of that court.

In general, trustees' fees are not a major concern to most of our clients. But a trustee's performance is the major concern of all of our clients. Your knowledge of trustees' fees, how they work, and what they are, will assist you in selecting your trustees.

20

Giving Property to Minors

Young Ones Are Tough to Give To

If ever an estate planning professional were to make a generalized statement, it would be, "Most people want their property to ultimately end up in the hands of their children and grandchildren."

Almost every simple will we have reviewed over the years has said, "I leave my property to my spouse. If my spouse does not survive me, I leave it equally to my children. If a child of mine dies leaving children, I want his or her share to go to his or her children, my grandchildren."

Almost every life insurance contract we have reviewed has named beneficiaries precisely like the simple will does: a spouse, children, and grandchildren, in that order.

The purpose of this chapter is to discuss the problems associated with giving or leaving property to minor children and grandchildren. Under our system of laws, giving your property to minor beneficiaries is neither easy nor wise.

Most states' laws define minors as persons who have not attained the age of either 18 or 21. There are a couple of states that use age 19 and at least one where it is 25.

Can you make an outright gift of property to your minor children or grandchildren? The answer is yes and no: yes, in that you can do anything you want; no, unless you follow the legal formalities under your state's law for the making of that gift. Under most states' laws, in order to make a gift of more than a nominal amount to a minor, you must take one of five actions.

1. **Set Up a Uniform Gifts to Minors Act Account or a Uniform Transfers to Minors Act Account.** Every state has a law governing these custodial accounts. Originally, custodial accounts under UGMA were used to make

a gift of money and stock or be a beneficiary of a life insurance policy. Now, in almost all states, with the advent of UTMA, they can be used to hold cash, securities, annuity contracts, real property, and virtually all other types of property. Even states that have a statute bearing the old UGMA name have liberalized their statutes to allow ownership of most types of property. An adult custodian must be named on the account with the minor or on the title of the property. The custodian manages the account until the minor reaches the state law age for termination of the custodial account. For almost all UTMA states the termination age is either 18 or 21; for UGMA states the termination age is generally 18.

2. **Create a Savings Account Trust.** The savings and loan association law provides liberalized handling of accounts created for a minor. These accounts can be established in the name of a minor, and the minor is entitled to make deposits or withdrawals in the same manner as an adult, without any liability to the savings and loan association.

3. **Establish a Totten Trust.** An account called a Totten trust can be established with a commercial bank or savings and loan association. An account of this kind is created by registering the account in a form such as, "John Jones in trust for Mary Jones." In states that recognize this technique, it is usually presumed that the account belongs to the adult person named as trustee, unless it can be shown that the trust was intended to be irrevocable. On the death of the adult trustee, the account proceeds belong to the minor beneficiary but are controlled by the local probate court on behalf of the minor until he or she reaches adulthood.

4. **Fund a Living Trust Created for the Benefit of the Minor Beneficiary.** A living trust that is used to give property to minors is called a 2503(c) trust or a minor's trust. It is named after the Internal Revenue Code section that allows this type of gift to a minor. The most important feature of a 2503(c) trust is that a gift made to it is a gift of a present interest that qualified for the gift tax annual exclusion. If you remember from Chapter 15, "Step-Up in Basis at Death," gifts made to an irrevocable trust generally do not qualify for the annual exclusion for gifts, but a minor's trust under Section 2503(c) of the Internal Revenue Code is one notable exception.

5. **Petition the Local Court, Usually the Probate Court, to Authorize a Custodial Relationship.** The court will name an adult custodian who will manage the property under the court's direction and supervision until the minor becomes an adult.

The techniques we have discussed represent, in the main, the alternatives available to you when you want to give property to minor children and grandchildren. If you think these living techniques are complex, can you imagine how difficult it is to get your property into the hands of these minors on your death?

If your will leaves property directly to minors or if your insurance proceeds are to be paid directly to minors, we can assure you that your minor beneficiaries will not directly receive anything. Every state in our country will require that those funds be subject to the supervision of a court-directed custodianship. The court that will supervise all matters relating to these funds will generally be the local probate court.

If you did not name a guardian for your minor children in your will, the probate court will select a guardian on its terms—not yours. If you have more than one child, the court could name a separate guardian for each child. Each court-appointed guardian will be totally responsible for all his or her actions to an already overburdened and extremely busy probate judge.

If you were prudent and named your choice of guardian in your will but, nevertheless, left property directly to minor children, the court will have to supervise the distribution of that property. The probate judge will appoint a custodian to administer your children's property. The custodian who is selected may be an adult person or a licensed institutional trustee. The person whom the judge selects will be responsible to the judge on an ongoing basis for all acts with respect to the children's property. The custodian may or may not be the same person named as the children's guardian.

A court-imposed conservatorship that results from leaving property directly to minors on death has, in our opinion, the following drawbacks:

- All your property and all the conservator's actions with respect to it are made public.

- The court will require that a bond be posted for each year of the conservatorship, and that it be paid for from the children's funds. The cost will be approximately 1 percent of the fund value each year, although that amount varies for jurisdiction to jurisdiction.

- The conservator will have to keep detailed records of his or her transactions and will have to show those records to the court. This takes time and costs money.

- The conservator will be paid out of the children's funds.

- The conservator is usually required to use the services of an attorney in working with the court; attorneys' fees will be paid out of the children's funds.

- The conservator whom the court appoints may not be experienced in the investment of funds and may not have the best interests of the children at heart.

Leaving property directly to minors on death involves a great deal of red tape; it depersonalizes the planning process and can create confusion and insecurity in your loved ones. It can also generate substantial expenses and unreasonable delays.

In talking with both parents and grandparents, we are convinced that they have very definite feelings with respect to how they want their children and grandchildren raised and provided for economically after their deaths; and yet so many people leave most of what they have directly to their minor children and grandchildren in the belief that somehow their property will miraculously be used to care for the children. This assumption is a mistaken one.

Any parent or grandparent who wishes to leave property to minor beneficiaries should always seek out a professional estate planner to accomplish those wishes through the creation of a properly drawn trust. Through the use of such a trust, the following are accomplished:

- Parents and grandparents can give what they have to minor beneficiaries in the way they want, and when they want those beneficiaries to receive it; they can control the disposition of their estates and create unique planning solutions to accommodate unique planning objectives.

- They can select the children's guardians and the person or persons who will invest and control the purse strings with respect to their property.

- They can avoid the active control and intervention of the probate court and keep their affairs and those of their beneficiaries out of the public eye.

- All expenses that result through a conservatorship are avoided; the only expense is the trustees' fees.

Chapters 21, 22, and 23 on trusts and planning for children should offer more than a glimmer of hope to parents and grandparents who want to plan properly for loved ones who are underage.

21

Planning for Children

Beliefs and Caring Can Survive Death

In discussing estate planning with our clients who have minor children, we have learned that most parents have very strong and definite ideas as to how their children should be raised and provided for. Our clients express significant concern with respect to who would raise their minor children and how the children would be economically provided for if neither parent were alive. Their fears and insecurities with respect to the reality that would follow a catastrophe have, in the main, been well-founded.

The responsibility of a professional estate planner includes helping parents plan for their children in the event that the unspeakable occurs. Planning in this area involves far more than mere economics. Planning for minor children involves creating an environment that will allow underaged loved ones to experience love and the care that goes with it, as well as the economic security that will provide more than the necessities of life as they grow to adulthood. The thought and sensitivity required to plan properly for potential orphans should not be taken lightly by any parent or professional advisor.

In this chapter we discuss the techniques you can use to provide a substitute lifestyle for your minor loved ones should a catastrophe occur. It is important to understand that your wishes can become reality after your death if you take the time to plan properly.

Selecting the Guardian

It is mandatory that you take the time to select and name the person or persons whom you wish to raise your children in your absence; these persons are called *guardians of the person*. Under the laws of most states, guardians are named in a will. When a revocable living trust is used, the guardians should be named in the pour-over will that accompanies it.

Many of our clients become exasperated when asked, "Who do you want to raise and care for your children in your absence?" In attempting to respond, they can generally think of no one who, as a replacement parent, would do as good a job as they. Several names are usually discussed and discarded because of one deficiency or another. Often the result of this process is no result at all. The parents, in frustration, come to this conclusion: "We don't know anyone who could raise our children as well as we would."

Our advice is always: "We understand, but please, after giving it much thought and after discussing it together, give us the best of the worst." You must select your children's guardian because, regardless of its drawbacks, your choice will in all likelihood be far better than the choice of the probate judge. If you do not name a guardian, the court will. The selection of a guardian is a painful process, but it must be done. In going through the process, you should always:

- Provide for a succession of guardians in your will. There is no guarantee that any guardian will be alive when needed or that your chosen guardian will agree to serve.

- Always spell out your first, second, and, if important to you, third choice of guardians in your will.

- Always discuss the situation with the guardians you would like to name before you name them. Be sure that they will, in fact, serve if named.

- Share your estate plan with the guardians you have named so they will know and understand what they may be getting into.

- Select your guardians on the basis of their beliefs, morality, and lifestyle, not on their ability to manage a financial portfolio. Management of the children's funds will not necessarily be the responsibility of the guardians. Others can be named to manage the children's property as trustees. If you choose, however, the guardians and the trustees can be the same.

- If you elect to name a married couple as guardians, use both of their full names in describing them in your will. If you use a "Mr. and Mrs." designation, there could be a different "Mrs." at the time they are needed.

In most states, the guardians who are selected and named in a will do not serve automatically. The probate court judge, after independent inquiry, must approve and name the guardian who will ultimately serve. In some states the parents' choice is presumptive; in others it is not. Regardless of the laws of the state in which you reside, always include your choices in your will to give the judge some help and direction.

Leaving Property to Children

Do not leave your property or insurance proceeds directly to your minor children. We discussed the problems that occur when this is attempted in Chapter 20, "Giving Property to Minors."

Always use a trust vehicle to leave your property to minor loved ones. As we discuss in the chapters on trusts, you may elect to use either a trust in your will (testamentary trust) or a revocable living trust. We believe that a revocable living trust should be used, for all the reasons we have already discussed.

By using a trust, you can spell out in great detail precisely how you wish your children to be taken care of and when you wish them to receive the balance of your property. You can also name the individuals or institutions you would like to manage the property for the benefit of your children. The trustees or financial guardians can and will work closely with the personal guardians in following your instructions to provide for your children's well-being. The rest of this chapter describes many of the techniques that are used in a trust by professional estate planners to care for minor children.

When Property Is Divided Among the Children

Many wills and trusts we have reviewed on behalf of our clients divide the property into equal but separate shares for each child immediately upon the death of the maker. This technique reflects the maker's intent to treat the children equally, and as a result, each child has a separate trust share that can only be used for that child's benefit.

We believe that planning of this sort is ill-conceived and does not accomplish what the parent had in mind. What happens if one or more of the children have extraordinary needs for funds because of sickness or other unforeseen emergencies? The answer is that, under this technique, once their individual trusts are depleted, they will become wards of the state. This would be true even though their brothers or sisters still have significant sums remaining in their trusts that they do not need.

A better technique, in our opinion, is to leave all your property in a common trust for the benefit of all your children for their health, support, maintenance, education, and general welfare. Once all your children become adults, whatever is left can be divided equally among them and given to them or placed in a separate trust for each of them to be distributed in accordance with your wishes.

The statement that "there is nothing so unequal as the equal treatment of unequals" certainly applies here. In reality, most parents, while alive, care for their children based on need. That is to say, their resources are used based on the needs of the individual children, rather than on a dollar-for-dollar accounting parity. After death this reality should be no different.

When the common trust for the children will be divided into shares is a matter of individual preference. Many of our clients believe it should be divided when the youngest child attains the age of 23 or even 25 years of age. One technique we find particularly intriguing divides the common trust into separate shares when the youngest child attains the age of 23 or, alternatively, upon graduation from college, whichever happens first. When you choose to divide the common trust is your decision. The important consideration in your estate plan is to make sure all your children are provided for while they are minors, and that they are provided for from all your resources.

One of the questions this technique frequently raises is: "Do my older children have to wait until their youngest brother or sister reaches that magic age before they can get some of their money to invest in a business or for any other good purpose?" The answer is no, if the trust document is carefully written. Instructions can be given to the trustee to advance money to any older child for the purposes enumerated in the trust instructions. In advancing the money, the trustee should be instructed to first be sure that enough common trust funds will be left to feed, clothe, educate, and care for the minor brothers and sisters. A provision can also be included in the trust document to provide that upon ultimate division of the common trust into separate and equal shares for each of the children, any amounts advanced to adult children will reduce the amount of the shares those adult children actually receive.

The choices available to you are limited only by your imagination. If we have spurred your thinking, we have accomplished our purpose.

When Property Is Distributed to Children

Many of our clients believe that when all their children reach adulthood, the property in the common trust should be given or distributed to them outright. This approach may have been all right in the past, but given our economic outlook today, it may not be as sound as some other alternatives.

Wealth is a strange phenomenon; it is a concept that is relative to the perception of the wealth holder. Whether a person's wealth is acquired quickly or over a long period of time appears relevant to whether they consider themselves wealthy. Most of our clients are wealthy when measured against world or national averages; yet with few exceptions, they do not view themselves as financially secure, and are prudent and relatively conservative in their lifestyles. They are concerned with the need to always have enough for the tomorrows in their lives.

Whether a young adult will exercise good judgment with regard to inherited property is always uncertain; most young adults do not have the experience or maturity to handle what are to them large sums of money. People do make mistakes, and generally the frequency of their mistakes is tied directly to their experience or lack of it. Property left to a young adult all at one time is frequently lost through poor investment or spent as if there were no tomorrow. Parents know too well what tomorrow may bring and are generally very concerned about when and how their children receive their funds.

Parents concerned about when their children will receive funds can provide for a pattern of distribution in the trust documents. These might state that when the youngest child attains a certain age, the common trust property will be divided equally among the children. Rather than giving it to them outright, however, the funds are placed in each child's separate trust to be distributed in accordance with the parents' wishes. How that property is distributed and when it is distributed always depends on the wishes and beliefs of the parents. While the property is in the child's trust, however, the trustee will always be instructed to care for the child with both the income and principal of the trust in accordance with the written instructions of the parents.

Here are some distribution techniques selected by many of our clients:

> The child will receive the trust proceeds in two distributions. These distributions will be half at 21 and half at 25; or half at 25 and half at 30; or half at 30 and half at 35.

Regardless of the ages used, the concept is to ease the child into the money, so that if a mistake is made with the first half, time and experience will be on the child's side when the second half is received. This distribution method should enable the child to learn from previous mistakes. This technique also manifests the belief that there is a certain age below which the child should not have the opportunity to exercise judgment with regard to the inherited funds. The advantage of this technique is that there will always be two or more distributions.

The problem with the multiple-age technique is that if the child is already over the last distribution age specified by the parent, the funds will be received at one time. Many people believe that age does not a wise person make, but rather, experience does. These people obviously would not use this approach.

Parents who do not like a distribution pattern predicated strictly on age could use a pattern of distribution similar to this:

> The child will receive half the funds upon attaining a minimum age or, if over that age, immediately on the death of the parents. The balance of the trust fund will be distributed five, 10, or 15 years later.

Many of our clients prefer that their children receive their property in three or more distributions, which may be tied to certain ages or time intervals. Some parents like a plan of distribution that uses both time intervals and attained ages. These parents reason that if the distributions are spread out, each child will gain more experience and wisdom with every additional distribution. The disadvantage to this approach is that in waiting to receive the funds, the child might think the deceased parent was not confident of his or her abilities, or was trying to exercise control from the grave. An example of this distribution pattern:

> One-fourth at 25 or one-fourth immediately if the child is over 25 on the death of the parent, with additional equal distributions every five years thereafter until all the trust principal has been distributed.

Some of our clients create uneven distributions, patterns such as one-third of the property at 25 and the balance at age 40.

The important point to recognize is that you can control how you wish your property to pass to your children. When you think about your preferences, remember that you can also create different patterns of distribution for each of your children. For example:

> To my sons, one-half of their share at 25 or immediately on my death if they are over 25, and the balance five years later. To my daughters, one-fourth of their share at 25 or immediately on my death if they are over 25, another fourth five years later, and the balance of the trust property is in trust for the lifetimes of each of my daughters.

Parents who select this pattern of distribution believe that a daughter may need more protection in our society than a son. If that is their belief, this pattern might suit them. Obviously, this concern could be directed at sons, and if so, the pattern is reversed.

Please understand that you can leave your property equally to your children and, through the use of trusts, create different patterns of distribution with regard to each child's individual share. This technique is of major importance when planning for handicapped or disadvantaged children. Disadvantaged children may never have the ability to handle their own affairs; they may require lifetime care with respect to the property in their trusts. Trusts can be tailored to fit the needs of any child.

Most parents know their children, and all parents know their own minds; they should plan accordingly.

A growing number of clients elect not to make outright distributions of property to their children, or at least keep a large part of the inheritance in trust. These parents usually instruct the trustee to care for their children from their respective separate shares of both the income and principal of their trusts in accordance with the terms of the trust, and provide that on the child's death the balance of the trust principal will go to that child's children. If that child has no children, the balance will go to the trusts created for the child's brothers and sisters.

The reason that this "trust for life" alternative is being used more and more is that it reflects uncertainty about the future of our children and grandchildren. It may be that the next generation or two, for the first time in the history of the United States, will have a lower standard of living than the prior generation. There is also concern about the long-term viability of Social Security, Medicare, and other government programs that previously could be relied upon to offer a safety net for people in need.

By retaining property in trust, parents can at least attempt to provide a personal safety net. The trust can act as a retirement plan, allowing children and grandchildren to get money out for necessities, such as health care, education, purchasing or starting a business, and other needs. A trust maker can draft in as many instructions as he or she wants to ensure that children and grandchildren will be cared for.

Lifetime trusts also have the ability to protect beneficiaries from the claims of creditors. If you create a trust for your children and your trust contains a so-called "spendthrift clause," your children's creditors cannot take trust assets to pay liabilities. Spendthrift trusts also offer some protection in divorce actions. While not 100 percent foolproof, they are close to that for most creditor protection purposes. It is imperative that your lawyer includes a spendthrift clause that protects your beneficiaries from the claims of creditors.

A final word about long-term trusts. To make them effective, they must have fuel. If you do not have enough assets to protect your children or grandchildren over a long period of time, read Chapters 27, 28, 29, and 30 about how you can obtain the fuel to run your trust vehicle. It makes no sense to create a wonderful security net for loved ones and then not have enough assets to ensure the results you want.

Special Needs Children

The odds are very high that you or another family member have a child that has special needs. Special needs range from social, developmental, and educational problems to health, mental, and drug problems. Some needs are medically diagnosed while others are personal to the family.

If you are in this situation, you should consider creating a separate trust or a separate trust share for your special needs child. As you can imagine, there are infinite ways to draft a special needs trust. An experienced lawyer will be able to offer you many alternatives. Here are a few ideas you can think about and discuss with your lawyer and other advisors.

1. Do not accept boilerplate drafting; your lawyer must tailor the trust to the needs of your special needs child.

2. Explain in detail to your lawyer what challenges your special needs child has; do not hold back any information.

3. Bring literature to your meeting with your lawyer if there is a particular disease or diagnosis for your child, so the lawyer will be able to understand the needs and challenges.

4. Make sure your lawyer includes language, usually based on your state's laws, that will allow your child to qualify for any state or federal benefits offered for your child's needs or condition.

5. Discuss how much money or property the trust will need to sustain your child for his or her life expectancy.

6. Absolutely avoid using a software program or an Internet service to draft a special needs trust.

The discussion on planning for children can be summarized as follows:

• Select a guardian for your minor children.

• Leave your property in a trust for your children, not as an outright bequest.

• Use a common trust for minor children.

• Divide your property when all your children are adults.

• You can make several distributions to your children or you can leave property in trust for them for life.

• Create a separate trust for your special needs child that truly reflects those needs.

22

Per Stirpes versus Per Capita

Serious Latin

In reviewing estate plans with clients over the years, many of our clients have asked, "What does *per stirpes* mean?" or "What does *per capita* mean?" For years we have vowed that if we ever wrote a book on estate planning, we would explain these important terms to our readers.

Per stirpes and per capita are Latin phrases, either of which can almost always be found in a will or trust. The use of the terms by an attorney provides a precise way to create a property distribution pattern. In employing them, an attorney reduces the use of words considerably.

Per stirpes means "by roots or stocks; by representation." This distribution pattern means that beneficiaries get what their immediate ancestors had, or were to receive. Some professionals use its English phrase, "by representation."

Per capita means "by the head or polls; according to the number of individuals; share and share alike." This distribution pattern means that all beneficiaries are counted, irrespective of generation, and their number divided into the property at hand, with each beneficiary receiving a resulting equal percentage interest in the property.

In Figure 22-1 on page 142 we have created the same family tree twice. If the father, Jim, and his son, John, were both dead, notice how differently Jim's property would be distributed under each method.

Under the plan with a per stirpes pattern of distribution, Jim's son, Herb, received one-half his father's property, and Herb's nephew, Dick, and niece, Jane, each received equal shares of the half that was to pass to John. Dick and Jane each received one-half of what was supposed to pass to their father, John.

Under the plan that used a per capita pattern of distribution, Herb, Dick, and Jane each received the same distribution: one-third of Jim's estate.

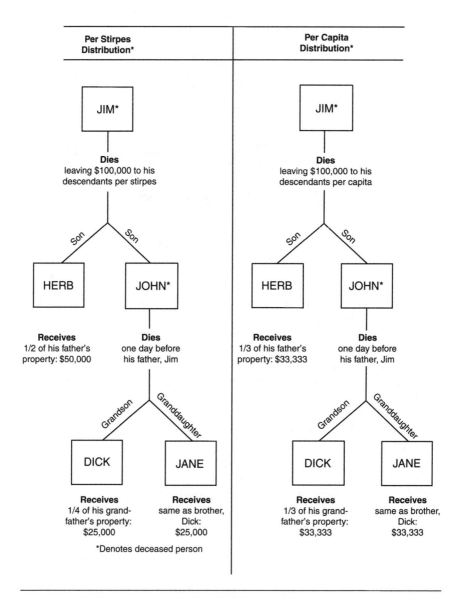

Figure 22-1 (Left) Per stirpes distribution. (Right) Per capita distribution (illustrated through grandchildren).

If Dick died in the same accident that took his father's life, and Dick had no children, the result under both distribution plans would be the same; Jim's son, Herb, would receive half of Jim's property, and Jim's granddaughter, Jane, would also receive half.

If Dick died in the same accident that took his father's life and left two living children, each plan would provide a dramatically different result.

Under the per stirpes plan, Herb would receive one-half Jim's property, or $50,000. Herb's niece, Jane, would receive $25,000: one-half of the property that would have gone to her father. Herb's great-nephews, Chip and Dale, would each receive one-half of the $25,000 that was supposed to pass to their father, Dick, or $12,500 each.

Under the per capita plan, Jim's son would receive one-quarter of his father's property, as would Herb's niece and great-nephews. Under the per capita method they each would receive the same amount, $25,000.

These results are illustrated in Figure 22-2 on the next page. As trusts last longer and longer, some clients are deciding to combine per stirpes and per capita in one estate plan. The two are combined when a trust maker wants to treat children and grandchildren equally.

In our example of Jim, Herb, and John, if Herb had three children, then under a per stirpes distribution Herb's three children would share Herb's half equally. Each of them would end up with one-sixth of Jim's estate. John's children would each end up with one-fourth of Jim's estate. One way of looking at this (and a lot of clients do), is that Herb is being penalized for having more children.

Jim may decide to create a plan that keeps his assets in trust equally for Jim and Herb (per stirpes), but when one of them dies, the remaining trust funds of the one who dies are divided equally among all the grandchildren (per capita). The net result is that the grandchildren each receive one-fifth of Jim's assets after both Jim and Herb die.

Another aspect of the "who will receive what" discussion is the definition of the beneficiaries. Wills name heirs, and trusts name beneficiaries. Both refer to children or descendants. Consideration must be made as to who is included in the family line. What if you have an adopted child or one of your children adopt a child? You may want to include the child or grandchild in your family line or you may not. In either event you must state your intentions. A clause we use in our estate plans is:

> A person's descendants shall include all of his or her lineal descendants through all generations. A descendant in gestation who is later born alive shall be considered a descendant in being throughout the period of gestation. An adopted person, and all persons who are the descendants by blood or by legal adoption while under the age of 18 years of such adopted person, shall be considered descendants of the adopting parents as well as the adopting parents' ancestors.

Another consideration is children of in vitro insemination occurring after the death of a parent. For example, if a married couple's daughter has a child that is conceived after the death of her husband from the deceased

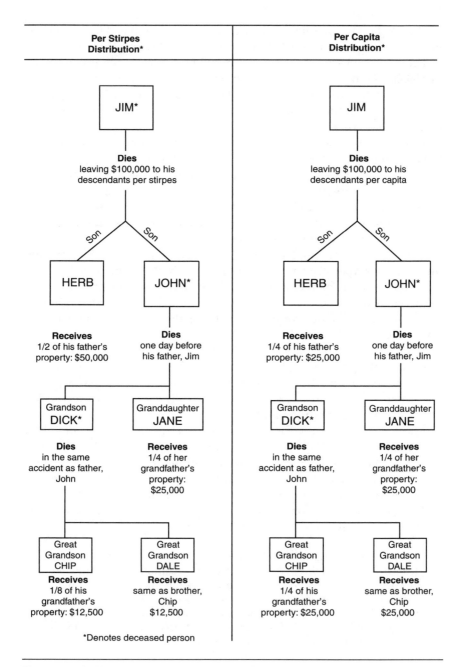

Per Stirpes Distribution*	Per Capita Distribution*

JIM*

Dies
leaving $100,000 to his
descendants per stirpes

Son   Son

HERB   **JOHN***

Receives
1/2 of his father's
property: $50,000

Dies
one day before
his father, Jim

Grandson
DICK*

Granddaughter
JANE

Dies
in the same
accident as father,
John

Receives
1/4 of her
grandfather's
property:
$25,000

Great
Grandson
CHIP

Great
Grandson
DALE

Receives
1/8 of his
grandfather's
property: $12,500

Receives
same as brother,
Chip
$12,500

JIM

Dies
leaving $100,000 to his
descendants per capita

Son   Son

HERB   **JOHN***

Receives
1/4 of his father's
property: $25,000

Dies
one day before
his father, Jim

Grandson
DICK*

Granddaughter
JANE

Dies
in the same
accident as father,
John

Receives
1/4 of her
grandfather's
property:
$25,000

Great
Grandson
CHIP

Great
Grandson
DALE

Receives
1/4 of his
grandfather's
property: $25,000

Receives
same as brother,
Chip
$25,000

*Denotes deceased person

Figure 22-2 (Left) Per stirpes distribution. (Right) Per capita distribution (illustrated through great-grandchildren).

husband's sperm, is that child a descendant? Or, if a daughter chooses not to marry but conceives through artificial means, is that child a descendant?

Finally, if a child is born out of wedlock, is that child a descendant or not?

While these issues may seem a little esoteric, it is surprising how many lawsuits are conceived and born from incomplete or overlooked drafting. Issues like this are why having an attorney draft documents is so important.

It is absolutely critical that you understand these distribution concepts and that you understand what Latin and English words go with them. If your attorney does not use the right words to accomplish your desires and you do not catch the mistake, your property will go in the wrong amounts to your beneficiaries and may go to beneficiaries whom you do not want to include.

People involved in planning their estates should understand the results that each distribution pattern creates and how descendants are defined. Other than your review, there may be no checkpoint that will ensure that the right words have been used. Mistakes in their use cannot be corrected after death.

We have listened to clients describe how they wish to distribute their property on death. We have also reviewed the existing wills and trusts of these same clients and have discovered that the wrong words were used. This does not happen often, but it can and does happen. Know your Latin, or at least four words of it.

23
Generation Skipping
Geometrically Increasing Your Estate

As property passes from one generation to the next, it is subject to the federal estate tax. Before 1976 it was possible to avoid the federal estate tax when property passed to subsequent generations. The avoidance of federal estate tax was usually accomplished by the use of a *generation-skipping trust.*

A generation-skipping trust allows the maker of the trust to skip federal estate tax as property passes from generation to generation. Here is how it works:

- The maker of the trust creates a trust, which receives the assets at the maker's death.

- The trust provides that the maker's spouse receives all income from the trust. The spouse receives principal from the trust if needed.

- At the death of the trust maker's spouse, the trust maker's children receive all the trust income. They too can receive principal from the trust if they need it.

- Upon the deaths of the trust maker's children, the principal of the trust passes to the maker's grandchildren.

- Alternatively, the trust maker could, at the death of the trust maker's spouse, provide that the trust property go directly to the trust maker's grandchildren, bypassing the trust maker's children completely.

Generation-skipping trusts have historically accomplished three basic objectives:

- Provide support for the maker's spouse, if any, and children, if the maker so chooses.

- Prevent the maker's spouse and children from "wasting" the maker's property by having the property controlled by a trustee.

- Limit federal estate tax payments to one on the maker's death and one on the death(s) of the grandchild(ren). (The maker's spouse and children paid *no* federal estate tax on the generation-skipping property on their deaths.)

As you can see, the middle generation (the children) was skipped; it did not pay any estate or gift tax when it passed to the grandchildren.

Generation skipping was very popular, especially among the very wealthy. The federal estate tax savings from generation to generation were significant. Because generation skipping was considered a tax loophole for the rich, its use was severely restricted by the Tax Reform Act of 1976.

The current generation-skipping transfer tax subjects to tax almost all transfers of property from an individual in one generation to a person or persons at least two generations below the transferring individual's generation. The simplest example of a generation-skip is a gift made by a grandparent to a grandchild. The generation-skipping tax can apply whether this gift is made during the grandparent's lifetime, at death, or by a trust or other method that delays the gift until some future time. Thus, not only are the traditional generation-skipping methods covered by this tax, but so are all other methods that have the effect of skipping the federal estate tax in one or more generations.

Under the generation-skipping tax for 2011 and 2012, everyone has $5 million with which to generation-skip. The 2012 amount was indexed for inflation to $5,120,000. This base amount of $5 million ends in 2013, when it is scheduled to go down to $1,060,000, plus inflation adjustment since 2001. In this chapter, because of the ease of using $5 million, that is the amount our examples are based on. You should always find out from your estate planning professionals the current amount of generation-skipping transfer tax exemption that is in effect.

Because a husband and a wife each have a $5 million exemption, they can, if they so choose, treat a generation-skipping transfer by one of them as being made one-half by each of them. Combined, then, they have at least $10 million to work with.

The $5 million exemption applies to lifetime generation skips or those occurring at the death of the trust maker. The $5 million can be allocated to one generation-skipping transfer, or it can be allocated in any manner the trust maker chooses among several generation-skipping transfers. If it is not specifically allocated by the trust maker, then the Internal Revenue Service provides automatic allocation rules. Sometimes these work just fine; other times they can be disastrous.

If a child of a trust maker dies before a generation-skipping transfer is made, then any transfers to that child's children by the trust maker are *not* considered to be generation-skipping transfers. This is called the *predeceased ancestor exception.*

The generation-skipping tax is due when the recipient of the generation-skipping property receives property, when the recipient has the right to the property (even when it is in a trust), or when a direct gift is made from a grandparent to a grandchild. The applicable tax rate is the highest federal estate tax rate: 35 percent for 2011 and 2012, and as high as 55 percent beginning in 2013, unless the law is changed. As you can see, this tax is extremely high.

There is a common misconception about the generation-skipping transfer tax exemption. Many people think that they can leave the generation-skipping exemption amount to their grandchildren entirely free from tax. However, the property is also subject to federal estate tax. Here is how the federal estate tax and the generation-skipping transfer tax work in tandem:

> Bill Anderson is not married; his wife died several years ago. Bill's only son, Ed, has one child, Andrea. Ed is wealthy in his own right, so Bill wants to leave his $10.5 million taxable estate to Andrea. On Bill's death, the applicable exclusion amount is $5 million. Because Bill's estate is $10.5 million and his applicable exclusion is $5 million, his taxable estate is $5.5 million. The tax is $1,925,000. The federal estate tax rate is 35 percent. That means there is $8,575,000 left to pass to Andrea. Then the $5 million generation-skipping exemption is applied. The generation skipping tax is imposed at a 35 percent rate on the net amount received by Andrea after payment of the estate and generation skipping tax. There is an additional tax of $926,852 (amount received by Andrea of $7,648,148 − $5 million generation skipping exemption × .35%). Andrea will end up with $7,648,148. A total of $2,851,852 went to taxes.

A similar result occurs if Bill makes a direct lifetime gift to Andrea. The gift tax and the generation-skipping tax are imposed, making the gift much more expensive. Let's assume Bill wants to use his entire $10.5 million to make the gift to Andrea and to pay all transfer taxes associated with the gift. Here is how that works:

> Bill makes a gift of $8,017,816 million to Andrea. Bill owes a generation skipping tax of $1,425,918, which he has to pay. Now a gift tax is imposed on the combined amount given to Andrea plus the generation skipping tax paid by Bill ($8,017,816 + 1,425,918), unlike at death when it is imposed on the amount left over after paying the federal estate tax. So, another $1,425,918 must be paid. The total tax is $2,428,918. The only good news is that Andrea ends up with more ($8,017,826 rather than $7,648,148) and Bill's estate is reduced by the $8,017,816 gift and the $2,482,918 in gift and generation skipping taxes that he had to pay.

For those who want to pass more than the generation-skipping tax exemption amount to their grandchildren, some planning techniques are available that avoid the gift tax, the federal estate tax, and the generation-skipping tax. For example, certain gifts of life insurance allow the generation-skipping tax to be leveraged. By making gifts of life insurance premiums, at worst, the amount of the premiums reduces the generation-skipping exemption. At best, the premiums do not even reduce the exemption. The following example shows how this leveraging can work:

> Charlotte McCarthy's grandchildren buy a $6 million life insurance policy on her life, naming themselves as the beneficiaries. Each year, Charlotte gives her grandchildren enough money to pay the premiums on the life insurance, but does not require them to pay the premiums. Because the gifts to the grandchildren are gifts of a present interest and their combined value is less than the annual exclusion gift amounts per year, there are no adverse federal gift tax consequences. The gifts do not reduce Charlotte's generation-skipping exemption because they are annual exclusion gifts to Charlotte's grandchildren.
>
> On Charlotte's death the $6 million in life insurance proceeds that passes to her grandchildren is not included in her estate for federal estate tax purposes. In addition, *none* of the $6 million counts toward her generation-skipping exemption. Therefore, she still can leave another $5 million (or whatever that amount is at her death) to her grandchildren free from the generation-skipping tax.

The generation-skipping tax is aimed at wealthy individuals who want to pass a substantial amount of property to younger family members without paying federal estate tax when intervening generations of family members die. While this tax has made it more difficult to generation-skip, some methods still exist to maximize the amount that can pass from grandparents to grandchildren or great-grandchildren.

To illustrate the importance of using the generation-skipping exemption amount, Table 23-1 presents estate tax numbers for an estate that passes through three generations. *It assumes that the family has used its estate tax applicable exclusion amount of $5 million* ($10 million combined) and that the estate is taxed at 35 percent. We use a $10 million taxable estate to make our point. After three generations, 72.5 percent of the value of the estate has gone to federal estate tax. We know this is an oversimplified example, but in larger estates, even taking into account that the inherited money is invested, each generation's estate will diminish by 35 percent, assuming federal estate taxes stay at this low rate. If estate tax rates increase, the amounts increase significantly.

Table 23-1
Federal Estate Tax over Three Generations at 35 percent on $10 million

Generation	Beginning Estate	Estate Tax	Remaining Estate
Grandparents	$10,000,000	$3,500,000	$6,500,000
Children	6,500,000	2,275,000	4,225,000
Grandchildren	4,225,000	1,478,750	2,746,250

Table 23-2 demonstrates the results of simple generation-skipping planning. If children are skipped and the $5 million generation skipping exemption of each grandparent is used for the transfers to the grandchildren, much more goes to the grandchildren and great-grandchildren.

Table 23-2

Generation-Skipping over Three Generations at 35 percent on
$10 million

Generation	Beginning Estate	EstateTax	Remaining Estate
Grandparents	$10,000,000	$3,500,000	$6,500,000
Children	0	0	0
Grandchildren	6,500,000	2,275,000	4,225,000

Planning can be done that will theoretically leave some of your property free from any gift, estate, or generation-skipping tax for as long as the grandparent would like. It is called *dynasty trust planning*. Since the inception of the United States, every state has adopted a rule that we inherited from England called the *Rule against Perpetuities*. Many legal treatises have been written about this rule, but in essence it says that you cannot leave your property in trust forever. Over half the states have now either repealed this rule or have extended it to at least 360 years. By creating a trust in one of these states, it is possible to allow all of your succeeding generations to use a portion of your wealth and, at the same time, avoid any gift, estate, and generation-skipping tax on it. You do not have to live in one of these states to create a trust that falls within its law.

If you have a large estate, you should explore dynasty trust planning. Over time it can save literally millions of dollars in taxes, and can also be used to help all of those family members who come after you.

Generation-skipping transfer tax affects only those taxpayers who have large estates. However, if used properly and coupled with sophisticated planning, the generation-skipping exemption can be used to geometrically increase the amount of property passing to other generations.

24

Disinheriting a Spouse

Spouses Have Rights Too

In planning estates over the years, we have often been asked, "What happens after my death if I disinherit my spouse?" And, "If I disinherit my spouse, can my spouse contest my will or trust, and get my property?" The answer to both questions is that in all states, disinherited spouses have the right to receive some of the property or other rights that was not left to them.

We must stress that each state has its own unique laws with respect to a surviving spouse's rights in the property of a deceased spouse. Most states give a surviving spouse the right to receive far less than half of the deceased spouse's property.

The name in which ownership of property is taken can become of critical importance on the death of a spouse, because ownership rights not established during life will not be meaningfully restored on death under the laws of most states. Even in states with liberal laws in bestowing rights to a surviving spouse, the rights are usually limited to a spouse receiving a maximum of one-half of the deceased spouse's property.

If you are thinking about disinheriting your spouse, *be careful.* After your death, your spouse will still have all the rights given under your state law to elect against your will and perhaps even your trust. It may also have a significant impact on federal estate taxes. Read Chapter 12, "The Marital Deduction," and Chapter 25, "Planning for a Spouse," to understand the federal estate tax ramifications of disinheriting a spouse.

If you choose to disinherit your spouse totally or partially, your estate planning needs can be determined only after you are aware of the rights your state gives your spouse after your death. After you finish this chapter, read the introduction to Appendix C and then read about your state's law with respect to you and your spouse's rights. It is important that you read the introduction to Appendix C because it will familiarize you with the

terms you will need to understand as you read your state's law. Knowledge
of your state's law will also enable you to better apply the techniques of
spousal planning that we discuss in Chapter 25, "Planning for a Spouse."
Laws change in states all the time. *Do not rely on Appendix C for the definitive
law in your state.* Always consult with a knowledgeable attorney in your state
prior to making decisions as to how much or how little you would like to
leave your spouse. Making a mistake because you fail to get good advice
could have a huge impact on how your estate will pass at your death.

Two techniques are generally used to assure persons that their spouses
will not successfully elect against their wills or trusts. The first technique is
called a *premarriage contract.* Attorneys refer to this contract as a *premarital,*
or *antenuptial,* contract. The second technique is called an *after-marriage contract* and is referred to by attorneys as a *postnuptial agreement.*

A premarriage contract is used by persons who wish to marry but who
also want to establish their right to leave property to their loved ones prior
to taking their marriage vows. The right of potential spouses to enter into
premarriage contracts is recognized in every state. Premarriage contracts
have been in use for centuries and are used more than ever today, particularly in second marriages. In order for these agreements to be valid, the following requirements usually must be met:

- Each party must be bound to the agreement and consent to it.
- Each party must totally disclose all assets.
- The agreement must be in writing.
- Both parties must understand what they are signing.

Premarriage contracts make it possible for spouses to protect the inheritance rights of their respective children by prior marriages, and as a result,
prevent strife over the disposition of their estates. The laws of all states favor
these contracts if they are properly prepared.

After-marriage contracts can also be used to set forth the spouses' inheritance wishes. They are not legally recognized to the extent that premarriage contracts are. The laws of each state are unique as they apply to the
after-marriage contract. Most states that recognize these contracts require
that:

- They be negotiated in good faith and reduced to writing.
- There is complete and frank disclosure of all the economic facts of each
  party.
- The provisions are fair and reasonable.
- The circumstances leading up to the signed agreement are free of fraud,
  duress, and undue influence of any kind.

After-marriage contracts are looked upon with suspicion by courts, and as a result, must be entered into very carefully. Because of this suspicion, the requirements for an after-marriage contract, where permitted, are much more complicated and rigorous than for a premarriage contract.

Given a choice between signing a premarriage contract or an after-marriage contract, always opt for the former; they are valid and binding if fair and fairly made, and have always been favored by the laws of most states.

Second marriages offer the most troublesome of estate planning challenges. The trouble arises because many people have children from their first marriages and want to assure that all or most of their estates go to those children. Alternatively, if there are children from one, two, or more marriages, making sure the children and the current spouse are all taken care of can be very difficult.

The best way to plan for a second marriage is through the use of a premarriage contract. Most problems concerning who gets what can be solved. If a premarriage contract was overlooked, an after-marriage contract may solve the problem.

What happens if neither premarriage nor after-marriage contracts can be used? Spouses in a second marriage have rights too. As a matter of fact, absent those contracts, their rights are exactly the same as a first spouse's rights given under your state's law. Please refer to Appendix C to get an idea as to your state's law with respect to your spouse's rights.

When you are planning your affairs, whether you are married or are contemplating marriage, remember: spouses have rights too!

25

Planning for a Spouse

An Incredible Number of Choices

Planning for a spouse starts with an initial decision of whether federal estate tax planning is necessary. If a married couple's estate is not going to be subject to federal estate tax planning, then there are fewer choices, making the decisions somewhat easier and straightforward. When federal estate tax planning is added, the planning choices are expanded considerably.

Will You and Your Spouse's Estate Need Federal Estate Tax Planning?

Believe it or not, deciding if federal estate tax planning is appropriate is not easy to do. It used to be, when there was some certainty as to the federal estate tax laws. Since Congress has not yet put in place a permanent federal estate tax, there is a lot of conjecture as to which estates need federal estate tax planning.

As we discussed in Chapter 9, "The Federal Estate Tax," in 2011 and 2012 the applicable exclusion amount (the base amount not subject to federal estate tax) is $5 million for an individual and $10 million for a married couple with the 2012 amount indexed for inflation. The inflation-adjusted amount in 2012 is $5,120,000. To simplify the illustrations in this chapter, we will ignore the inflation adjustment amount in 2012. In 2013, absent congressional action and presidential approval, that amount will revert to $1 million for an individual and $2 million for a married couple.

Of course, the next question has to be, "So, which law do I plan for?" The answer, if you want to protect your estate, is that you plan for the worst-case scenario, which is the $1 million and $2 million applicable exclusion amount.

The absolutely worst thing that you can do is to wait and see what Congress will do. If you do that, you may as well not plan at all. Odds are that you will be long gone before you can anticipate what Congress and the President will do. In the meantime, life and death will certainly go on and you may wait just long enough until you cannot do anything for your family. The time to plan is now.

If you and your spouse have combined assets that approach $2 million, we highly recommend that you go to the section below that explains planning for federal estate tax. If you do not, then your heirs may end up paying federal estate tax when they didn't have to.

Planning for a Spouse without Federal Estate Tax Considerations

Traditional planning for a spouse without the complexity of planning for the federal estate tax has been with an "I love you" will or an "I love you" trust. "I love you planning" means that each spouse has a will or trust that leaves all of the deceased spouse's property to the surviving spouse. The surviving spouse then has his or her own will or trust, which leaves property to children, grandchildren, relatives, friends, or charity. Each will or trust is an exact copy of the other.

This is pretty easy and standard planning that has been used for centuries. It is what almost all married couples desire, and a lot of time it works, but some of the time it does not. Before you think to yourself that this is no big deal and this is what I want, consider a few issues.

"I love you" planning is pretty much like joint tenancy planning. You can quickly review Chapter 3, "Jointly Held Property," to understand the advantages and disadvantages of joint property with right of survivorship. The only difference between "I love you" planning and joint tenancy is that with will planning, there could be a probate on each death. With trust planning, there is no probate on either death. In virtually every other way, "I love you" planning and joint tenancy planning are identical. Our conclusion with joint tenancy planning was that for most people joint tenancy is about the worst way to own property.

"I love you" planning with a will has several disadvantages. Property left to a surviving spouse in a will must pass through the probate process. This is one disadvantage that joint tenancy property does not have. If you want to leave all your property to your spouse, at the first death, joint tenancy is definitely easier.

Leaving property to a spouse outright by will allows the surviving spouse to use the property without any restraints. You may want your property to pass to your spouse and then your children. Leaving property outright to a spouse allows the spouse to give the property away during his or her lifetime and leave it to whomever he or she wants at death. There is also no protection from creditors, if that is an issue. This loss of control worries some people; others do not mind it.

When your spouse dies, the property you left him or her, as well as your spouse's own property, must go through probate once again, no matter where it passes. This is always true with a will.

If you leave property to your spouse in trust, you can control where that property passes at the death of your spouse. Your instructions will dictate where the property goes and when. Property held in trust does not have to go through probate; it can pass directly to beneficiaries without court supervision.

If you are concerned about your spouse's creditors, leaving property outright to him or her is a mistake. When a person inherits property under a will, that property is owned by the heir. His or her creditors can take the property. If property is left in trust for a spouse, there is creditor protection.

Property left outright to a spouse may have disability planning implications. If your spouse becomes incapacitated, maybe even from the same car accident that you died in, his or her assets may be subject to a living probate. If your spouse has the proper disability planning—including a Health Care Power, Living Will, and Durable Power of Attorney—the issue may be reduced, but it is highly likely that some court intervention will be needed even if your spouse has all the right documents. The best way to reduce the chances of court supervision is to leave property in trust.

There is one issue that you and your spouse need to consider when you create a revocable living trust. As we saw in Chapter 24, "Disinheriting a Spouse," surviving spouses have the right to receive part of a deceased spouse's assets when that spouse passes away. In the living trust planning that you do, make sure the surviving spouse has the right to receive the amount required by state law. In the absence of this provision, you and your spouse can prepare a postnuptial agreement where you each waive this right. Doing so can be expensive, so when you have an attorney draft your documents, find out what they would suggest.

For estates of $2 million or less, there are many planning variations. If your estate is under $2 million, you can accomplish your planning motives and always keep your estate free of federal estate tax on the deaths of both you and your spouse. How your objectives will be accomplished can be determined through the advice and counsel of your estate planning professionals.

If you wish to leave property to your spouse in trust, you should read the next section dealing with the marital trust to get some ideas on what is typically contained in a marital trust. For more restrictive trusts, read the section below on family trusts. It will give you even more ideas about what can be done when leaving property in trust for your spouse with the idea of protecting those assets so they ultimately pass to your heirs rather than being controlled by a surviving spouse.

Planning for a Spouse with Federal Estate Tax Considerations

When property is left to a U.S. citizen spouse, there is an unlimited marital deduction. No matter how much is left to that spouse, it is not subject to federal estate tax *at that time*. When a person who is unmarried dies, all of his or her property, even though it may have been inherited from a spouse and not taxed, is subject to federal estate taxation. There are special rules for property that passes to spouses who are not U.S. citizens. These rules are discussed later in this chapter. For purposes of the figures that follow, all references to spouses are to surviving spouses who are U.S. citizens.

There is interplay between the unlimited marital deduction and the applicable annual exclusion amount. To fully understand how they work together for a married couple, let's begin with what the law is supposed to be in 2013. Then we will come back to 2011 and 2012 to see how the rules changed for these two years.

In 2013 and after, you could leave all your property outright to your spouse and be assured that your estate would pay no federal estate tax on your death. The reason, of course, is that you can always leave all your property to your spouse entirely free of federal estate tax because of the unlimited marital deduction.

Figure 25-1 illustrates the federal estate tax consequences of leaving all your property directly to your spouse in 2013 and after. In our example, we are assuming that you have $1.5 million of property in your name and your spouse has no property. As you can see, the result of leaving the entire $1.5 million estate to your spouse is that $500,000 of your spouse's estate will pay federal estate tax when he or she dies.

The reason that tax is generated is that you used the unlimited marital deduction to shelter your estate from tax. Because you chose to leave all of your property to your spouse, the unlimited marital deduction applies to the full amount. You did not use any of your $1 million applicable exclusion amount.

When your spouse dies, there is no unlimited marital deduction (unless your spouse has remarried and wants to leave your property to his or her new spouse). Your spouse can shelter $1 million from federal estate tax because of the applicable exclusion amount. The other $500,000 will be taxed. The amount of the tax will be $210,000.

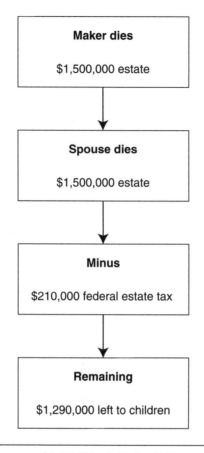

Figure 25-1 Outright-to-spouse, $1,500,000 estate after 2012.

If your spouse dies before you do, the result is the same, unless you leave all of your property to a new spouse. If you die unmarried, then the tax would be $210,000 because you will have an estate that is $500,000 over the applicable exclusion amount. Without additional planning or without a new spouse, the order of death of you and your spouse does not matter.

Contrast this with the result that would occur under what is known as the traditional two-trust plan, illustrated in Figure 25-2. This plan assumes that you want to leave one-half your estate to your spouse outright or in a marital trust for the benefit of your spouse, and one-half your estate for the benefit of your spouse and children in a separate family trust, both of which will be discussed later in this chapter.

If you used a traditional two-trust plan, there would be absolutely no federal estate tax on the death of either you or your spouse on a $1.5 million estate if you die first. (Later in this chapter, under the heading "Gifts between

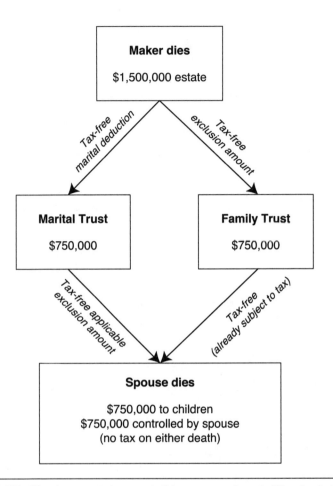

Figure 25-2 Traditional two-trust plan, one-half to spouse and one-half to a family trust after 2012.

Spouses," we discuss how you can eliminate estate tax in this situation no matter which one of you dies first.) There would be no tax on your death because the half of your estate that passed to your spouse is sheltered by the unlimited marital deduction. The half that passed to the family trust is sheltered by the applicable exclusion amount of $1 million, although only $750,000 would be needed.

Upon the death of your spouse, the $750,000 left to him or her outright or in trust would be sheltered by the spouse's $1 million applicable exclusion amount. The amount in the family trust was subject to tax at your death, but was sheltered by your applicable exclusion amount. Because of the way the family trust is drafted, it is not included in your spouse's estate, so it too passes tax-free to your children. The two-trust plan would save

$210,000 of federal estate tax. On a $2 million estate, the tax savings would be $435,000.

If your spouse had property of his or her own, or the $750,000 you left to him or her grows to over $1 million, the excess would be subject to federal estate tax.

One of the most beneficial results of using a family trust is that no matter how large it grows, it will not be taxed in your spouse's estate. If that $750,000 grows to over $1 million, there would still be no federal estate tax imposed on it when it passes to children or even grandchildren.

Before we go forward, let's delve into the two-trust plan just a bit.

Chapter 12, "The Marital Deduction," explained the unlimited marital deduction. It is available if you pass your property to your spouse outright or in trust. If you use a trust, the spouse, at a minimum, must receive at least annually all the income from the marital trust. The spouse must be given the right to convert the trust property to income-producing property so there is income for her or him to take. Finally, no person can have the power to give any part of the marital trust property to anyone other than the surviving spouse. The terms of the marital trust can be more liberal, but not more restrictive to take advantage of the marital deduction.

The family trust is an entirely different animal. Because its assets are subject to federal estate tax (but sheltered by the applicable exclusion amount of the first spouse to die), it can have almost any terms. Your spouse does not have to be a beneficiary, for example; you could name your children, grandchildren, friends, and relatives. The family trust still would not be subject to federal estate tax. The only thing you cannot do is give your spouse too many benefits, such as the right to leave the family trust property to whomever your spouse wants or the right to take out principal for any reason If you do, the family trust would be included in your spouse's estate, which would defeat the purpose of the family trust.

The most common type of family trust names the spouse, children, and grandchildren as the beneficiaries of the income and the principal of the family trust. Often the spouse is given first priority as to income and principal if he or she needs it. Sometimes the spouse is given the right to all income. The most liberal terms you can grant a spouse in a family trust and not have the trust included in your spouse's estate are:

- The right to all of the family trust income.
- The right to withdraw the greater of $5,000 or 5 percent of the family trust's principal each year.
- The right to receive principal distributions at the discretion of the trustee, usually limited by the standards of health, maintenance, education, and support.
- The right to change the amount each beneficiary receives on the spouse's death and the right to change the beneficiaries.

This last spousal right is called a *limited power of appointment*. If you give your spouse the right to name his or her estate or creditors as a beneficiary (this right is called a *general power of appointment*), however, then the full amount of the family trust will be included in your spouse's estate.

As you can see, the family trust's provisions can be very generous to a spouse.

Once you understand how the marital trust and the family trust work together, other issues have to be addressed. Right now you may be asking yourself, "What should I do if I do not want to leave one-half of my estate to my spouse?" The answer depends on whether your planning motive is to give your spouse the maximum benefits from and control over your estate (Figure 25-3) or whether your motive is to give your spouse the least benefit from and control over your estate (Figure 25-4). Figures 25-3 and 25-4 illustrate how you can accomplish either of these aims and still reduce federal estate tax.

You can see the dramatic difference in the results for the surviving spouse between the two scenarios. In both illustrations there will be no federal estate tax on the death of either you or your spouse, unless the marital share grows to exceed the applicable exclusion amount ($1 million beginning in 2013, subject to any legislative changes) or if your spouse has assets of his or her own.

In Figure 25-4, our minimum-to-spouse diagram, the only right your spouse has is the right to the income from the $500,000 in the marital trust. Do not forget, however, that under state law your spouse may have the right to elect against your plan. Good planning for estates when a spouse is to receive minimal benefits is to create a marital trust that would equal but not exceed the spousal rights accorded that spouse under state law. For example, assume you died a resident of a state that provides that if your spouse and children survive you, your spouse is entitled to one-third of your estate. A plan that would accomplish your objectives and not be inconsistent with state law is illustrated in Figure 25-5.

Planning in 2011 and 2012

We need to digress a bit before moving on to other planning possibilities. The law in 2011 and 2012 is different in some respects, so it too has to be looked at for planning opportunities and issues.

Before 2011 the *applicable exclusion amount* (which has had other names over the years) was treated the same for individuals and married couples. That is, each person received the applicable exclusion amount. If an individual received that amount, so did each spouse in a marriage. Prior to 2012, if a single individual or the first to die of a married couple did not use his or her applicable exclusion amount during lifetime or at death, it vanished.

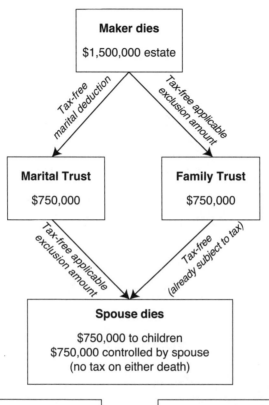

Figure 25-3 Maximum-to-spouse motive after 2012.

Terms of Marital Trust

All income to spouse.

Principal to spouse whenever desired.

Trustee gives principal to spouse as needed if spouse unable to ask for it.

Spouse has right to leave principal on death.

If spouse does not leave principal elsewhere, it will go automatically to children.

Terms of Family Trust

All income to spouse.

Spouse receives $5,000 or 5% of principal, whatever is greater, each year.

Spouse is cotrustee and spouse is primary beneficiary of principal.

Spouse can leave principal among select beneficiaries.

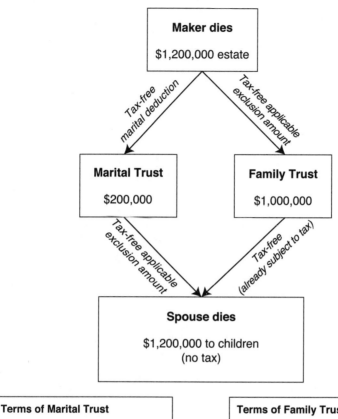

Figure 25-4 Minimum-to-spouse motive after 2012.

Congress deviated from this approach for 2011 and 2012. The $5 million applicable exclusion amount applies to an individual. In contrast, a couple in essence is given a $10 million applicable exclusion amount, which they may share for federal estate and gift taxes. Tax planning professionals call this concept "portability." Spouses cannot share the $5 million generation-skipping transfer tax amount. When the first spouse

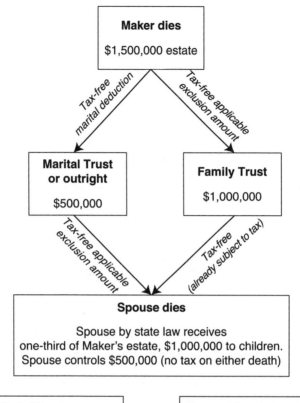

Figure 25-5 Minimum-to-spouse under state law after 2012.

dies, he or she can leave to the surviving spouse the deceased spouse's remaining applicable exclusion amount. The surviving spouse claims the deceased spouse's unused applicable exclusion amount by filing a federal estate tax return.

Figure 25-6 illustrates a simple scenario where one spouse has a $10 million estate and the other spouse has no assets. If you contrast this with

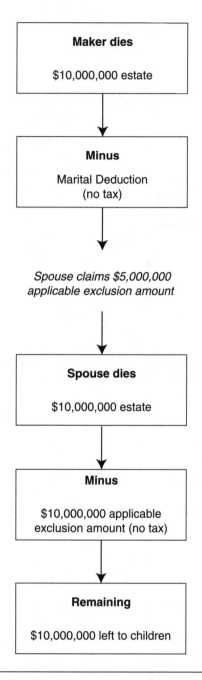

Figure 25-6 Outright-to-spouse, $10,000,000 estate in 2011 and 2012.

Figure 25-1, you will see that the surviving spouse gets the benefit of the combined $10 million applicable exclusion amount. When the spouse with all the assets died, even though he or she used the marital deduction and not a dime of the applicable exclusion amount, the surviving spouse could use the full $10 million applicable exclusion amount to pass the $10 million to children tax-free. All the surviving spouse had to do was file a federal estate tax return and elect to "inherit" the $5 million applicable exclusion amount.

This sharing concept is true even if the spouses die in the wrong order. If the spouse with no assets died first, the spouse with all of the assets could inherit the deceased spouse's $5 million applicable exclusion amount, leaving the surviving spouse a full $10 million applicable exclusion amount.

The ability to share the $10 million amount could be especially helpful if one spouse had more assets than the other and the poorer spouse dies first. For example, in Figure 25-7 the husband has $3 million in his name and the wife has $7 million. The husband could shelter his $3 million using a portion of his $5 million applicable exclusion amount and leave the excess $2 million exclusion amount to his wife. The wife could shelter her $7 million with her $5 million applicable exclusion amount plus the $2 million amount transferred from her husband at his earlier death. The combined estates just have to equal $10 million or less.

While there are many complexities to this planning, some of which remain unresolved, the bottom line is that a married couple, if they both died in 2011 and 2012, could use the full $10 million applicable exclusion amount no matter which of them owned the property.

What is not known at this time is the effect of this planning after 2012. It may be that if one spouse dies in 2011 or 2012 but the other spouse survived, this sharing of the applicable exclusion amount is lost. So planning for 2011 or 2012 has to be done in such a manner as to preserve the most tax benefits no matter how the federal estate tax laws are changed.

To help you with this planning, the first action we would recommend is to use two-trust planning. When each spouse leaves his or her entire estate to the deceased spouse, as we have discussed earlier, there is loss of control and loss of creditor protection. It also is not the best way to maximize federal estate tax planning, since there is a risk that the surviving spouse will lose the 2011 and 2012 sharing of the applicable exclusion amount or the applicable exclusion amount will be lowered after 2012. And, of course, there is the very real possibility that both spouses will be living after 2012, in which case, they would have to redo their planning to meet the requirements of yet another federal estate tax change.

The ideal planning under the 2011 and 2012 law would be to maximize the use of each spouse's applicable exclusion amount by allocating it to the family trust, no matter which spouse died first. In order to accomplish this

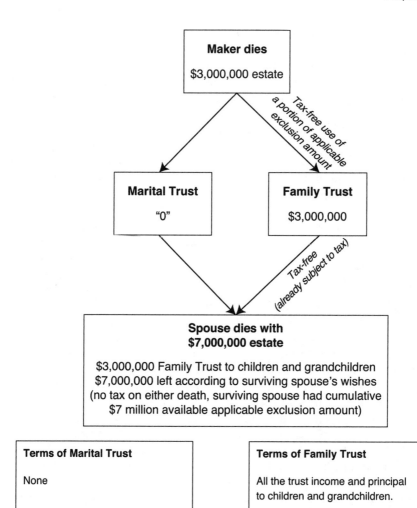

Figure 25-7 Maximum-tax-savings motive in 2011 and 2012.

planning, it is necessary in larger estates for the poorest spouse to have assets of at least $5 million. The family trust is irrevocable, so the hope would be that once the maximum amount was put into the family trust, it would not be subject to federal estate tax until it was included in the estate of the maker's children, and to the extent of the $5 million generation-skipping tax exemption, for many generations. Figure 25-8 shows an estate of $10 million, all of which is owned by one spouse with a motive to reduce the maximum federal estate and generation-skipping taxes.

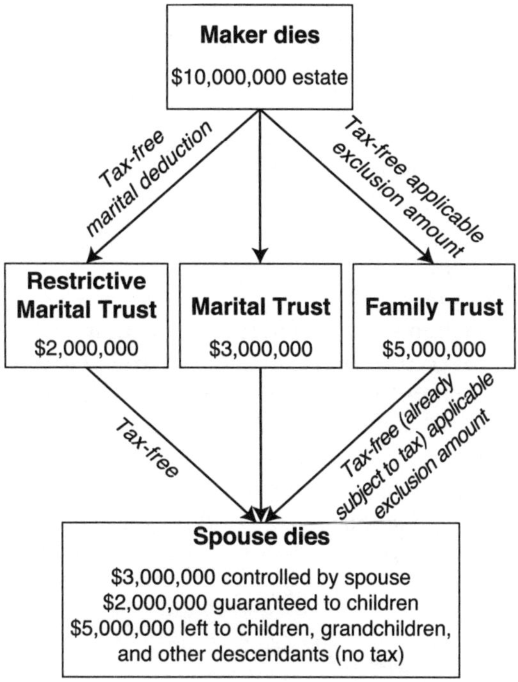

Terms of Restrictive Marital Trust	Terms of Marital Trust	Terms of Family Trust
All income to spouse.	All income to spouse.	All the trust income and principal to children.
Spouse has no right to use principal during life.	Spouse has right to use principal during life.	Spouse has no rights to trust.
Spouse has no right to leave principal at death.	Spouse has right to leave principal on death.	
Principal automatically goes to children on spouse's death.		

Figure 25-8 Minimum-to-spouse under state law in 2011 and 2012.

For estates over $10 million, after the estates are "equalized" by gifts to the poorer spouse to fully utilize the applicable exemption amount available at death, all the excess property of the deceased spouse would be left outright to the surviving spouse, or, as we would recommend, to a marital trust. There would be no tax on the amount left to the marital trust. On the death of the surviving spouse, the amount in the marital trust and any other property owned by the surviving spouse would be subject to federal estate tax, but sheltered by the applicable exclusion amount that was then in place. The surviving spouse could use his or her $5 million generation-skipping to pass property to grandchildren and other descendants.

Remember that there is no guarantee that the amounts left to the spouse in the marital trust will avoid federal estate tax. If the spouse should die in 2013 or later under the current law, some part of the property in the marital trust could be subject to federal estate tax.

For those couples who have estates that approximate $2 million or more, there is no difference in planning than the couple that has $10 million. The more that is allocated to the family trust, the more likely it is that a greater amount can be preserved for children and grandchildren. The important principle to understand is that it is highly unlikely the family trust will be subject to federal estate tax when the surviving spouse dies, no matter how the federal estate tax laws have changed.

Other motives, of course, may dictate a different allocation to the marital trust and the family trust.

Protecting Your Estate from Federal Estate Taxes

If you believe that your estate has a value in excess of $2 million in 2013, or if you are reading this book in 2013 or later and the applicable exclusion amount is such that your estate may be subject to federal estate tax, there are many planning opportunities available.

Planning your estate in order to minimize federal estate tax on your death and the death of your spouse will always depend on your objectives.

Here are the parameters you must follow:

- Property left to a spouse outright or in a properly drafted marital trust qualifies for the marital deduction.

- You must take into account your state's law regarding how much you must leave your spouse.

- If the surviving spouse dies unmarried, all of his or her property, including property in the marital trust, is subject to federal estate tax, but is sheltered from tax to the extent of the applicable exclusion amount then in effect.

- A family trust is not subject to federal estate tax, because it is sheltered by the applicable exclusion amount in effect in the year you die.

- The surviving spouse does not have to be a beneficiary of the family trust.

- A properly structured family trust is not subject to federal estate tax when the surviving spouse dies, no matter how large the family trust grows, as long as the spouse does not have a general power of appointment.

- A family trust can be used to skip generations, thereby delaying the application of a generation-skipping tax for many generations, depending on state law.

A living trust or a will with a testamentary trust (not our favorite planning technique) can contain the instructions you and your spouse want. The document can have language that allocates property between a marital trust and a family trust. Almost all plans for a married couple contain a formula clause that allocates property between the marital trust and the family trust based on the federal estate tax marital deduction, the applicable exclusion amount, and the generation-skipping tax exemption amount in effect on the death of the first spouse to die.

Because of the many choices based on motives, it is imperative that this planning be implemented with the help of an experienced estate planning attorney, an accountant, and financial and insurance advisors. The laws are far too sophisticated and complex for anyone to rely on a form, a software program, or an Internet-based planning system.

Gifts between Spouses

In a noncommunity-property state, when a married couple owns most or all of their property in the name of only one spouse, or in a community property state when a spouse owns most of his or her property as sole and separate property, another technique can be used to reduce federal estate tax. In using this technique, the asset-owner spouse gives property free of federal gift tax to the other spouse, who must be a U.S. citizen. The value of the gift should be large enough so that when added to the poorer spouse's other property, their total estate is equal to the full applicable exclusion amount. If the spouse already has property equal to or greater than the applicable exclusion amount, a gift is not necessary.

If the poorer spouse then dies first, an amount up to the applicable exclusion amount will not generate federal estate tax. If this property is left in a family trust for the benefit of the asset-owner spouse and children, there will be no federal estate tax on the death of the asset-owner spouse. If this technique is not used and the non-asset-owner spouse dies first, that non-asset-owner spouse's exemption equivalent is lost. The loss of the applicable exclusion amount could cost hundreds of thousands or even millions in additional federal estate tax on the death of the asset-owner spouse.

Planning for a Spouse Who Is
Not a U.S. Citizen

If your spouse is not a U.S. citizen, some significant marital deduction planning advantages are lost. First and foremost is the unlimited marital deduction for gifts. Gifts between spouses who are U.S. citizens qualify for the unlimited marital deduction. For these spouses there is no limit on the amount of tax-free gifts. Gifts from a spouse to a noncitizen spouse were originally tax-free up to $100,000 annually. This amount is adjusted annually for inflation and is $139,000 in 2012. If gifts exceed this amount in any one year, the excess is a taxable gift. The $139,000 amount does increase with inflation, so check with your estate planning professional for the current allowable amount.

Sometimes, unintended taxable gifts are made between spouses where one of them is a noncitizen. For example, if one spouse purchases a home using his or her own funds and titles the property in joint tenancy with rights of survivorship, a gift of one-half of the value of the property has been made. If the amount paid is in excess of double that year's annual exclusion ($278,000 in 2012, $139,000 × 2) for a noncitizen spouse, then a gift has been made. It is very important to consult a competent estate planning advisor if either your spouse or you are not a U.S. citizen and you want to make interspousal gifts.

There are a number of restrictions on the standard marital deduction when a spouse dies and leaves property to a noncitizen spouse. To qualify for the deferral of estate taxation on property left in trust for the noncitizen spouse, these rules must be followed:

- Property must be left in a special type of marital trust requiring income to be paid to the spouse for life, paid at least annually; this trust is called a Qualified Domestic Trust (QDOT).

- Principal distributions are subject to estate taxes when made to the spouse, unless made for hardship reasons.

- At least one trustee of the marital deduction trust must be a U.S. citizen or a domestic corporation with trust powers. (In case of assets above $2 million, the trustee must be a U.S. bank.)

- No principal distributions are allowed unless the U.S. trustee has the right to withhold any tax imposed on distribution.

- After the death of the surviving spouse, the assets held in the QDOT are subject to estate tax as if they were included in the estate of the first spouse who died.

It is difficult to get principal out of the QDOT without taxation. The only way to get it out tax-free, other than for the spouse to become a U.S. citizen, is for hardship reasons. *Hardship* is defined as an immediate and substantial financial need relating to the spouse's health, maintenance, education, or support, or that of any person the spouse is legally obligated to support. Any other distributions are taxable at the highest marginal rate applicable to the estate of the spouse who created the marital trust.

If you do not set up a trust that qualifies as a QDOT, there are methods to have the trust reformed to qualify. It is better by far to have your attorney create a QDOT trust to avoid costly and stressful action after the death of a spouse. But if the surviving spouse becomes a U.S. citizen after the death of his or her spouse and prior to the date the federal estate tax return is due (nine months after date of death), a QDOT is not necessary.

We must reiterate the importance of seeking proper planning if your spouse or you are not a U.S. citizen. The penalties for not planning can be costly, so seeking out experts is a necessity.

In this chapter we have highlighted some basic planning techniques that you should be familiar with when planning for your family. This discussion of techniques is not exhaustive, however. The number of planning alternatives available to you and your professional advisors is staggering.

26

Planning for Unmarried Couples

Protecting the Rights of Both Parties

Much of financial and estate planning focuses on planning for married couples. Little is written concerning the planning issues, challenges, and solutions for unmarried couples. There are a number of safeguards and protections under state and federal law for married couples that do not apply when the couples are not married as recognized by federal law. This chapter does not address specific planning for same sex couples, nor does it discuss the laws in those few states that do provide certain rights and privileges to domestic partnerships or civil unions under state law. Rather, we deal here with a number of issues common to all unmarried couples, opposite sex and same sex.

Unmarried couples who wish to provide for each other and to be legally able to make decisions for each other face myriad challenges and obstacles generally not faced by married couples. We have discussed why it is so important for married couples to engage in comprehensive planning. It is as important for unmarried couples to do so.

Unfortunately, many unmarried couples living together in long-term relationships have not engaged in any formal planning. The unmarried couple often pool their earnings and resources to pay their ongoing expenses and even to save for the future. The income earned by each partner may be deposited in a joint account to pay for the couple's everyday expenses and save for their futures. Often, couples title their accounts and property jointly to further the concept of the family unit and for convenience. Pooling of resources and joint account ownership is no problem for married U.S. citizens because of the unlimited gift tax marital deduction. However, unmarried couples pooling their resources and titling property jointly may result in immediate, unintended gifts for gift tax purposes. Here is an example of what we mean:

> Mary and John have been living together for 10 years in a home that Mary purchased before she and John began dating. They decided several years ago that they would never marry, but planned to spend the rest of their lives together. Recently, they decided they'd like to live in a larger home in the country. Mary sold her existing home and used the proceeds and some of her savings to purchase a new home for $500,000. When she took title to the new home, she thought it was only fitting that they own the home jointly with rights of survivorship. Up until this time Mary and John owned all of their assets individually. They then decided it would be easier if they titled all of their assets jointly with rights of survivorship, including their bank and brokerage accounts.

Let's examine more closely what Mary and John did.

Because they were not married, there was no unlimited marital deduction to prevent taxable gifts from occurring on transfers between them. When Mary paid the entire purchase price for the new home with her own money and then added John's name to the deed, she made an immediate taxable gift to John. The amount of the gift for federal gift tax purposes depends on their ages. The IRS uses life expectancy tables to determine this type of gift. Mary and John are the same age, so one-half of the value of the new home, $250,000, is a taxable gift to John. (If John were younger than Mary, the gift would be more than one-half the value. If he were older, the gift would be less than one-half.) Assuming this is the first gift of the year from Mary to John, the $250,000 taxable gift is reduced by the annual exclusion amount, $13,000 in 2012. Mary adding John onto the deed has reduced her lifetime gift tax applicable exclusion amount by $237,000.

Recall in Chapter 3, "Jointly Held Property," we discussed the few benefits and the many pitfalls of creating joint tenancy with rights of survivorship property. In Mary's case, in addition to the adverse gift and estate tax consequences, potential pitfalls include her inability to sell the home without John's signature. In addition, upon her death the home will pass outright to John. These consequences may present substantial problems if Mary and John's relationship terminates for any reason.

John and Mary also named each other as joint account holders on their individual brokerage and bank accounts. Generally, this action alone does not create a taxable gift to the person who is added to the account. A taxable gift does occur when the newly added person withdraws funds from the account. John and Mary have created a situation in which a taxable gift can occur every time one of them withdraws funds from these accounts. Under most joint account agreements, one joint owner has the right to withdraw all of the funds from the account at any time without the consent of the other owner. If things go well in their relationship, this feature of joint accounts may not be a problem, but it is not good planning to merely hope for the best.

Before unmarried couples begin to treat their financial affairs and ownership of assets similar to those of married couples, it is incumbent upon them to enter into a legal agreement that sets forth the rights and responsibilities between them upon the occurrence of certain events, such as termination of the relationship, disability, or death. With proper planning, the unmarried couple can also avoid many of the pitfalls of joint ownership.

Proactive Planning for Unmarried Couples

Unmarried couples in long-term relationships should discuss and plan for a number of things that are typically addressed by married couples more routinely. For example, an unmarried couple should discuss how they want their property to pass when they die. Without will, trust, or other planning, most property other than joint tenancy property owned at death is distributed in accordance with state intestacy statutes.

When a married person dies with no children and without planning, most intestacy statutes give the entire estate to the surviving spouse. If there are children, then many intestacy statutes provide for one-half of the estate to pass to the surviving spouse and one-half to the children. When an unmarried person dies intestate, most states provide that the property passes to any children. If there are none, then the property passes to surviving parents. If there are no surviving parents, then property typically passes equally to surviving brothers and sisters. The person totally omitted from intestacy statutes is the surviving member of the unmarried couple!

Unmarried couples must plan in order to leave property at their death to their surviving partner. They also need to plan if they want to provide financially for their partner on their disability and if they want their partner to be able to manage their affairs upon disability. In Chapter 17, "The Revocable Living Trust," we discussed our strong preference for revocable living trust based planning over will based planning. For unmarried couples, revocable trust based planning may be even more important for accomplishing their goals and objectives with the least amount of hassle and resistance. Will based planning for unmarried couples may lead to disappointment. As we discussed, wills are generally more easily challenged than are revocable living trusts. When a partner dies leaving assets to the surviving partner, the deceased partner may have disgruntled relatives who believe they were "deprived from what was rightfully theirs." If a disgruntled relative wishes to bring legal action to set aside the planning, such action is often easier to commence and to succeed when the planning is will based.

Let's look at an example of a plan that successfully accomplishes the goals and objectives of Jack and Jill.

They have been in a relationship for five years, decided they want to be together "forever," but have no desire to get married. They want to organize their affairs to best deal with future circumstances to make sure they can each take care of the other while they are both alive, and that when the first of them passes away the survivor is well taken care of. Jack and Jill also want to avoid the tax problems and potential land mines that Mary and John caused when they created joint accounts and took title to assets jointly with rights of survivorship.

Jack and Jill shared all these matters with their estate planning attorney, who asked them a number of questions to more fully understand and refine their intentions. After carefully listening, the attorney prepared living trusts, pour-over wills, durable powers of attorney, health care powers with HIPPA provisions, and living wills for them.

For Jack and Jill, their individual living trusts are the foundation of their planning. With the assistance of their attorney, they transferred their separate assets to their own living trust following the advice provided in Chapter 18, "Funding a Revocable Living Trust." They each retained the right to add property to their trust, remove property from their trust, to change the terms of their trust at any time, and to totally revoke their trust if they choose to do so. Each trust provides specific instructions for the management of their assets in the event of their disability.

In Jack's living trust he is the initial trustee, and he has named Jill and his CPA as his successor trustees. Jack's trust provides that upon his disability, his successor trustees—Jill and his CPA—are to use his trust assets to take care of him by providing whatever care he needs, to pay all his expenses, to pay his and Jill's joint living expenses, and to pay for Jill's basic personal needs if she can't afford to do so.

Jill's trust is very similar to Jack's, except she wants to be sure that she is not placed in a nursing home if there is any possibility for her to remain at home. Her aunt was in a nursing home for a number of years before she died, and Jill has bad memories of her time spent visiting her aunt in the home. Upon Jill's disability, her successor trustees are Jack and her financial advisor, Maryrose, a close personal friend and confidante.

Upon death, Jack and Jill's living trusts each establish a trust for the benefit of the survivor of the two of them. The successor trustees are instructed to invest the assets for the benefit of the survivor, and to make distributions of income and principal for the survivor's health, maintenance, education, and support. When both Jack and Jill are deceased, their trusts provide for different distributions of the remaining trust assets. Upon Jack's death, if he survives Jill or upon her death if he predeceased her, all of his remaining trust assets are to be distributed to the National Wildlife Foundation. Upon the last to die of Jack and Jill, all of the assets remaining in Jill's trust are to be distributed equally among her then living brothers and sisters.

Jack and Jill also signed pour-over wills that primarily address the appointment of executors or personal representatives and provide that any property owned at death not titled in their living trust will be transferred to their trust.

In Chapter 4, "Disability," we discussed the importance of durable powers of attorney, health care powers with HIPPA provisions, and living wills. These documents are even more essential for unmarried couples who want their partner to be involved with any of the matters these documents are created to address. Jack and Jill are determined that they are involved in making any health care decisions when they are unable to make those decisions for themselves. Absent properly drafted health care powers naming each other as the decision maker, there is very little chance that either of them would be able to participate in those critical decisions. In fact, there are a number of articles describing a partner in an unmarried couple relationship being barred from even visiting with his or her disabled partner by the family members of a disabled partner. These unwanted results can only be avoided by unmarried couples planning ahead and stating clearly their desires in the proper legal documents.

Jack and Jill implemented a plan that achieves their desires. It allows both of them to maintain control of their own property and determine how each will be cared for while alive and the survivor taken care of after the first death. They have engaged in the ideal estate planning we describe in Chapter 1, "What Is Estate Planning?"

Let's compare the outcome of John and Mary's lack of planning against Jack and Jill's comprehensive planning.

Mary made a taxable gift to John when she titled the new home she purchased in their joint names with rights of survivorship. Mary lost control over the home, since John has the ability to prevent its sale by refusing to sign a deed. Upon Mary's death, if she is survived by John, the home passes to him outright, to do with whatever he pleases. In addition, the full value of the home at Mary's date of death is included in her estate for estate tax purposes, since she provided the entire purchase price for the home.

When John and Mary added each other's names to all of their bank and brokerage accounts, they each lost control of those assets. The noncontributor to each account has the immediate ability to withdraw some or all of the assets from the account. Worse yet, the "taker" causes the contributor partner to make a taxable gift for gift tax purposes of the assets withdrawn from the account. Since neither John nor Mary engaged in any real planning, if one of them becomes disabled, a guardianship proceeding will be commenced in court to appoint a guardian for the person and the property of the disabled person. The petition to appoint the guardian will likely come from a family member of the disabled partner, and the judge will be inclined to appoint a family member (not the partner) as the guardian. The family member guardian would then marshal the disabled partner's assets and decide how the assets are invested and spent. The guardian would likely petition the court to have all of the accounts that the disabled partner funded, and added the other partner's name on closed and open accounts in the disabled partner's name only.

Under the law, the disabled partner's assets can only be spent for the benefit of the disabled partner. The guardian decides where the disabled partner lives and who is allowed to visit the partner. In addition, the court would stay involved in overseeing how the disabled partner's assets are invested and spent by the family member guardian. This scenario could easily result in the nondisabled partner being "left out in the cold" with no ability to see the disabled partner, and certainly no right to any financial benefits from the disabled partner.

Effective Transfer Tax Planning for Unmarried Couples

Unmarried couples with estate tax concerns can greatly benefit by engaging in transfer tax planning in addition to the good estate planning exemplified by Jack and Jill. At what threshold level of net worth does an unmarried couple have an estate tax issue? Under current law, when one of the partners has an estate in excess of $5 million in 2011, $5,120,000 in 2012, his or her estate may be subject to federal estate tax.

Beginning in 2013 that threshold amount drops to $1 million, unless Congress changes the law before then. A married couple engaging in the planning we describe in Chapter 25, "Planning for a Spouse," can have a combined estate of double these threshold amounts ($10 million today, $2 million beginning in 2013) without incurring federal estate tax at the second death. The unlimited estate tax marital deduction allows a married couple to avoid any estate tax at the first death no matter how large the estate. Unmarried couples with a combined estate today over $5 million ($5.12 million in 2012) or over $1 million beginning in 2013 who leave their estates to the survivor will have an estate tax issue at the second death and will also have an estate tax issue at the death of the first partner if their estate exceeds $5.12 million with death occurring before the end of 2012, and $1 million if death occurs after 2012.

Since unmarried couples do not have the benefit of the unlimited marital gift tax deduction, or the unlimited marital estate tax deduction. They often need to engage in more sophisticated planning to maximize assets available to the surviving member of the couple by minimizing taxes. But there are many tax planning strategies and techniques available to unmarried couples. Some of the following techniques require making life transfers, which can result in loss of control over the property transferred. You will want to work closely with your planning advisors to make sure you don't take action today that you will regret in the future.

Annual Exclusion Gifts

One easy method of estate tax planning is establishing a program of annual exclusion gifts. This strategy works best when one partner is slightly over the estate tax threshold amount and the other is well below it. The wealthier partner makes annual exclusion gifts to the poorer partner and does so either outright or in a trust. Remember, if the gifts are made in trust, the partner who is the beneficiary of the trust is given the right to withdraw the gifts to qualify them for the annual exclusion. We discuss trust beneficiary demand rights in Chapter 30, "The Irrevocable Life Insurance Trust." Over time this simple plan may reduce the wealthier partner's estate below the estate tax threshold.

Life Insurance Owned by an Irrevocable Life Insurance Trust

Life insurance owned by an irrevocable life insurance trust (ILIT) is a great way to leverage annual exclusion gifts between unmarried couples. Cash in amounts as much as the annual exclusion in the year of the gift ($13,000 in 2012) can be given to the ILIT. The trustee of the ILIT uses the annual cash gifts to purchase life insurance on the life of the donor. Upon the donor's death, the life insurance proceeds are paid to the ILIT and can be spent for the benefit of the surviving partner. The life insurance proceeds will be out of the estate of the insured, and the ILIT can be structured to keep the proceeds out of the surviving partner's estate as well if that's desired. See Chapters 27 through 30 to review the structure and benefits of incorporating life insurance owned by an ILIT into an estate plan.

Limited Partnerships and Limited Liability Companies

Unmarried partners can often obtain several advantages by transferring a portion of their assets to a Limited Partnership or Limited Liability Company (LLC). Let's look at an example using an LLC.

Rich Partner contributes rental property with a fair market value of $900,000 to a newly formed LLC in exchange for a 90 percent member interest. Poor Partner contributes $100,000 cash in exchange for a 10 percent member interest. The LLC's operating agreement provides that Rich Partner is the operating manager, restricts a member's ability to make transfers of LLC interests, and provides for all matters regarding the ongoing operation of the LLC. Over time, Rich Partner may wish to give some of his or her LLC interests to Poor Partner. The amount of the gift would be less than the pro rata interest in the underlying assets, and it would be determined by an appraiser who has special qualifications in the area of valuing entity interests.

If structured and administered properly, this situation allows Rich Partner to maintain control over the assets of the LLC and allows Rich Partner to make discounted gifts to Poor Partner, thus leveraging Rich Partner's applicable exclusion amount and reducing the taxable value of his or her estate. For more information regarding LLCs and limited partnerships, see Chapter 33, "Discounting the Value of Your Estate."

Grantor Retained Income Trusts

In Chapter 33 we discuss how at one time Grantor Retained Income Trusts (GRITS) used to be a great planning technique until Congress virtually eliminated them back in 1989. However, even today there are transfer tax benefits to using a GRIT when the beneficiaries of the GRIT are not family members. The good news is that unmarried couples are not within the definition of "family members" in the Internal Revenue Code. If the wealthier partner wishes to make a gift today that will benefit his or her partner in the future, a GRIT may be the answer.

Rich Partner, age 50, transfers ranch land valued at $1 million to a GRIT. The land is leased to a cattle rancher for $20,000 per year. Rich Partner retains the right to all the income from the GRIT for 10 years. After the end of the 10-year term, the ranchland goes outright to Poor Partner. Let's further assume that the percentage rate the Internal Revenue Service requires Rich Partner to use to value the retained right to receive all GRIT income for 10 years is 5 percent. Rich Partner has made a taxable gift to Poor Partner of $574,580.

Let's assume that the value of the land increases 5 percent per year during the 10-year period it is owned by the GRIT. At the end of 10 years Poor Partner receives the ranchland valued at approximately $2,079,000, even though the taxable gift was only $574,580.

Combining Gifts to a Partner
with Charitable Planning

Charitable remainder and charitable lead trusts can be a good way to transfer assets from Rich Partner to Poor Partner while supporting Rich Partner's philanthropic causes. The specifics of these strategies are discussed in detail in Chapter 42, "Giving It to Charity."

Charitable remainder trusts and charitable lead trusts can be created either during lifetime or at death. If they are created at death, there is no loss of control over the assets used to fund the charitable trust during lifetime, and the planning can be easily changed if circumstances change. When a member of an unmarried couple has a taxable estate, that partner may wish to incorporate a testamentary charitable remainder trust or charitable lead trust in his or her revocable living trust that is not actually funded until that member's death. A portion of the assets funded into the charitable remainder trust or the charitable lead trust will qualify for the estate charitable deduction and may be structured to eliminate most if not all estate taxes. Let's take a closer look at how these charitable strategies work for unmarried couples.

Charitable Remainder Trusts

If a testamentary charitable remainder trust is created by one partner of an unmarried couple, upon the death of that partner the surviving partner will begin receiving an immediate income distribution from the charitable remainder trust in addition to whatever other assets are left to the surviving partner.

> Rich Partner has a $6 million estate. If Rich Partner left his entire estate to his partner when the estate tax applicable exclusion amount was $5 million, there would be an estate tax liability of $350,000. However, if Rich Partner leaves one-half of his estate to the surviving partner and one-half to a charitable remainder unitrust (CRUT) paying 7 percent annually to the surviving partner for life, with the balance going to Rich Partner's alma mater at the surviving partner's death, there may be no estate tax due. The amount of the charitable estate tax deduction is dependent upon several factors, including the age of the surviving partner at Rich Partner's death, the applicable federal interest rate then in effect, and the percentage payout from the CRUT.
>
> Let's assume that when Rich Partner dies, surviving partner is age 65 and the applicable federal interest rate is 3 percent. Three million dollars funded into this CRUT would generate a charitable estate tax deduction slightly in excess of $1 million ($1,015,470), resulting in no federal estate tax. A $6 million estate less a $1,015,470 charitable deduction equals a taxable estate of $4,984,530, just under the $5 million threshold. The surviving partner would receive 7 percent of the income from the CRUT for his or her life.

Charitable Lead Trusts

A charitable lead trust (CLT) pays an annual amount to a charity for a term of years, and following the term, pays the balance of the assets then owned by the CLT to the remainder beneficiary. The maker of the CLT can receive a charitable deduction for the present value of the income interest paid to charity. When the CLT is funded during the maker's lifetime, he or she receives a charitable gift tax deduction. When the CLT is funded at death, the maker receives a charitable estate tax deduction. The charitable deduction allows a member of an unmarried couple to leverage his or her gift or estate tax applicable exclusion amount by making gifts into the CLT during their lifetime or commencing at death to the other member of the unmarried couple.

> Rich Partner decides to immediately transfer $1 million to a charitable lead annuity trust paying 8 percent ($80,000) annually for 15 years to the University of Florida. At the end of the 15-year term the balance is held in trust for the benefit of Poor Partner. Let's assume the transfer occurs when the applicable government rate is 3 percent. The value of the gift tax charitable deduction is approximately $955,000, leaving a taxable value of the remainder interest of approximately $45,000 for gift tax purposes. Alternatively, Rich Partner could incorporate the same charitable lead annuity trust into his or her revocable living trust and have it funded at his or her death as a means to reduce or eliminate federal estate taxes.
>
> When a testamentary charitable lead trust strategy is used, it is common to have Rich Partner engage in the ILIT strategy so Poor Partner has the benefit of the insurance proceeds immediately upon Rich Partner's death.

Unmarried couples need to take planning for their present and their future seriously. First, it is very important for unmarried couples to work closely with their advisors to determine their individual and joint goals and objectives. If those goals and objectives include providing for each other, then they need to follow up with their professional advisors to put in place the planning needed to accomplish their individual and combined objectives. By failing to take these steps, it is more likely than not that there will be adverse tax, legal, and practical results.

27

Life Insurance

Estate Planning Fuel

When we first wrote this book, the most important issue in the estate planning field was the lack of understanding and proper use of fully funded revocable living trusts. Over the years, revocable living trusts have become mainstream planning vehicles, taking the place of wills as the primary way to plan for loved ones. Now we believe that the most important issue in estate planning is the failure of consumers and their advisors to properly fund estate plans.

All of the documents we have addressed up to now are important and should be considered in everyone's planning. That being said, all the documents in the world will not help you or your loved ones if they are not funded. Having a wonderful estate plan without funding is like buying a great new car and having no gas. Neither your estate plan nor your car will take you anywhere if it doesn't have the fuel to make it to its destination.

Life insurance, for most people and their families, is the best and most economical method of fueling an estate plan. It is so important that we devote this and the next three chapters to life insurance and how it is used in estate and wealth planning.

Most of our clients and the noninsurance professionals whom we teach (lawyers, CPAs, and financial advisors) have almost universally expressed a desire to know more about life insurance and how its proper purchase facilitates planning objectives. They have been and continue to be confused about the amount of life insurance that should be purchased and the type that is best. They do not understand its pricing and have a very difficult time comparing product costs between companies and even between products offered by the same company.

They *do* understand that life insurance seems expensive and does not represent a current benefit to them or their families. Many feel that it is money gone to waste because they cannot see its immediate benefit.

In addition, they are often reluctant to make a purchasing decision and are concerned they may be overinsured.

Why People Are Reluctant to Purchase Life Insurance

We have been in practice for many decades. We have represented the super-wealthy and people with modest or nonexistent estates. A vast majority of them needed life insurance. That same vast majority wanted nothing to do with life insurance. The bottom line is that most people just don't like the idea of life insurance.

Why is that? Having participated in the placement of billions of dollars of face value life insurance, it is our conclusion that people do not hate life insurance, but they sure do hate how it is sold. They feel pressured and are confused as to what they need and why. Not surprisingly, after they buy it, they do not know what they have and why they bought it. They either decided it was easier to buy the insurance and end the sales process or felt guilty if they did not buy the insurance.

Over 70 percent of people's life insurance policies have not been reviewed in the last two years. The greatest reason is that life insurance agents themselves have a short shelf life. They turn over quite a bit. The policyholders they abandon are called "orphans," and it is unlikely that another agent will take them over.

Another reason life insurance agents do not come back to see their customers is the way life insurance commissions are structured. There is a substantial first year commission, some small "trailing" commissions for a few years, and then the revenue for the agent ceases. With so little economic incentive to support existing policies, but with so much economic incentive to sell a new policy, it's no wonder that life insurance agents often stop seeing their old customers.

We are not implying there are no life insurance agents who service policies after they sell them. There remains a strong cadre of professionals who do a great job. There are just not very many of them, at least in our experience. And their numbers are growing smaller. Life insurance companies and insurance agencies find it hard to recruit and retain agents, making it even more difficult to service existing customers.

Now that you see some of the problems, the good news is that a decision as to whether to buy life insurance does not have to be painful or confusing. It does not have to be part of a sales process. Life insurance should only be purchased if there is a demonstrable need. After that need is clearly identified, then it is up to an insurance or other planning professional to find the best companies and products that fit that need. In this and the next three chapters you are going to learn how that happens.

Who Needs Insurance and Why?

We believe that in estate and wealth planning, life insurance should be purchased for two reasons: to create an estate or to protect an estate. It is that simple.

Life insurance purchased to create an estate should be looked upon as casualty insurance—insurance purchased to replace economic loss resulting from the death of the family wage earner. The problem resulting from a wage earner's death is lost income. The solution that life insurance provides is to create a fund of invested money that can be used to sustain family members who do not have an alternative source of income.

We often use the analogy of the goose that laid the golden eggs. What is more valuable, the goose or the eggs? Well, the eggs can be replaced if they are lost; that goose will keep on laying those golden eggs. If the goose dies, there are no more golden eggs. And when the existing golden eggs are gone, it could be very difficult to get any more. So it's better to insure that golden goose so there is a way to continue to collect those eggs.

In addition to replacing golden eggs (income), life insurance is also used to replace the monetary value of the non-wage-earner's contribution to a marriage. There are substantial costs involved in replacing the parent who cares for the children and the home. Loss of a marriage partner or significant other can cause hardship if sufficient funds are not available to hire someone to replace his or her functions.

Once a client understands the "why" of estate creation insurance, they want to know the amount they need. In the next chapter we will provide you with a short, effective process for determining how much life insurance you need. To truly understand this process, read about life insurance to protect an estate. You may be surprised about what needs to be protected.

Life insurance purchased to protect an estate is intended to pay real or potential obligations of that estate. These obligations include debts, taxes, and inheritances.

If you have debt, it will not go away when you die. Your estate is still liable for the debts you accumulated during your life, including mortgages, credit cards, notes payable, and virtually any other obligations you had. If your estate does not have the cash needed to pay off the debts, then your creditors can foreclose on your property, just as if you were still alive. If you are single with no children and do not want to leave an inheritance, this may be all right. If you are married, have children, or want to leave an inheritance, then to protect your estate you may want to pay off those debts. Leaving a spouse and children with house payments or loan payments may not be ideal.

A lot of people do not have the liquid assets to pay their debts when they die. Life insurance is an excellent method of providing immediate cash that can be used to pay off or pay down these obligations.

Earlier in this book we discussed federal estate taxes, state inheritance and estate taxes, and generation-skipping taxes. We emphasized the need not to rely on existing federal and state exemptions or tax rates. Since we do not know what taxes will be when we die, prudent planning dictates that we at least consider having funds available just in case there is a tax due.

Those lucky people in the 1 percent of the population that have taxable estates even with the exemptions now in effect know they will have a liability. Often clients who have an estate that will generate tax and other death expenses believe, incorrectly, they have no need for life insurance. They envision that their property will be sold to pay the estate bills and that the balance of the property will be sufficient in value to accomplish their planning objectives. Too often clients believe their estate assets can be sold at their fair market value to pay death costs when due. In our experience this assumption is not practical and seldom proves true.

We have previously discussed the fact that federal estate taxes are due and payable nine months from the date of death, in cash. Nine months does not represent a great deal of time, particularly when the survivors have other matters on their minds. Death's aftermath is always frenetic, even with the best of estate plans. Buyers are usually aware of the time constraints placed on estate sellers. The more aware the buyer, the more likely the price offered will be reduced. Panic sales are seldom fair market value sales. They are usually distress sales.

Prudent estate owners should always plan to pay their estates' debts with cash. Estate property should be sold at the highest price, and that price should be negotiated without timing constraints. Life insurance should be considered a planning alternative to create instant estate cash. This entire discussion, and the problems it describes, is referred to by estate planners as the "liquidity problem." The more nonliquid the estate, the greater the potential need for life insurance.

An obligation that is often overlooked—and represents a growing concern —is the liability that accompanies most retirement plans. Other than Roth IRAs and a few other types of plans, the entire amount in an IRA or other type of retirement plan is fully subject to ordinary income taxation. That amount can be delayed and may not have to be paid when the account owner dies, but someone, someday, will pay the taxes.

There is a concept in the Internal Revenue Code called *Income in Respect of a Decedent (IRD)*. It says that if a person did not pay income tax on income that was earned but not yet received, then whoever inherits that income must pay income taxes on it. IRD comes in a few different forms, but the primary two are retirement plans and installment notes. If a person dies who sold land, for example, over a period of time prior to his or her death, then whoever inherits that note must pay the income tax on it. The same is true for retirement plan proceeds.

For example, let's say you have a retirement plan with $500,000 in it. As you take the proceeds out, you declare those proceeds on your income tax return and pay taxes at whatever rate you are currently in. When you die, whoever your beneficiary is will at some point begin taking out the proceeds. He or she will declare those proceeds as taxable income and will pay taxes on them.

If we assume the average tax bracket is 35 percent, then there will always be liability against those proceeds of 35 percent. It is not uncommon for individuals and families to purchase life insurance to make up for the taxes due. If the expectation is that 100 percent of the proceeds will go to your beneficiaries, then the only way that expectation will be met is with life insurance.

Retirement plans are also subject to federal estate tax and generation-skipping transfer tax. When you die, the value of the plan (before any income taxes are due) is included in your estate. If you have a taxable estate, federal estate taxes will be due. Assuming the federal estate tax rate is identical to the income tax rate—35 percent—then there are two taxes due. Nine months after you die, your estate will have to come up with $175,000 (35 percent of $500,000). If your estate has to take the money from the plan (because it has no other funds), it will have to take out $269,230 and pay a 35 percent income tax, leaving $175,000 to pay the federal estate tax. The plan will have $230,770 left. That means an effective overall tax rate of just about 54 percent. The remaining amount will still be subject to 35 percent income tax, based on our assumption of a 35 percent income tax rate. If that too is distributed, then another $80,770 of tax is due, leaving $150,000 out of $500,000. That is an overall tax rate of 70 percent.

It is also possible, but not likely, that the remainder could be subject to a generation-skipping transfer tax of another 35 percent. The overall tax rate would then be well over 80 percent.

With good tax advisors and good financial and estate planning, there are a few ways to reduce at least some of the taxation, or at least delay it. Our example is, however, reasonable and possible.

If you have a retirement plan other than a Roth IRA, you should understand how income and estate taxes will affect your plan and your beneficiaries. We highly recommend that if you want to protect your estate and enhance its value to those you love, consider the purchase of life insurance. It can be far less expensive and far more effective than any other planning.

The purpose of this chapter is for you to understand why your planning needs fuel. Life insurance, in our experience, should always be explored as a cost effective and efficient method of creating an estate or protecting an estate.

In the next chapter we explain the types of life insurance and how you decide which kind to buy and why.

28

Life Insurance

What Kind of Fuel Do You Need?

Life insurance does not have to be complicated. It can appear to be complicated, but only if you get bogged down in the details. In this chapter we look at life insurance in the big picture. Once you understand a few basic concepts, then the professional with whom you work can address and take care of the details. We highly recommend that you work through a professional. You will not pay substantially more for the coverage you purchase, and the help you get will be invaluable. Life insurance is too important to try to do it yourself. In the long run it will cost you and your family more in terms of time, money, and stress if you attempt to purchase it without a professional's help.

The Big Picture

There is a 100 percent chance that you will die. The only question is when. Based on a huge amount of statistics, insurance companies have developed mortality tables that predict with uncanny accuracy what percentage of an age group will die in any one year. So, while life insurance companies do not know who will die in any one year, they know what percentage will die.

As a class of people gets older, the percentage of who dies in that class increases. For example, in a group of women aged 45, .23 percent will die that year. At age 65, 1.14 percent will die in that year. Thus, the risk of dying increases by fivefold in that 20-year span.

Actuaries—specialized mathematicians who work for insurance companies—decide how much the insurance company has to charge customers in the form of premiums to pay the death claims in any one year and still make a profit. To make an accurate prediction of the premium costs, actuaries look at a broad range of variables, including gender, age, health, how many people will buy a particular policy; the expenses the insurance company will pay to create, market, and distribute the policy; and how much profit the company wants to make on that policy. When each premium is paid, some of the premium is put into a reserve account so the insurance company will be able to pay the predicted death claims. The remainder is used to pay expenses and return a profit to the company.

Over the last 150 years, insurance companies have gotten very good at pricing policies. Those who were not have gone out of business. To stay in business, insurance companies have developed a few different types of insurance policies that make it easier for consumers to buy them and easier for the companies to sell them.

Types of Life Insurance

Life insurance policies come in two basic varieties: *term* and *permanent.* The difference between the two is not what they do—both are life insurance— it is the manner in which premiums are paid.

Term insurance is life insurance that provides a pure death benefit. It has no frills; the owner just pays the premium for pure life insurance protection. The cost of this protection goes up each year, because the odds of dying increase with each additional year of age. Term insurance is not very expensive when someone is young. However, it can get very expensive as a person ages. Here are some typical annual premiums for a male who wants to buy a $500,000 term policy at various ages:

Age 45	$707
Age 55	$1,710
Age 65	$4,510
Age 75	$15,245
Age 85	$49,355

Because term policies get so expensive when people get older—just when they need the insurance—it is estimated that less that 2 percent of all term policies ever pay a death benefit. Term is inexpensive at younger ages because the odds of death are low. When the odds of death increase as the insured ages, term policies price themselves out of the market, so the odds of a death claim are low.

Term insurance has three other characteristics that are important to understand. First, once you qualify medically for one-year renewable term insurance, as long as you pay the premium it does not lapse, no matter the state of your health. Second, it is possible to convert some types of term policies into a permanent policy, although this may be affected by your health condition at that time. Finally, you can buy term insurance on a level premium basis. This means you can purchase a 10-year level term policy that has level premiums for 10 years. After that, the premiums can go up quite a bit, and to get new insurance you have to qualify medically. Generally, the level term premium is an average of the 10 years of term premiums, so you pay more in the early years and less in the later years.

There are other variations of term life insurance. For example, there is *decreasing term*. This type of term has a decreasing benefit over a period of time. It is used for mortgages and other obligations that become smaller over time. A good insurance professional can help you if you need this type of term insurance or others that are more specialized.

Permanent life insurance is still term insurance. How the premium is paid is the difference. The classic type of permanent insurance is called *Whole Life insurance*. In a Whole Life policy, actuaries create a level premium for the life expectancy of the insured. During the early years, the premium is significantly higher than a term life insurance premium. In later years, when the term premium is quite high, the Whole Life premium remains at the same level.

In order for the insurance company to make this all work mathematically, the excess amounts paid in the early years (after expenses) are invested by the insurance company on behalf of the owner of the Whole Life policy.

Let's say the Whole Life premium is $5,000, but the term premium is $500 in the first year. The insurance company takes the difference, less any expenses, and invests it in safe investments. The insurance company guarantees a certain rate of return on this invested side fund. As long as the owner of the Whole Life policy pays the premium, the insurance company guarantees that it will pay the death benefit when the insured dies and that the side fund will make a certain rate of return. The term premium inside of the Whole Life policy will continue to go up every year, so the insurance company takes out that premium every year. At some point the cash value of the side fund will go down as the term premiums increase, but the insurance company takes on this risk so long as the insurance owner continues to pay the same premium.

Whole Life premiums are expensive because the insurance company is making a lot of guarantees and the owner of the policy has to pay for those guarantees. To reduce the premium costs, insurance companies invented a second type of permanent life insurance policy called *Universal Life*, which offers the policy owner more options to decrease the premium and add flexibility.

Universal Life allows the owner to select the premium amount for a certain death benefit within a range. The lower the premium, the less is invested in the side fund. When we discussed Whole Life insurance, we said that in a $5,000 Whole Life premium, maybe $500 would go to the term cost and the remainder, after expenses, would go to the side fund. In a Universal Life policy the owner may choose to pay a $2,000 premium. The term cost would remain the same, but less would go to the side fund. Since the side fund is smaller, as the term cost increases with age the fund will be used up faster. The owner may then have to pay a higher premium in later years to make up the shortage. If the owner decides not to pay, then the policy will eventually lapse, leaving the owner with no insurance protection.

One of the reasons Universal Life policies were looked on with disfavor in recent years is that life insurance agents and companies projected that the side fund of a Universal Life policy would generate a very high rate of return in their sales illustrations. If the side fund makes this type of return, then there would be plenty of money in the policy to pay the term premiums. Unfortunately, the side funds did not create a high rate of return, so policy owners had to pay in a lot of additional money to keep these policies afloat. Consumers did not read the fine print that said that the illustrations showing a high rate of return were not guaranteed. A much smaller return was guaranteed, and this smaller rate of return required higher premium payments.

Today, there have been numerous changes in the laws that require more disclosure with respect to illustrations. Even then it is important to understand that the only relevant illustration of premiums and how long the policy will last is the illustration that is *guaranteed*. Universal Life is a great way to buy insurance, but you still have to exercise great care in understanding what you are getting and why.

There are Universal Life policies that offer more guarantees than their traditional counterparts. Under these policies, if the owner of the policy pays certain premiums over a certain amount of time, the policy is guaranteed to pay out even after the owner stops paying the premiums. This sounds a lot like Whole Life, but there is a distinct difference. In a Whole Life policy the insurance company creates a real reserve of money to pay death claims. So the life insurance company backs up its guarantee with real funds. In a guaranteed Universal Life, the life insurance company makes the promise to pay but does not have to back up that promise with fully funded reserves. Universal Life shifts some of the risk that the life insurance company was taking when selling a Whole Life policy and puts it back on the consumer. That is why premium payments for Universal Life are less expensive than premiums for Whole Life.

There is another type of Universal Life policy, called *Variable Universal Life*. A Variable Universal Life policy shifts even more risk to the consumer. Just like regular Universal Life, it has a flexible premium and a side fund. In a Variable Universal Life policy, however, the owner of the policy decides how the side fund is invested. In Whole Life and Universal Life, the life insurance company made the investment decisions. In Variable Universal Life, the owner is offered a number of different investment options for the side fund. These vary from money market accounts to more risky equity accounts.

If the owner chooses the policy investments correctly, the side fund can grow at a very good rate. If the owner does not choose correctly, that side fund could decline or disappear. If the side fund cannot support the term premiums inside the policy, then the owner must pay extra premiums. As we learned in the recent Great Recession, the stock market can plunge. Those people who owned Variable Universal Life policies that were invested in the stock market lost a great deal of the value of their side funds, forcing them to either cancel the policy or pay significantly higher premiums.

The lesson learned is that a Variable Universal Life policy must be constantly reviewed to make sure it is invested in a manner that preserves the policy over time. Our view is that risky investments do not belong in a Universal Life policy. For those who choose this route, it usually pays to make conservative investment choices so that life insurance proceeds will be available to fuel the estate planning car.

Just as in term insurance, there are variations of Universal Life. There is Indexed Variable Universal Life and some other hybrids. Before choosing any of these products, it is extremely important that you understand what you are getting into. We recommend that you stay away from those products you do not understand. The best way you can ensure that your insurance will work is to keep it simple, rely on the basics, and use a professional advisor whom you know and trust.

Your Health Determines the Cost of Your Fuel

Before we address the question of what type of life insurance you need, there is one more important issue that must be addressed: your health. While age is one of the most important aspects of the cost of life insurance, your health is just as important and maybe even more important when it comes to the premium you will have to pay.

The mortality tables that predict life expectancy do not discriminate between healthy and health-impaired people. It takes into account only age.

Life insurance companies know that the healthier you are, the more likely you are to live until your life expectancy or even longer. The longer you live, the more the life insurance company makes because it delays paying a death benefit and it continues to collect premiums on which it can make a profit.

Over the years, life insurance companies have determined that it is better to offer lower premiums to healthy people and higher premiums to those who are not so healthy. Life insurance companies have different categories of health-based risk. A person can be a preferred health risk (very healthy), standard health risk, or a rated risk (not healthy as compared to the standard risk), and each one of these designations have a premium associated with it. The less healthy you are, the more you will pay in premiums, because your risk of dying earlier than normal life expectancy is greater.

Just as an aside, insurance companies also take into account those of us who are engaged in risky activities. If you sky dive, fly an airplane, race cars, or even scuba dive, you may have to pay more for life insurance. Remember, your insurance company is interested in keeping you alive as long as possible.

The process of determining your health and activity risk is called *underwriting*. When you hear this term, it means that your insurance company is investigating your health and other activities to determine the premium they are willing to accept to insure you.

Term or Permanent: Which Is Better?

Almost every client and professional we talk with wants to know which type of insurance is better, term or permanent? Before we address this question, it is important that we share a few additional insights into our views of planning, and the fuel it takes to make that planning work.

Estate planning is a journey, just as life is a journey. A particular person's planning needs today may be far different that that person's planning needs next year or in the next decade. We can only plan for today taking into account what we think may happen over time. By the same token, there are some planning needs that will be short-term and some that will be long-term. Term life insurance is designed to take care of short-term needs because it is much more like renting than buying. A person who buys term insurance is betting that the need will go away when the insurance gets too expensive to be viable.

Permanent insurance is just that: a type of insurance designed to last. It is owning rather than renting. It is recognition that an estate plan needs fuel no matter what happens in the future. It is protecting an estate over time and enhancing an estate that may not have the fuel it needs at any one time.

From our perspective as planners, given a choice between term and permanent insurance, we would almost always choose permanent. Experience has taught us that most real life insurance needs do not go away. Those that do are invariably replaced by another need that crops up after the original need has gone. Here is an example:

Harvey and Lydia have a home with a mortgage, two teenage children, and some savings. Both work and have growing 401(k) retirement plans. If one of them should die, they worry about the ability to continue making house payments—or maybe even paying off the mortgage. They also worry that there will be enough money to pay for college and graduate school for their children.

Based on these facts, it appears that Harvey and Lydia need term life insurance to pay off some or all the mortgage, and to pay for college, if one of them dies. Both of these potential events are limited in time. The mortgage has a limited life, and the children have a limited time for the parents to pay for their education.

Just about the time these needs run out, Harvey and Lydia should be thinking about having insurance to take care of the survivor if one of them dies. It is highly likely they will need income replacement insurance or insurance to protect their 401(k) plans from taxes, or even to assure an inheritance for their children and grandchildren. We see this all the time.

When the so-called "term" need expires, they will have to buy additional life insurance to take care of these new needs. The downside is that they will be 20 or 30 years older then and may be far less healthy. As a result, their insurance will cost substantially more, if they can even get insurance based on their health at that time. Had they only looked at their short-term need as a continuing need they could have paid more on the front end for permanent insurance and guaranteed that its face amount would be locked-in until death.

Once you have determined that you have a need for life insurance and how much life insurance you need, you need to determine the price. Before you make any decision, you should get a quote for both term and permanent insurance so you can compare the costs in both the short and long term. To get an accurate quote, you must give as much health information as possible. Do not fall into the trap of trying to do this yourself, because an insurance quote that you receive that is not based on underwriting is not going to be accurate. Work with an insurance professional so you will know the actual price for term and permanent insurance as they apply to your specific situation.

If you have taken the steps we outlined, you can then make the appropriate decision. In general we believe that our clients and you should buy as much life insurance as they and you are willing or can afford to purchase. If having a higher death benefit is important to you but you cannot afford to get that benefit with permanent life insurance, then buy some term and some permanent, with the idea of converting the term to permanent when you can afford to do so. If absolutely having insurance locked-in is important to you and the death benefit is of second importance, you should buy only permanent insurance. You do not have to buy only one kind or another. You can and should blend your life insurance to meet your budgetary and planning needs.

Your decision may not be perfect, but then, in our decades of planning experiences, nothing is. You should do the best you can do based upon your unique circumstances. The key to making a good decision is to understand a little bit about life insurance and then seek a professional who has the expertise and the interest in you personally to take the time and effort necessary to provide you with the best type of life insurance from a quality company for your particular circumstances.

29

Life Insurance

How Much Fuel Do You Need?

Determining the amount of fuel you need for your estate and wealth planning is not an exact science. In fact, it is generally no more than an educated guess. It is likely that you have never heard this before, but it is true.
There are many variables that affect life insurance needs, many of which are totally unknown. Here is a list of some of the variables:

- Date that you will die
- How much income your family will need when you die
- Inflation rate from now until you die
- Rate of return on any invested assets from now until you die
- Income, estate, and generation-skipping taxes that will be in effect when you die

There are numerous computer programs that take into account these variables and more. However, you and your advisors have to make assumptions (guesses) as to each of these unknowns. All of these assumptions can be based on statistics and prior history, but as we have seen over the last few years, historical assumptions can be misleading and often end up being dead wrong.

With this uncertainty implanted in our planning consciousness, we will explore how you can realistically come up with the amount of life insurance you need. When we lecture to professionals and they ask us the same question, "How much insurance do I or my clients need?" we answer with straight faces, "As much as you can afford or are willing to pay." Let's test the veracity of our answer.

How to Understand the Unknowable

We believe that the place to start deciding how much life insurance you and your family need is to look at now rather than to the future. For example, what effect, if any, will the death of the breadwinner have on his or her family if death occurred today?

Here are some important questions you must answer. They come from a process we have developed over many years that we think is the most effective way to determine real life insurance needs:

* How much after-tax income would your family have if the breadwinner died today?
* What would your family's annual expenses be if the breadwinner died today?
* What is the shortfall, if any, between after-tax annual income and annual expenses?
* If you invested money today, what after-tax rate of return could you realistically receive on those invested funds?

How Much After-Tax Income?

Once your family loses a breadwinner's income, the surviving family members will need other sources of income. There may be existing life insurance that can be invested. Maybe there are Social Security benefits. There could be existing savings or investment accounts. Many people have IRAs or pensions. All of these other income amounts should be listed and then an income tax rate should be applied. The income tax rate can be a ballpark figure. If you want a more exact amount, talk to your CPA or tax advisor. You can even go online, where a number of Web sites will give you income tax rates, both state and federal.

What Are the Annual Expenses?

Next, decide what expenses will continue after the death of the breadwinner. This is where many families make mistakes. After going through this exercise with thousands of clients we have learned that families invariably underestimate these expenses. Unless a family is willing to completely abandon its current lifestyle, the loss of the breadwinner does not reduce annual expenses significantly. These expenses may even increase!

Our experience tells us that expenses upon the loss of a breadwinner will not go down by much, if at all. If you think differently, we would suggest that you reduce expenses by 10 to 20 percent at the most.

What Is the Shortfall?

If the annual after-tax income is less than the annual expenses, there is a need for more income. Life insurance will fill this need. If there is not a shortfall, your family probably does not need insurance, but do not stop reading, because you will find there may be other compelling reasons to have life insurance.

What Is the After-Tax Rate of Return?

If life insurance is part of your planning, its proceeds need to be invested to create spendable income. In taking this into account, you need to decide on a realistic but conservative basis what after-tax rate of return might be expected to generate income. For example, you may be making 6 percent on your money now. If you are in a 35 percent income tax bracket, the after-tax rate of return would be the product of multiplying 6 percent by 65 percent, which is 3.9 percent.

Computing the Need for Income Replacement

To demonstrate the computation that you need to make to determine how much life insurance you and your family need to replace your after-tax income shortfall, let's look at an example:

> Terrence and Kathleen are married and have three children under the age of 18. They both work outside the home. Terrence makes $80,000 a year as a manager of a clothing store and Kathleen is a part-time teacher making $30,000 a year.
> If Terrence died today, the $80,000 a year would be gone. Kathleen would likely continue to work but does not wish to work full time. After taking into account the income from savings, a small life insurance policy that Terrence has through his company, and some other benefits, the total income of the family would approximate $43,000. The amount left after income and other taxes would be about $35,000.
> Terrence and Kathleen spend most of what they make, although they do save some in the form of a 401(k) and savings account. They own a house and have house payments, plus real estate taxes and maintenance. Kathleen would not move if Terrence died because they are close to their neighbors and are in a good school district. Terrence likes to fish and play golf. Those are his only forms of entertainment, other than family events. They estimate that their expenses would be about $80,000 a year if Terrence were to die.
> Terrence and Kathleen have a shortfall of $45,000 a year. They agree that if they had money to invest, a reasonable after-tax rate of return would be 5 percent.

Now, here is what we need to compute. How much money would it take, invested at an after-tax rate of return of 5 percent, to generate $45,000 per year? If you divide $45,000 by .05, you will find that it is $900,000. This formula to divide the amount of money needed by the projected rate of return always works in determining the amount of insurance required.

We would suggest to Terrence and Kathleen that this is the necessary minimum amount of life insurance if Terrence died today. We would then do the same exercise for Kathleen, taking into account that expenses may increase because of additional day care and the necessity to replace her contributions to the marriage.

There are certainly holes and inaccuracies in our computations. We do not take into account an inflation rate. We do not take into account that Kathleen could spend down principal and interest, rather than retaining the $900,000 for life. We do not take into account excess expenses for health issues or college. If we did, it is likely the insurance need would be far greater than $900,000.

To further refine a life insurance need, there are other questions to address:

- Would you like to create a fund for education or other special needs?

- Would you like to ensure that a charity or others receive a guaranteed inheritance?

- Would you like to create a fund to pay income or death taxes on retirement plans?

Education or Other Special Needs

It is not uncommon for a family to add education or other special needs to their life insurance needs. Other special needs can include debts or a fund to care for a special needs child. These are in addition to needs for income. If you assume the fund for income can also be used for special needs, your family may need to choose between education and income. When determining needs, it is like all other planning: it's better to be safe than sorry.

Amounts added here are educated guesses, just like any other planning assumption, because you will not know if your children or grandchildren will enroll in higher education or the educational costs at that time.

Guaranteed Inheritances

Another fund that some families wish to create is one to insure for a guaranteed inheritance or for a donation to charity. We have run into situations where even a family of very modest means wants to make sure that the children receive an inheritance that can only be created with life insurance.

The same is true for charity. If you have a cause you care about, and want to preserve a legacy for you or your family, a life insurance policy may be the answer. By buying a life insurance policy on your life and naming a charity as the beneficiary, you can fulfill this desire.

You can also have the charity purchase the insurance policy on your life and then you can donate the premiums to the charity. If you do this, you can take a charitable income tax deduction on your income tax return. In Chapter 42, "Giving It to Charity," you will find information about making charitable contributions.

Taxes

As with all other assumptions, there is no way to know what estate, income, or other taxes will be when you die, or when other members of your family die. As you know from our earlier chapters, the odds of taxes going down are not as great as are the odds of them going up.

Since there is no telling if your estate will be subject to death taxes, we would recommend two courses of action. The first is that if your estate is in excess of $1 million, or the combined estate of you and your spouse is in excess of $2 million, you should consider creating a reserve to pay death taxes. Second, if you do so, then please read Chapter 30, "The Irrevocable Life Insurance Trust."

Life insurance proceeds are included in your estate for purposes of the federal estate tax and in many of the states that have their own death taxes. It is important to keep those death proceeds out of your taxable estate, and that is what an Irrevocable Life Insurance Trust does for families whose estates may be taxable.

If you do not use an Irrevocable Life Insurance Trust or some other method to keep the life insurance proceeds out of your estate, then a large portion of the life insurance you bought to pay taxes will additionally generate even more death taxes!

As we mentioned in Chapter 27, "Life Insurance," most people do not understand that their traditional IRAs and retirement plans will be subject to income taxes. It may be later as opposed to sooner, but those proceeds will be taxed. To protect your heirs from having to use retirement plan proceeds to pay those taxes, it may be wise to use life insurance as the means of paying them.

For those who have larger estates that may be subject to estate taxes, there is a double whammy. Not only are income taxes going to be paid on the proceeds, but the entire amount of their IRAs or retirement plans are going to be included in their estate. The taxes can reach into the 60 percent brackets and higher. At this time there is no legitimate way to avoid death taxes on retirement plans short of giving them away while you are alive. If you do that, you will likely generate even more taxes.

If you decide to leave your IRA or retirement plan proceeds directly to your grandchildren, the proceeds may be subject to a third tax, the generation-skipping transfer tax. This tax, which is currently the same as the top federal estate tax rate, can result in a loss of over 80 percent of the plan proceeds when income and death taxes are also taken into account. Obviously, this is a situation to be avoided, but short of that, it certainly should be planned for in terms of creating the money to pay the taxes.

Federal estate tax rates have varied over the years. They have been as high as 90 percent. Income taxes have the same history. They have been as high as 70 percent. Since there is no way for anyone to know what the tax rates are going to be when you die, the amount of the reserve to be set aside is conjectural at best. Our best estimate is to consider anywhere from 20 to 40 percent of the value of your retirement plan will be lost to after-death income taxes.

How Much Fuel Do I Need?

After you have answered the questions posed in this chapter, you will have a dollar figure of what your need for life insurance is today. It could be a small number or a very large one, depending on the size of your estate and the extent of your particular planning desires.

The primary limit on how much insurance you should buy is your ability to pay premiums. The first step in finding out how much your insurance will cost is to work with an insurance agent. It may be a full-time agent for a particular company or perhaps an independent agent serving a number of companies. The agent could be your CPA, your financial advisor, or your property and casualty insurance agent. No matter who you turn to, it should be someone you feel is trustworthy and has your interests ahead of theirs.

Insurance agents make a pretty good commission on many of the products they sell. We only say this to remind you that you should take the time to discuss your needs with your agent, and not be afraid that you are imposing upon his or her time. Most agents want to do a good job for you so you will appreciate their professionalism and help. They would also like you to refer other clients to them, which you would be inclined to do if your agent does a good job.

As a matter of fact, you can ask your friends and colleagues for recommendations if you do not know an agent. You do not have to settle on the first one you meet. We prefer agents who are more technical in nature rather than in the selling mode. A good agent will spend time finding out your needs and teaching you, with the goal of placing your business with a good company. If at any time during the process you feel pressured, you should terminate the relationship and move on.

Ask your agent to quote prices for term and permanent products so you have a range of costs. Some agents represent one company, so you will get one set of quotes. Other agents may bring you quotes from several companies. Discuss the viability and competitiveness of the company or companies your agent recommends. You should be satisfied that the quoted products and companies are top-notch. It is here where your trust in the agent must be placed. We have said it before and we will say it again: "If you don't know your jewels, know your jeweler." You are not an expert in life insurance (jewels), so you will have to rely on your expert agent (jeweler) to produce the best product for you.

Once you know the cost of the insurance you need, it is decision time. Buy what you can afford. If you can afford the insurance but would rather trust that your investments can do better over time and that you will be alive then, you can purchase less coverage. This is not a strategy we would recommend as estate planners, because a person's date of death is unknown. You can die before your investments grow large enough, and you can die when your investments have gone down in value. It is life insurance that protects your estate from risk and enhances your estate by providing spendable income.

You might want to buy all term insurance because that is all you can afford, or you might want to buy all permanent because you want to make sure your family is covered. You might want to buy some of both so you can reach your goal for a more reasonable price. In the end, if you have the need for the insurance, it is up to you how much to spend and for what type of insurance.

Underwriting

Earlier we discussed underwriting, and would now like to discuss it in terms of your premium. As we noted, your insurance agent should gather as much health information as possible before he or she gets quotes for premiums. As also noted, your health has a huge effect on the premium. Be totally honest when answering the questions insurance companies will ask. They will find out anyway when they research your medical records, and you will do better along the way if you are the one to disclose your health issues. Insurance companies, like all of us, are more sympathetic toward honest people.

You will need to have a medical examination. Your agent will help you prepare for that examination so you will be in the best physical condition the day you take it. It is important that you present your health in the best light possible, because the results of your examination will have a direct and impactful effect on the amount of your premiums.

Finally, once you have your life insurance in place, you will need to make sure you review your insurance every two or three years, because the life insurance industry often changes in terms of products and pricing. Health standards change also. As you review your coverage, you will want to shop your policies under new conditions, because even though you will be older, you still may be able to buy a better policy for less money given better underwriting considerations in the industry at large.

How your life insurance is owned is a critical component of life insurance planning. In the next chapter we will share some ownership ideas that will help you plan better with your life insurance.

30

The Irrevocable Life Insurance Trust

Having Your Cake and Eating It Too

As we have said, life insurance proceeds provide the fuel that powers many an estate planning car, but most of the time the fuel mixture is taxed at the pump before it finds its way into the estate planning vehicle.

A disadvantage generally associated with the purchase of life insurance is that its proceeds usually increase the taxable estate of the policy owner. Upon the death of the insured owner, life insurance proceeds are included in the insured owner's estate for federal estate tax purposes. Most people buy life insurance with the belief that insurance proceeds can be used by their beneficiaries free of federal estate tax. If the insured owns a life insurance policy on his or her own life, all the life insurance proceeds are included in the estate for federal estate tax purposes.

In order to avoid federal estate tax, many people have the life insurance on their lives owned by their spouses or others—*cross-ownership*—then upon the death of the insured, the policy proceeds are paid to the owner's beneficiary free of federal estate tax.

There are problems with the cross-ownership technique:

- The insured loses control of the life insurance policies.
- Proceeds are usually taxed on the death of the policy owner if he or she is the beneficiary and dies after the insured.
- Few people plan for the contingency that the owner-beneficiary may die first.
- If the proceeds are payable to other than the insured or the owner, there is a gift of the entire insurance proceeds to the beneficiary from the policy owner.

We discuss these problems at length in Chapter 31, "Some Estate Planning Solutions."

An ILIT Avoids Federal Estate Tax on Life Insurance Proceeds

The goal sought by insurance policy cross-ownership—to avoid federal estate tax on life insurance proceeds—is a noble one. But there is a better way to accomplish this goal. You can use an irrevocable life insurance trust (ILIT) to own life insurance policies that insure your life. By using an ILIT, the insurance proceeds will be free of federal estate tax on your death. In addition, if you plan for your spouse, the ILIT will keep the proceeds out of your spouse's estate as well.

The ILIT has been used as an estate planning technique since the federal estate tax laws were permanently implemented. These trusts were designed to keep life insurance proceeds free of federal estate tax. Because the government was losing tax revenue, the Internal Revenue Service attacked their use on many grounds, and as a result the ILIT fell into disuse. Since World War II, however, their use has come back into vogue. Today they are frequently used and in fact are enjoying a heyday. It is important to understand how an ILIT works. Once you understand them, you will appreciate why they are so popular.

Generally, if a life insurance policy is given away, the value of the life insurance proceeds will not be included in the estate of the person who gave the policy away. Whoever gives a life insurance policy away must be careful not to retain incidents of ownership in the policy. This means that the person giving the policy away must not retain control over the use of the life insurance policy in any way.

Using an ILIT, three estate planning objectives can be achieved:

- Insurance proceeds can be kept free of federal estate tax upon the deaths of both spouses.

- Because of the terms provided in the trust document, the trust maker can control the insurance proceeds received by the ILIT to care for the maker's beneficiaries.

- The life insurance proceeds received by an ILIT can be used to pay the death expenses, including taxes, of both the maker and the maker's spouse.

Irrevocable Is Not Always Irrevocable

The ILIT is used to own an insurance policy, whether it is purchased by the ILIT or given to it. As its name implies, the ILIT must be irrevocable. Once the trust is drafted and signed, it is difficult to change. A court can change some provisions of an ILIT, but only under very special circumstances.

An ILIT can have a provision allowing an independent trustee, sometimes called a *trust protector*, to make changes without court approval, but this provision must be carefully drafted and administered. If an ILIT is *not* totally irrevocable or if the maker retains direct control over it, the insurance proceeds will *not* be free of federal estate tax.

While an ILIT must be irrevocable, its assets do not have to be. You can name an independent person other than the trustee, as the holder of a special power to remove the life insurance policies owned by the ILIT, as well as any other assets owned by it, and distribute them to the beneficiaries of the trust. The independent person needs to be someone who is not related or subordinate to the maker or any of the ILIT beneficiaries. This special power can be exercised at the holder's discretion, allowing for flexibility in your planning. This power must be drafted carefully by an experience attorney to avoid any adverse consequences. If your planning objectives change, the assets can be removed from your ILIT. The ILIT will continue because it is irrevocable, but it might not have anything in it. In reality, a properly drafted ILIT might not be irrevocable at all.

How an ILIT Works—or Doesn't

The beneficiaries of an ILIT are generally exactly the same as the beneficiaries of the maker's revocable living (main) trust. In fact, the terms of the ILIT are almost identical, and, believe it or not, the trustees under both the ILIT and the maker's revocable living trust are usually the same after the maker's death.

As we have discussed, assets receive a step-up in basis at death. To get cash (insurance proceeds) from the ILIT to the maker's main trust, a sale generally takes place. The ILIT buys nonliquid assets from the main trust, using cash provided by the life insurance proceeds. Because of step-up in basis rules, this sale can be accomplished income-tax-free. Another technique often used to transfer the ILIT's cash to the main trust is a loan. Regardless of which approach is used, the net result is the same: the main trust has cash and can pay expenses. The ILIT has the nonliquid property either as collateral for the loan or as the owner after the sale. There are no distress sales or unreasonable borrowing requirements, and because the beneficiaries of the main trust are identical to those of the ILIT, there is no loss of asset value or control.

Too good to be true? Not if the ILIT is properly drafted and implemented by an estate planning professional. Irrevocable trust drafting is no place for rookies or do-it-yourselfers. One small mistake made in an ILIT and all the tax benefits can be lost; remember, irrevocable is irrevocable. Good advice on the front end is essential so flexibility can be incorporated into the ILIT, making irrevocability less ominous.

Your spouse can be the trustee of your ILIT as long as it is properly drafted. An ILIT that gives your spouse too much control over its terms may result in adverse tax consequences. Some professionals prefer to use an institutional trustee or another family member to alleviate potential adverse tax consequences.

How insurance policies find their way into an ILIT and how the premiums are paid on those policies are two issues of critical planning importance.

When an existing life insurance policy is transferred into an ILIT, a gift is made. Whether the gift is subject to federal gift tax is another matter. The value of the existing policy determines if it is.

The value of the life insurance policy is sometimes hard to determine, and valuing a policy should be done with caution. This value is *the replacement value of the policy.* If you do not know the value of an existing life insurance policy, your insurance professionals can easily tell you.

You can transfer your existing policies into your ILIT, or you can have your ILIT purchase life insurance policies on your life. The latter is easier because you may not have to be concerned with policy values for federal gift tax purposes or about the three-year rule, discussed later in this chapter.

Through gifts of cash from you or others, the ILIT receives funds so it can pay premiums on life insurance policies it owns on your life, or it can pay those premiums from the income generated by other property you have already transferred into your ILIT. The federal gift tax consequences of these transfers must be examined.

The annual exclusion for gifts is $13,000 per recipient each year, although this amount is subject to inflation adjustment, allowing it to rise if inflation increases. The annual exclusion can be used only when there is a gift of a present interest in property. A *present interest* is a gift of which the recipient can have the current use and benefit. A gift of a life insurance policy or the money to pay its premium is generally not a gift of a present interest when given to a trust. If there is no annual exclusion available for life insurance, the use of an ILIT may not be attractive, but this apparent problem has been solved.

The Demand Right

A man named Mr. Crummey established a special irrevocable trust for the benefit of his beneficiaries. Under his trust, his beneficiaries were to receive property from the trust sometime in the future. Crummey claimed the annual exclusion for the gifts he made to this trust, and the IRS took him to court. Crummey beat the IRS. He won because his irrevocable trust had an added feature: a *demand right.*

A demand right is the ability of a beneficiary, for a limited period of time, to ask for and receive from a trust the value of the current gifts made to it.

For example, on November 1, Dee Fox gives $5,000 to her ILIT. The trustee, pursuant to the terms of Dee's trust, notifies the beneficiaries that they have until December 1 to demand their share of the $5,000. If they choose not to make this demand, the demand right ends. This demand right can be given even if the beneficiary is a minor, because the minor's guardian may exercise the demand right for him or her.

Because of the demand right, a present interest is created in the property given to the ILIT, and the annual exclusion is available. Because of Mr. Crummey, your gifts to your ILIT can qualify for the federal gift tax annual exclusion.

There may be a practical problem with giving others a demand right. The beneficiaries may demand their share of the premium money, though in our experience this has not been a problem. The demand right is refused by the beneficiaries and the money is used to pay life insurance premiums. After all, the beneficiaries are your family members, and even though they are free to exercise their rights, they will likely understand that by not exercising them they are helping the family's overall tax situation.

Despite Mr. Crummey's groundbreaking efforts, when you give money or property to your ILIT, you can use only $5,000 of your annual exclusion for each beneficiary of your ILIT. Why? Because of a technical quirk in our federal estate and gift tax laws, use of more than $5,000 of the annual exclusion per beneficiary in an ILIT does create gift tax problems. There are ways to circumvent the $5,000 limitation. An understanding of these methods, however, is beyond the scope of this book. If you want to exceed the $5,000 limitation, consult your planning professionals.

A Window of Opportunity

The Tax Relief, Unemployment Insurance Reauthorization, and Job Creation Act of 2010 created a wonderful window of opportunity in the use of ILITs. If you remember from Chapter 11, "The Gift Tax," for 2011 and 2012 the lifetime exemption for gifts was increased from $1 million per person ($2 million for a married couple) to $5 million per person ($10 million for a married couple). The 2012 amount was indexed for inflation and is $5,120,000. This large gift tax exemption was unique in the history of the federal gift tax.

The exemption means that a wealthy family can pass a huge amount of wealth by using an ILIT. For example, if a married couple were to make an $8 million gift to an ILIT and the trustee of the ILIT were to purchase a second-to-die policy so the life insurance proceeds were received by the trust when the second one of them died, the death benefit could be huge.

If the husband was 64 and the wife was 60, the death benefit would be around $50 million for a couple in fairly good health.

The huge estate planning opportunity created by the 2010 law is a certainty for no more than two years. Those who can take advantage of it will be able to pass a great deal of wealth to children, grandchildren, and more distant generations without paying gift or estate tax on the death proceeds (and the subsequent growth) held in the ILIT. Even for an individual or a couple who wants to make a much more modest gift, the opportunity is almost too good to pass up.

Other ILIT Rules and Ideas

If the terms of an ILIT require that its income be used only to purchase life insurance on the maker's life, then any income or available deductions of the ILIT are included in the maker's income tax return. This rule is just one example of the income tax rules associated with the ILIT. The technical term for an irrevocable trust that is drafted in such a way that the trust's income and deductions are included in the maker's income tax return is a *Grantor Trust*. Grantor is another name given to the maker of a trust.

There are some other income tax ramifications of trusts, many of which affect the ILIT. For example, if you name your spouse as a trustee or beneficiary of your ILIT, the income of the trust will be taxed to you. Usually this does not present a problem, because an ILIT is generally not designed to create taxable income when all it owns is an insurance policy. However, this provision, as well as others, may have an effect on your planning. The income tax issues of an ILIT provide a good reason to check with an experienced professional before establishing one.

Having a friendly trustee is important. A second reading of Chapter 19, "Trustees," is probably a good idea. Trustees and their successors must be provided for in the original ILIT trust document and cannot be changed.

There is one last pitfall in giving life insurance policies to an ILIT. If a life insurance policy is given to your ILIT within three years of the date of your death, the life insurance proceeds are brought back into your estate for federal estate tax purposes. This could also be true for insurance policies purchased directly by your ILIT if the ILIT is drafted or administered incorrectly. It is best for the trustee to apply for the life insurance policy as the owner, to reduce the risk that the insurance policies will be included in your estate if you die within three years after the date the insurance policy becomes effective.

Almost any type of insurance can be used in an ILIT. Term, Whole Life, Universal Life, Variable Life, group, or corporate insurance, properly structured, can all be used. We recommend that if at all possible you should use a permanent policy such as Whole or Universal Life. Since the needs for which an ILIT is created are long-term, it is essential that the life insurance is permanent so the proceeds will be in the ILIT when they are needed.

Creating an ILIT that will meet your objectives and will really work requires the hands of both an expert estate planning attorney and an expert insurance professional. To use less than the best is to invite disaster. If you use competent advisors, your ILIT will allow you to have your tax cake and eat it too.

The discussion on an irrevocable life insurance trust can be summarized as follows:

- Keeps life insurance proceeds free from federal estate tax upon the deaths of both spouses.
- Allows the maker to control life insurance proceeds.
- Allows the life insurance proceeds to pay the death expenses and taxes of both the maker and the maker's spouse.

31

Some Estate Planning Solutions

Techniques and Gimmicks That Do Not Always Work

There are many estate planning techniques that do not always work. There are also some estate planning gimmicks that never work. In this chapter we discuss the following techniques and gimmicks that are frequently tried as solutions in the estate planning process:

Techniques

- Cross-ownership of life insurance
- Joint tenancy
- Minors Act custodial accounts
- General powers of attorney

Gimmicks

- Hiding property in a safe-deposit box
- Forms
- Do-it-yourself estate planning
- Constitutional trusts

Cross-Ownership of Life Insurance

The proceeds of life insurance are subject to federal estate tax in the estate of the owner of the policy. They are not necessarily subject to federal estate tax in the estate of the insured. As a result, many insurance salespeople suggest that spouses purchase and own insurance policies on each other. For example, the husband is the owner of the policy insuring the wife, and vice versa. By doing this, each spouse is the beneficiary of the death proceeds from the policy he or she owns on the other's life. On the death of one spouse, the insurance proceeds are paid to the other free from federal estate tax.

Let us take a closer look at this technique. Under current law the proceeds going to a U.S. citizen spouse would be tax-free anyway because of the unlimited marital deduction. On the second death, the entire amount of the remaining insurance proceeds will be included in the estate of that spouse and will be subject to federal estate tax, unless sheltered by the applicable exclusion amount. This amount is inflation indexed to $5,120,000 in 2012 and will go down to $1 million in 2013 unless Congress changes the law.

The tax consequences of cross-ownership are even worse if the insurance proceeds are payable to someone other than the spouse who owns the policy. If this occurs, there is a gift under federal law of the entire insurance proceeds to the beneficiary from the spouse who owns the policy.

Cross-ownership is not a good technique for avoiding federal estate tax. In reality it does not accomplish a thing for spouses. There are better techniques available to avoid death taxation on insurance proceeds, techniques that can keep the proceeds free of federal estate tax on both deaths.

Cross-ownership also results in loss of control over the policy and the proceeds. The owner of the policy, not the insured, controls the policy. What if a divorce occurs? The insured may be left without insurance. On the death of the insured, the owner-beneficiary will receive the proceeds without any requirement as to how, why, or for whom the proceeds should be used.

Cross-ownership between nonspouses is equally dangerous. Here, though, the benefit is potentially greater: There will be no federal estate tax on the death of the insured where there might otherwise be if the insured were the owner. But remember, the insured loses all control in the policy and its proceeds.

The better technique to avoid federal estate tax is establishing an irrevocable life insurance trust, which can keep control of the policy and its proceeds in the insured. This technique was discussed in Chapter 30, "The Irrevocable Life Insurance Trust."

Joint Tenancy with Right of Survivorship

Because of its importance and frequent use as an estate planning technique, we have discussed joint ownership in several other chapters. However, a summary of its weaknesses is apropos here.

Putting property in joint ownership with a nonspouse creates a gift for federal and some state tax purposes. This is true when one party paid for the property or already owned it.

Joint ownership results in loss of control of the joint property, because the other owner can require that it be split up or sold. On death there is no control; it is a mini estate plan. The entire property could be subject to the other owner's creditors. The property cannot be planned. There is a loss of step-up in basis that is particularly detrimental in spousal planning.

Joint tenancy is an estate planning technique that should be avoided, because other techniques can accomplish estate planning goals far better.

Minors Act Custodial Accounts

Uniform transfers to minors' custodial accounts can be created in all states. These custodial accounts come in two forms. Which kind you can use depends on the state's law in effect where the account is set up.

The original form of special custodial accounts for minors was the Uniform Gifts to Minors Act. This legislation was essentially passed to allow an adult to give stock to minors; some states' acts also apply them to savings accounts and annuity contracts. The gifts to minors law allows an account to be created for the benefit of a minor child in the name of an adult, and in some states, in the name of a bank or trust company. The adult or institution in whose name the account is created is called a *custodian*.

Gifts to minors laws allow certain property to be given to minor children without necessitating the creation of a trust. In most states, when a child reaches the age of either 18 or 21 the account is closed and the property transferred to him or her.

Almost all states have adopted a newer version of the Uniform Gifts to Minors Act, called the Uniform Transfers to Minors Act. The newer version is aimed at eliminating some of the shortcomings of the old act. Essentially, the new law allows all types of property to be held in the custodial account, rather than only the limited types allowed under the older act; and the new version broadens how custodial accounts can be established and used. For property that cannot be held in an account, such as real estate or personal property, the new law allows title to the property to be placed in the name of a custodian on behalf of a minor. In most other respects both versions of the law are the same, with almost the same problems and pitfalls.

The problems resulting from these accounts and other custodial transfers can be weighty:

- If the dividends or other income generated by the stocks are used to support the child and the person who created the account is legally obligated to support the child, the income will be taxed to the person who created the account.

- If the person making the gift is the custodian of the account, the entire value of the account will be taxed in that person's estate on death.

- The custodian cannot invest in property other than stock in some states, but may put the income in a savings account for the child's benefit. There is little investment flexibility in these accounts.

- The custodian is liable to the child for the negligent handling of these accounts and must, on the child's request, make a complete accounting with respect to the transactions in the account.

- The child must receive the account property, including the income earned from the account, when he or she reaches adulthood, which is either 18 or 21 in most states. What they do with the account proceeds is then the recipient's business.

- The creation of these accounts is a gift under both federal and state gift tax laws. If the value of the gift to a minor exceeds the annual exclusion amount ($13,000 in 2012, plus any adjustments for inflation) in any given year, gift tax may have to be paid.

We believe that this technique usually does not accomplish the objectives of the account creator. Too often these accounts are abused, cannot be controlled sufficiently by their makers, and result in adverse tax consequences.

Another way to accomplish your objectives in this area is to establish a minor's trust. Estate-planning professionals call this a 2503(c) trust. The use of this trust provides much greater flexibility as to the investment of your funds, because the trust investments are not limited to stock and the trust property is not included in your estate on death. Gifts to a minor's trust qualify for the annual exclusion under federal gift tax law. In addition, the 2503(c) trust allows the maker more control over the property in the trust and over the income it earns. However, a 2503(c) trust must allow the beneficiary to take out the funds at age 21, so it too has its pitfalls. The better alternative is to create an irrevocable trust, which is similar to an irrevocable life insurance trust, the subject just discussed in Chapter 30. Always be wary of making gifts to a custodial account, and consider a 2503(c) trust or an irrevocable trust as better alternatives.

General Powers of Attorney

Many older people concerned about their ability to conduct their affairs grant a general power of attorney to loved ones. By doing this, these mature adults hope to avoid the confusion that could occur should they become ill or mentally incompetent. They want their children or other loved ones to be in charge of their affairs, not attorneys or courts of law. Their objectives are sincere and patently reasonable.

However, a general power of attorney may not accomplish the objectives of its maker. Under the laws of most states, a general power of attorney is invalid upon the death or adjudicated incapacity of its maker. Thus, when the event the maker feared occurs, the envisioned solution will not work without language that converts the general power of attorney into a durable general power of attorney.

The granting of a general power of attorney can be exceedingly dangerous. The person who has this power of attorney can control all the property of the maker. This means the holder can spend or dispose of the property for the holder's own benefit.

The concerns that motivate individuals to use these general powers of attorney are real, however, and should be addressed. If you are concerned about your affairs, create a revocable living trust, spelling out how you wish to be taken care of in case of incapacity. Name a trustee you can trust, whether child, friend, or advisor. If these alternatives are not available or acceptable to you, name an institutional trustee.

By using a revocable living trust, you can reduce the likelihood that others will appropriate your property for unauthorized purposes. This alternative is discussed at length in Chapter 17, "The Revocable Living Trust."

General powers of attorney should not be confused with limited or durable special powers of attorney. A discussion of these powers can be found in Chapters 4, "Disability," and 18, "Funding a Revocable Living Trust."

Hiding Property in a Safe-Deposit Box

We have found that many of our clients believe that if assets are placed in safe-deposit boxes, family members can go to the bank after their deaths, take the assets out, and nobody will be the wiser.

This kind of thinking could not be further from the truth. Our public officials are not so naive. The first public act, generally through each state's death tax division, is to lock or freeze a safe-deposit box upon the death of the owner. The box stays frozen until the proper public official can inventory every asset in the box.

On being informed of this, many clients do not relent, but become even more creative: "I'll put my assets in someone else's box so the state won't know about it." Not a bad idea, except for the fact that a gift has been made without a receipt, total control over the contents has been lost, and a potentially fraudulent transaction has been entered into. Not reporting assets for federal estate tax purposes is like not reporting income; it is a crime. Need we say more?

Forms

In 1965, Norman F. Dacey authored *How to Avoid Probate.* The book was a national best seller. In it, as we have indicated elsewhere, Mr. Dacey viciously attacked attorneys and the probate process. His thesis was that probate should be avoided. This book remains in print, even though Mr. Dacey died years ago.

Most of the Dacey book represented his views and suggestions—complete with tear-out forms—on how probate should be avoided and how estate plans should be drafted. Mr. Dacey was not an attorney; his forms were to be filled in and used by the readers of his book to effectuate their estate planning goals. He did not encourage his readers to seek the advice and counsel of attorneys, accountants, insurance professionals, or other estate planning advisors in using his forms.

We partially agree with Mr. Dacey: probate should be avoided. We do not believe, however, that his "forms" approach represents a sound estate planning process. We do not believe that the reading of one book (including this one) qualifies anyone to properly plan an estate without the additional help and knowledge of experts in the field. We believe that filling out forms is a gimmick that should be avoided.

Do-It-Yourself Estate Planning

An extension of the use of forms is the growing industry of buying estate plans through the mail, through software, through the Internet, or by having advisors other than lawyers prepare estate plans. These are gimmicks that should be avoided at all cost.

Wills, trusts, and all other aspects of estate planning almost invariably involve legal and tax rules. The rules apply in certain ways based on an individual's particular personal and financial situation. For an individual to plan his or her estate without legal counsel is akin to performing brain surgery without the aid of a physician.

Mail order, software, or Internet planning and planning provided by those who are not lawyers may sound attractive, but engaging in it is a big mistake. Lawyers are the only professionals who can, by law, draft legal documents and render legal advice. They are trained in the information that is critical to perform certain legal tasks.

Some of the people who sell forms or provide mail order or Internet planning make the claim that their documents have been drafted and reviewed by lawyers. This is a weak and misleading statement. For a lawyer to draft a form for a particular fact situation without having any specific information about the client's family, financial situation, and particular wants and needs is unethical. These boilerplate plans that have not been tailored to the needs of a particular client do not result, for the most part, in responsible planning.

The definition of estate planning is giving what you have to whom you want, the way you want, when you want, and if possible saving every fee and tax possible. Mail order or other long-distance planning and estate plans sold by nonlawyers do not even begin to meet that definition.

Attempting to circumvent lawyers in estate planning may cost more money in the short run—many software, Internet, and mail order trusts are more expensive than those drafted by lawyers. It may cost more in the long run too. When do-it-yourself, mail order, Internet, or software plans, or plans drafted by nonlawyers, are put to the test because of disability or death, it may well be that undoing them is much more expensive than doing the right plan in the first place. Do yourself and your loved ones a favor: use a lawyer as well as other professionals, and form an estate planning team that will clearly meet your planning needs.

As a final thought, remember this: if you use a form or any other type of do-it-yourself document and it is wrong, no one will be held accountable. The person who wrote the book, the owner of the Internet site, the manufacturer of the software, or anyone else who is not a lawyer will not be liable to your family. Each of these purveyors of bad advice will make you sign a disclaimer of liability or will have one in their literature.

While lawyers do make mistakes, they are liable for them. Your family has a good chance that the lawyer will either correct mistakes or pay for them. Your do-it-yourself plan, however, will not have this benefit.

Constitutional Trusts

Many of the techniques we refer to in this chapter have some basis in fact and in law. They are honest attempts at planning. The constitutional trust does not fall into this category.

The constitutional trust, or as it is sometimes referred to, the "pure equity trust," is an out-and-out fraud. It is a hoax promulgated by hucksters masquerading as professionals.

The hucksters claim that by using a constitutional trust (or some variation of it), estate tax can be avoided and no gift tax liability incurred. They even claim that income tax will be avoided through the use of their technique. Can you believe it? A triple play! They are selling these trusts and the planning kits that go with them at prices ranging from $4,000 to $25,000 or more. Generally, they present or sell their packages to professionals, with some emphasis, it seems, on the medical profession.

This scheme does not work, nor does it accomplish any of the benefits claimed. The Internal Revenue Service has watched these trusts for some time and has been coming down very hard on the often innocent participants taken in by this hoax. *Time* magazine exposed these devices as hoaxes. These trusts are shams and nothing more than page after page of nonsense.

If you have been taken in by this type of hoax, we strongly suggest you seek competent counsel immediately, or if you prefer, your local district or prosecuting attorney.

Beware of any income, gift, or estate tax scheme that seems too good to be true, because they are. There are many legitimate methods for saving substantial amounts of taxes. If you are willing to pay for the expertise, you will find out how to reduce or eliminate taxes in a safe manner that will hold up to scrutiny. When faced with a proposal from business hucksters that guarantees you will not pay taxes, get a professional opinion.

32

Freezing Techniques

Putting Your Estate in Cold Storage

Over the years, Congress has significantly reduced the number of estates that will be subject to federal estate taxation. Many estates, however, will continue to qualify for federal estate tax, and it is probable that inflation, real growth, and future changes in the estate tax laws will push estates that currently are not taxable into the realm of taxability. This chapter deals with traditional techniques that stop or at least control the growth of your estate by passing that growth to other family members. We explain how these *freezing techniques* have been radically altered by congressional attempts to prevent their abuse.

By using a freezing technique, you can accomplish the following with respect to your assets:

- Transfer future appreciation from your estate to your children and grandchildren while you are alive, with little or no federal gift tax implications.
- Keep control of your assets during your life.
- Continue to receive income from your assets.

Traditional Freezing Techniques

Prior to 1988 freezing techniques could be used for almost any asset, such as stock of closely held corporations, partnership interests, sole proprietorships, and real estate. Beginning in 1987, Congress began to enact tough legislation to address what was considered the abusive use of a tax-avoidance measures. As a result, Congress made two major revisions to the tax laws, enacting in quick succession two completely different methods to discourage the use of freezing techniques.

The Revenue Act of 1987 introduced a new section, 2036(c), to the Internal Revenue Code. That section substantially eliminated many of the freezing techniques used prior to 1988 by bringing the value of certain transferred interests back into the federal taxable estate of the person who made the transfer. Section 2036(c) was complex. It covered a broad spectrum of transactions, not just traditional freezing techniques, and was very difficult to administer.

In the Revenue Reconciliation Act of 1990, Congress completely repealed section 2036(c) but did not abandon trying to limit the use of freezing techniques. The 1990 Act replaced section 2036(c) with an entirely new set of rules. They focused on the valuation of transfers for gift tax purposes, rather than on interests retained under section 2036(c) that were taxed at the donor's death. The new provisions have a substantial effect on the use of traditional freezing techniques.

In order to understand the freezing techniques that are still available, it is important to understand the traditional freezing techniques. After an explanation of those techniques, as they were used prior to 1988, we will explain the new valuation rules introduced by the Revenue Reconciliation Act of 1990, which continue to be in effect.

One of the most popular freezing techniques was called a *recapitalization*. This restructures stock ownership in a corporation. For instance, exchanging growth stock for nongrowth stock restructures a corporation.

There are primarily two types of corporate stock: common stock and preferred stock. *Common stock* is the growth stock. As a corporation prospers and grows in value, so does its common stock. If the value of the corporation goes down, so does the value of the common stock. Owning common stock is risky because its value varies with the fortunes of the corporation.

Preferred stock is the nongrowth stock. Its value is fixed when it is issued. As a corporation prospers and grows in value, the preferred stock does not grow in value, and if the value of the corporation goes down, the preferred stock does not necessarily go down. Preferred stockholders get the first right to receive dividends paid by the corporation. If the corporation is sold or liquidated, preferred stockholders have the right to get paid for their stock before common stockholders. When a corporation issues preferred stock, it has a predetermined dividend. For example, 8 percent preferred stock with a face value of $100 means that if a corporation pays a dividend, the preferred stockholders will receive $8 of dividend income for each $100 of preferred stock they own.

Preferred stock can be issued so that the corporation is required to pay the agreed-upon dividend, or it can be issued so that the payment of the dividend is left to the corporation's discretion. If the preferred stock is *cumulative preferred stock*, the corporation must pay the agreed-upon dividend every year. If the corporation cannot afford to make a dividend payment to cumulative preferred stockholders, then it must make up the missed dividends in future years.

If the preferred stock is *noncumulative*, the corporation may or may not pay dividends each year. If dividends are not paid, they do not have to be made up in later years.

If a corporation is sold or dissolved, the preferred stockholders receive all the proceeds, after all creditors are paid, until the face value of their preferred shares, plus any dividends owed, is paid. Preferred stockholders get paid before common stockholders.

A *corporate recapitalization* occurs when a common stockholder exchanges common stock for shares of preferred stock. While there are many variations on how these tax-free trades are made, the following describes a typical exchange prior to 1988:

- An independent appraiser valued the existing common stock.

- The corporation issued preferred stock to the common stockholder in exchange for all or part of the common stock owned by that stockholder.

- The corporation issued new common stock to the preferred stockholder's children or grandchildren or other designated individuals; or the original stockholder gave the common stock to his or her children or grandchildren or to other designated individuals.

- The recipients of the common stock paid for their common stock if the corporation issued it. Because the corporation was only worth the value of the preferred stock, the price of the common stock would be very low.

The end result of this stock trade (recapitalization) was that the children or grandchildren had all the growth (common) stock. The original stockholder had no-growth (preferred) stock and had removed the future growth of the corporation from the stockholder's estate.

The most difficult and risky aspect of a corporate recapitalization is valuing the preferred stock. Because preferred stock in a closely held corporation is often structured in such a manner as to make its value problematical, it is not uncommon to have it valued significantly below the value of the corporation as a whole. When this occurs, the common stock is worth more, which may result in federal gift tax implications when the common stock is given to children or grandchildren. The IRS issued some guidelines in 1983 as to how preferred stock is to be valued in a corporate recapitalization. These guidelines should be adhered to in a recapitalization to avoid later problems.

Here is an example of how a recapitalization worked before 1988:

> John Walls, a man in his late sixties, and his wife Betsy, who is the same age, have spent all their lives accumulating an estate. They own a small print shop that designs and produces a line of greeting and Christmas

cards. Their business was incorporated years ago. All the corporation's common stock is in John's name.

John and Betsy have three children. Their son, Dave, works for the corporation. Their two daughters, Sally and Betty, have never worked in the business. Sally is a successful businessperson. Betty is a homemaker.

John and Betsy depend on their corporation for their livelihood.

Both John and Betsy want their son, Dave, to operate and own the business upon their deaths. They also want to be fair to their daughters. If John dies, Betsy needs to receive cash from the business. If the estate continues to grow at its present rate, the federal estate taxes that will ultimately have to be paid by the children may force the sale of the family business.

John and Betsy's advisors recommend a recapitalization. A report is issued by a professional appraiser stating that the common stock of the family's business is worth $750,000. After conferring with their appraiser and tax advisors, they agree that the preferred stock can be valued at $710,000. This will leave $40,000 worth of common stock to divide among Dave, Sally, and Betty.

John trades $710,000 worth of his common stock for $710,000 worth of 15 percent noncumulative preferred stock. The preferred stock has the right to vote on all corporate matters. John, however, still owns $40,000 worth of common stock, which he can divide up among Dave, Betty, and Sally in any manner he and Betsy decide. John and Betsy can give up to $20,000 (2 times the annual exclusion amount in the mid 1980s) a year to each of their children free of federal gift tax. If they want to give Dave more than $20,000 worth of stock, either they can use up part of the exemption equivalent or make a $20,000 gift in the current year and the remainder the next year. No matter how the gifts are made, any future growth in the value of the corporation will be passed on to John and Betsy's children, free from federal gift, estate, or income tax.

In our example, John transferred the future appreciation of the corporation to the children in the percentages he and Betsy wanted, free of federal income and gift tax. John and Betsy also retained control of the corporation because the preferred stock had voting rights. They continued to work in the family corporation and to take their salaries. They have also assured themselves that if the business does well, they can receive dividend payments upon retirement. On John's death, he can leave the preferred stock to Betsy so she can continue to enjoy all the ownership benefits. On Betsy's death, Dave will own and control the family corporation, as John and Betsy wish.

Figure 32-1 illustrates our example.

The example of John and Betsy illustrates how a recapitalization used to work. It could be structured to accommodate almost any family situation that involved a family-owned corporation. This technique was not commonly used, because only trained tax advisors understood it and knew how to implement it.

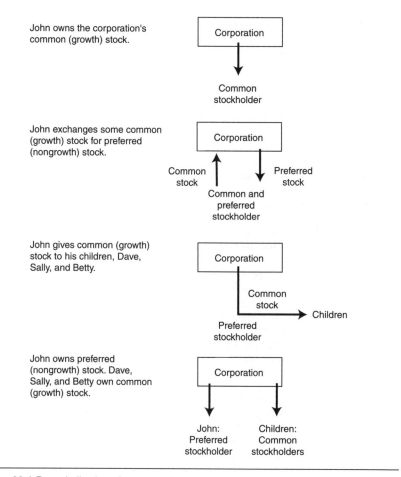

John owns the corporation's common (growth) stock.

Corporation

Common stockholder

John exchanges some common (growth) stock for preferred (nongrowth) stock.

Corporation

Common stock | Preferred stock

Common and preferred stockholder

John gives common (growth) stock to his children, Dave, Sally, and Betty.

Corporation

Common stock → Children

Preferred stockholder

John owns preferred (nongrowth) stock. Dave, Sally, and Betty own common (growth) stock.

Corporation

John: Preferred stockholder | Children: Common stockholders

Figure 32-1 Recapitalization of a corporation.

There is a second freezing technique known as a *partnership freeze.* It is used to freeze assets other than corporate stock. This technique accomplishes all the objectives that are accomplished by a recapitalization but is more advantageous. Because no corporation is involved, many of the valuation problems encountered in a recapitalization are avoided. In addition, there is no double tax on income when using a partnership.

The definition of a *partnership* is any endeavor entered into by two or more people with a view to making a profit. Profit can be made through operating a business or investing in assets for a later sale. Either way, the business or assets can be placed in a partnership. A partnership may either be general or limited. In a *general partnership,* all partners have an element of control and therefore have unlimited liability. A *limited partnership* has both general and limited partners. The general partners control a limited partnership and have the same liability they would in a general partnership. The limited partners do not have control and are liable only to the extent of their partnership investment.

Either a general or a limited partnership interest can be frozen for estate planning purposes. Just like no-growth preferred stock, partnership ownership can be established in such a manner that its value does not increase. Any nonfrozen partnership ownership then becomes growth ownership. To illustrate this concept, we will continue the example of John and Betsy.

> John and Betsy own a building in a joint tenancy. Like the corporation, it is increasing in value. They want the building's appreciation out of their estates but want to keep the income they receive from it.
>
> They have the building appraised. It is worth $650,000. John and Betsy then form a limited partnership and transfer the building into the partnership in exchange for a 50 percent general partner interest for each of them.
>
> They each owned 50 percent of the building before the partnership was formed, and nothing has changed except that there is a new name on the deed—the name of the partnership.
>
> The formal partnership agreement states that upon the sale of the building or the liquidation of the partnership, the general partners, John and Betsy, will receive the value of the building as it was appraised when put into the partnership. The value at that time was $650,000. Thus, the most they can receive in the future is $325,000 each. The value of the building is frozen in the same manner as a corporate recapitalization.
>
> After the partnership is formed, Dave, Betty, and Sally will buy limited partnership interests of their own. The price will not be high, however, because as in the recapitalization of the corporation, John and Betsy will decide the amount each can purchase. If they decide to sell $10,000 worth of limited partnership interests, $4,000 worth each may go to Betty and Sally and $2,000 to Dave. Betty and Sally would each have 40 percent of the future growth of the building, and Dave would have 20 percent.
>
> John and Betsy retain the income from the building. The partnership can provide an income to them before any of that income is paid to the children.

In the example of a partnership freeze, John and Betsy transferred the future appreciation on the building to their children in the percentages they decided, free of federal income and gift tax. John and Betsy also retained control of the building because they became general partners. As general partners, they control the partnership and continue to receive income from the building. On either John's or Betsy's death, the survivor will continue to receive this income from the building. On the deaths of both of them Betty, Sally, and Dave will own the partnership and therefore will own the building. The partnership freeze, like the recapitalization, has accomplished all of John and Betsy's planning objectives.

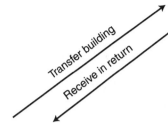

John and Betsy

Control as general partners.

Frozen (no-growth) partnership
interest.

First right to income.

First right to sale proceeds
up to frozen amount when
building is sold.

Children

Limited rights as limited partners.

Growth of partnership interest
as nonfrozen partners.

Income if some is left.

Sale proceeds only after
John and Betsy get theirs.

Figure 32-2 Frozen limited partnership.

The second example involving John and Betsy illustrates one of the many ways a partnership freeze was used prior to 1988. Like the recapitalization of a corporation, a partnership freeze was understood and properly used only by trained tax advisors. Figure 32-2 illustrates how this concept worked.

Changes Made by the Revenue Reconciliation Act of 1990

In the Revenue Reconciliation Act of 1990—which we will shorten to the "1990 Act"—Congress repealed code section 2036(c) retroactively to the date of its enactment and replaced it with a new set of rules. Every transaction that has the potential to freeze an estate must be analyzed in light of these new rules.

Traditional freezing techniques were based on the assumption that the value of future appreciation is very low and the value of the retained interest is very high. Under our earlier example of a traditional recapitalization, when John transferred common stock to his children, his advisors valued it much lower than the preferred stock he retained. By doing this, the cost of transferring the future appreciation of the business to John's children was very low.

The current rules take a different approach. Instead of allowing the taxpayer to value the property, the law sets out how property is to be valued. In addition, instead of imposing federal estate tax at the death of the person who makes the transfer, the current rules immediately subject the transfer to federal gift tax.

The current rules, in most situations, require John to value the preferred stock at a low or no value. Under John's plan to recapitalize the corporation, federal gift tax may well be generated when he gives the common stock to his children, because it will be valued at a substantially higher amount than it would have been prior to the current rules.

The same is true in a traditional limited partner freeze. Again, under the current rules the general partner interest is valued lower and the limited partner interests are valued at a higher amount. This allows Uncle Sam to subject the property to federal gift tax immediately. It also makes a recapitalization much less attractive from a planning point of view.

Under the current rules, some of the valuation issues are addressed under certain distribution rules for corporations and partnerships. Now, if an individual transfers an interest in a corporation or partnership and retains a right to distributions from a corporation with respect to its stock, or from a partnership with respect to a partner's interest in the partnership, that distribution right is given a zero value. The *transferred interest*—the part that will appreciate—is thus deemed to have all the value.

These distribution rules also apply to persons who control an entity immediately prior to the transfer. *Control* is defined as holding at least 50 percent, by vote or by value, of the stock of a corporation, or at least 50 percent of the capital or profit interests in a partnership, or having any interest as a general partner in a limited partnership. As with section 2036(c), the ownership of certain family members is lumped together for purposes of the 50 percent requirement.

For transfers of other types of interests, the valuation rules apply regardless of whether the person making the transfer or a group of family members has control. Some of these types of interests include rights upon liquidation and conversion, and puts and calls.

The rules recognize that a retained interest is not always worthless. If a corporation, for example, is paying periodic dividends to holders of cumulative preferred stock at a fixed rate and that stock is the retained interest, then the zero-value concept does not apply. These payments are called *qualified payment rights*. By properly structuring a recapitalization to include qualified payment rights, the value of the gift may be decreased to such an extent that the recapitalization may be attractive. There are other exceptions to the zero-value rule for other types of interests.

As usual, the 1990 Act came with its own complexities and introduced special valuation rules for different types of transactions. One set of rules applies to transfers of certain types of interests in corporations or partnerships. Another set of special valuation rules applies to transfers of interests in trust. Still another set of rules provides that the value of property is determined without regard to certain rights, options, or restrictions; this set of rules applies to buy-sell agreements. Another set of rules deals with the valuation of rights that terminate or lapse.

For transfers in trust, the valuation rules disregard the value of any retained interest that is not a qualified interest. A *qualified interest* is the right to receive fixed amounts, payable not less than annually; or the right to receive amounts that are a fixed percentage of the fair market value of the property, not less than annually; and any remainder interest that is not contingent on some event occurring in the future. Thus, if an interest retained by a person making a gift to a trust is not a qualified interest, the retained interest is treated as having no value and does not decrease the value of the gift. This concept is much like the qualified payment right for recapitalizations.

There are other exceptions to the valuation rules for transfers in trust. The valuation rules do not apply if there is no completed gift. This includes the situation in which a maker funds a revocable living trust. There is no gift made when transferring one's property to one's revocable living trust; it is an incomplete gift. Another exception applies to the holding of a personal residence in a trust.

Similarly, in the context of buy-sell agreements, the value of property being transferred is determined without regard to any option, agreement, or other right to acquire or use the property, at a price less than the fair market value of the property, or without regard to any restriction on the right to sell or use the property. This means that a price established in a buy-sell agreement to purchase the stock of a shareholder will not be binding for estate, gift, or generation-skipping transfer tax purposes unless the buy-sell agreement is a bona fide business arrangement and is not a device to transfer property to members of a person's family for less than full market value. Also, its terms must be comparable to similar agreements entered into by persons in arm's-length transactions.

The valuation rule for lapsing rights provides that if a person who makes a transfer fails to exercise any retained voting or liquidation rights in a corporation or partnership, then that failure to exercise lapses is treated as a transfer by the individual as a gift, or it may be included in the person's estate for federal estate tax purposes.

As you can see, the rules are extremely complex, and we have only scratched the surface of many of the provisions contained in the law that today significantly limit the use of estate freezing techniques. The general provisions of our federal tax laws often make it difficult to freeze estates and pass on any future appreciation in a business or other enterprise.

One of the most effective methods for avoiding the rules and shifting appreciation to family members is to plan ahead. Creating more than one class of stock in a new corporation may allow you to steer clear of the estate-freezing rules.

For example, Tammi decided to begin a new basket-decorating and gift business. Her children, Shayna, David, and Brian, will be running the business with her, and Tammi hopes they will take over the business one day.

Under the old rules, if Tammi incorporated her new business, she would own all the common stock. Now it may be appropriate to have preferred stock issued to Tammi and common stock issued to Shayna, David, and Brian before the business begins, especially if Tammi has a large estate. This would keep the growth in the value of the corporation out of Tammi's estate and there should be no gift tax consequences, assuming Tammi and the children each contribute their own funds to the business.

Putting your estate in cold storage has traditionally been a most effective estate planning tool. In certain situations it is still possible to freeze the value of property. The advice of your estate planning experts in the planning and implementation of family freeze techniques is of critical importance if you wish to put your estate in cold storage.

33

Discounting the Value of Your Estate

Reduce Value—and Taxes—by Restructuring Your Assets

In the previous chapter we discussed freezing techniques and the fact that they have been virtually eliminated in terms of estate planning. In this chapter we address a new generation of planning techniques that allow you to give your assets away for pennies on the dollar. Sound too good to be true? Not at all. However, the price you pay for discounting is some complexity and Internal Revenue Service frustration. These techniques work so well that the IRS has attempted to squelch their use by encouraging audits and issuing private letter rulings that are less concerned with the state of the law than with stopping the use of the techniques.

The techniques discussed here are *family limited partnerships* and special trusts known as *grantor retained income trusts*.

Family Limited Partnerships

Family limited partnerships are not new. In fact, an Internal Revenue Code provision specifically allows their use. This provision has been in the code for at least 60 years.

A family limited partnership (FLP) is structured in the same manner we explained in Chapter 32: a husband and wife (or a single parent) set up a limited partnership and own the general partnership interest and all of the limited partnership interests. Usually, the husband and wife own a 1 or 2 percent general partnership interest and a 99 or 98 percent limited partner interest. Recall from Chapter 32 that a general partner has full control of a limited partnership even if the general partner owns a very small percentage of the overall partnership.

When the FLP is formed, the husband and wife transfer assets into the partnership. The assets can be cash, stocks, bonds, or other investments. They can be real estate or a business. They can include stock in a closely held corporation (other than an S corporation), and other partnerships or limited liability companies.

Assets such as personal residences, vacation homes, or other personal assets should not be transferred into an FLP. The FLP must be a trade or business of some kind, even if that business is investments. It is important that the FLP agreement itself state the business purposes of the FLP and that the FLP does indeed have a business purpose. The Internal Revenue Service has tried to attack more than one FLP because they had no business purpose.

The FLP agreement must be carefully drafted. It must follow state law and generally should not create any restrictions on the actions of the limited partners that are in excess of state law. If extra restrictions are added, the FLP may fall under special rules that require the ignoring of those restrictions for valuation purposes, and it may even prevent making effective gifts of the limited partnership interests.

Even without extra restrictions, limited partners have rather limited rights in an FLP. By law, limited partners may not participate in the management of the FLP. They cannot force the general partner to pay them income that is generated by the FLP. In fact, limited partners can be prohibited from transferring their limited partnership interests to third parties without the consent of the other partners.

Because a limited partnership interest is subject to restrictions, its value is less than its proportionate share of the underlying assets. This reduction in value is a called a *discount*. It works in the following way:

> Sean and Jane have three children, and they own rental real estate. They would like to establish an entity to hold their rental real estate to provide them with asset protection and a formalized structure for managing the property. Sean and Jane have also discussed that someday they might want to make a substantial gift to their children of a portion of the rental real estate. However, they would like to continue to decide how their rental real estate is managed on a day-to-day basis. In addition, Sean and Jane would like to make sure their children do not give or sell their shares of the rental real estate to others, at least not without their consent.
>
> Let's assume that Sean and Jane, with the advice of their attorney and other professional estate planning advisors, decide to create an FLP. Initially, they name a newly created limited liability company (LLC) owned equally by Sean and Jane as the general partner and with the two

of them equal limited partners. This dual role is acceptable under all state laws, even though limited partners, in their capacity as limited partners, are not permitted to have management control.

Sean and Jane and their LLC fund the FLP by signing deeds transferring ownership of real estate worth a little over $4 million to the FLP. In exchange, their LLC, is named the general partner, receive a 1 percent general partner interest, and Sean and Jane, named limited partners, receive a 99 percent limited partner interest.

Several years later Sean and Jane decide that they want to give away about half of the limited partner interests to their children at a time when the underlying value of the rental real estate is still worth a little over $4 million. Of course, they would like to reduce the value of the gift to their children, if they can.

Sean and Jane want to give away 50 percent of the limited partnership interests equally to their children. However, the Internal Revenue Code requires that when an asset is given away, it must be valued at its fair market value for gift tax purposes. *Fair market value* is defined as the amount a willing buyer will pay a willing seller, each being under no compulsion to buy or sell and each having full knowledge of all relevant facts about the asset.

If a person were to buy a limited partnership interest, he or she would not pay full value for the interest if it were subject to restrictions. In fact, a buyer would not pay full value for the limited partnership interest if it would be hard to resell the asset.

To assess the fair market value of a limited partnership interest, it is imperative that an appraiser be used. The appraiser in this case has two jobs: value the assets put into the FLP, and value the general and limited partner interests. There is a difference. The assets put into the FLP have their own fair market value. However, the limited partner interest's fair market value must be adjusted for *lack of marketability* and *lack of control.* Lack of marketability means it will be hard to find a buyer for the limited partner because of its restrictions on ownership. As an incentive for a buyer to purchase the limited partner interest, it must be discounted. Lack of control is self-explanatory; a person will not pay full value for an asset that offers no control.

The fair market value of a limited partner interest generally ranges from 25 to 50 percent less than the value of the underlying assets. The overall discount is likely to beat the higher range if the assets inside the FLP are also restricted in some way. For example, if an FLP owns a minority interest in stock of a closely held business or another limited partnership.

Let's assume a qualified appraiser of 50 percent of Sean and Jane's limited partner interests determines it is subject to a total of 30 percent in discounts. That means they can make a gift of 50 percent of the limited partner interests to their children at a gift tax value of $1.4 million, while still controlling the assets within the FLP and how the income and principal are distributed to the limited partners.

It is possible to get similar discounts for gifts of stock in closely held corporations and ownership interests in limited liability companies. The latter did not exist in the United States prior to 1977, when Wyoming enacted the first limited liability company statute. Today there are LLC statutes in all 50 states. For a time following 1977 the laws favored the use of limited partnerships over limited liability companies. In the early years following 1977 there were many uncertainties regarding how existing law would be applied to LLCs. Today those questions have been answered in a very favorable way for LLCs, and as a result many planners use LLCs instead of or interchangeable with limited partnerships.

However, limited partnerships and limited liability companies are often preferred over corporations for a number of reasons.

Corporations must overcome many issues. A *C corporation*, which is a regular corporation with its own income tax structure, lacks the ability to pass through income to shareholders with only a single tax. Limited partnerships and most limited liability companies are pass-through entities; the partners or members include in income their pro rata share of partnership or LLC income. In a C corporation, the corporation has its own income tax liability. Any amounts paid to shareholders are subject to a second tax. When making gifts to children or grandchildren, most people would prefer that income be passed through without a second tax.

S corporations are pass-through entities. Their shareholders share income on a pro rata basis just as partners do. Voting can be restricted in an S corporation by the use of voting and nonvoting stock. However, there are many restrictions on S corporations, which sometimes make them difficult to deal with.

The state laws governing corporations are not as restrictive on value as the laws governing limited partnerships and limited liability companies. In addition, certain provisions of the Internal Revenue Code make it difficult to use restrictive provisions in a corporate shareholders' agreement to increase the amount of the discounts used in valuing the stock.

All in all, FLPs and LLCs tend to be the most effective structures for discounting gifts. State and federal law, as well as much legal precedent, favor the use of FLPs and LLCs for making discounted gifts.

If you are interested in forming an FLP or an LLC, seek expert advice. Because of the Internal Revenue Code and case law minefield surrounding FLPs and LLCs, only advisors with a thorough understanding of what can and cannot be done with an FLP or LLC should be hired to design and create these complicated entities. Also, make sure that you use a top-notch business appraiser. The old saying that an ounce of prevention is worth a pound of cure applies here.

Grantor Retained Income Trusts

Grantor retained income trusts (GRITs), like family limited partnerships, are not new. At one time a technique known as a statutory GRIT was used by many estate planners as a very effective way to transfer assets to children with little or no gift tax. The use of statutory GRITs has been curtailed, but other grantor retained interest trusts can be used effectively to make gifts to family members.

To understand how grantor retained interest trusts work, let's examine the old statutory GRIT, a trust that generally lasted for a term of years. A maker created an irrevocable trust, placed certain assets in it, and retained the income from those assets for the term of the trust. At the trust's end, the assets passed to the trust's beneficiaries.

The value of the gift to the GRIT's beneficiaries was the assets' fair market value at the time of their transfer into the GRIT, less the value of the maker's right to income over the term of the trust. The Internal Revenue Code provided a mechanism to compute the value of the income interest.

GRITs proved to be quite effective because the method of determining the value of the maker's retained income interest did not allow for the actual income generated by the assets. So, for example, a maker could place assets that were assumed to pay out a certain amount of income but actually did not. The net result was that a gift was made, over time, to beneficiaries. The value of the gift could be greatly understated.

Statutory GRITs are still allowed in limited circumstances. The Internal Revenue Code prohibits the use of GRITs if members of the maker's immediate family are beneficiaries. However, a maker can create a GRIT that names people other than immediate family members. Immediate family members include the maker's spouse, ancestors, lineal descendants of the maker or the maker's spouse, any brother or sister of the maker, and their spouses.

The use of GRITs even for nonfamily members is not as effective as in the past. There is a requirement that income-producing assets be used in the GRIT; if non-income-producing assets are used, then the Internal Revenue Service will attempt to increase the gift element of the trust to reflect that the income interest held by the maker is not worth very much.

GRITs can be used in one more area. It is possible to put certain tangible property in a GRIT, such as artwork, undeveloped property, or antiques. However, Internal Revenue regulations make use of these devices very difficult if not impossible. You may want to discuss using a Tangibles GRIT with your advisors to determine whether it may be applicable to your planning situation.

The most common type of grantor retained interest trust used today is called a grantor retained annuity trust (GRAT). A variation of this trust is a grantor retained unitrust (GRUT). Both of these trusts are specifically authorized under the Internal Revenue Code and have specific requirements on how they must operate.

A GRAT works very much like a GRIT except that the grantor retains an annuity interest rather than an income interest. An *annuity interest* is a periodic payment for a term of years that is based on the value of the assets initially put into the trust. For example, if $100,000 is transferred to an 8 percent GRAT, then the maker of the GRAT will receive $8,000 per year for the term of the trust. If the assets do not generate enough income to pay the $8,000 per year, then trust principal (part of the $100,000) must be paid to make up the difference.

In a GRUT, the income interest the maker retains is called a *unitrust interest*. This differs from an annuity interest in that the unitrust interest is a payment based on the fair market value of the trust's assets as valued each year. If $100,000 worth of assets is placed in an 8 percent GRUT, the payment the first year is $8,000. However, if in the second year of the GRUT the assets have grown to a value of $110,000, then the second year payment is $8,800 (8 percent of $110,000). If in the third year the value has dropped to $80,000, then the payment would be $6,400 (8 percent of $80,000).

For a number of reasons, GRATs are much more commonly used than GRUTs. The primary reasons are that GRATs tend to result in a lower gift to the beneficiaries, and their assets do not have to be valued each year to determine the amount of the payout.

The value of the gift to the beneficiaries of a GRAT or a GRUT is determined based on the following:

- Value of the assets initially transferred into the trust

- Length of time the trust pays its annuity or unitrust payment to the maker

- Payout rate to the maker

- Maker's life expectancy

- Interest rate provided the Internal Revenue Service for the month the trust was funded

- Timing of the payments (monthly, quarterly, annually, etc.)

The interest rate provided by the Internal Revenue Service is an assumed rate of return of the trust assets based on the applicable rate of interest for the month the trust was initially funded. For example, if the current rate published by the IRS is 6 percent, then it is assumed, for purposes of computing the value of the gift to the beneficiaries, that the trust will have a total rate of return of 6 percent for its full term.

In essence, the longer the trust pays its income interest to the maker, and the higher the payout amount is, the lower the value of the gift.

A simple example will illustrate how a GRAT works to discount the value of a gift:

> Margo Maker wants to make a substantial gift to her three children. Margo is 56 and has $1 million in stocks and bonds. She would like to retain an income interest of 8.5 percent ($85,000) a year paid on an annual basis for 10 years, at which time she would like her stocks and bonds to pass to her three children. The current interest rate for GRATs, as published by the Internal Revenue Service, is 3.2 percent. The amount of Margo's gift is about $282,000. Margo's gift will be sheltered by her applicable exclusion amount. Gifts to a GRAT do not qualify for the annual exclusion.
>
> Assume that the stocks and bonds actually grow at the annual rate of 10 percent over the 10-year term of her GRAT. The amount her children will receive from the GRAT at the end of the 10-year term will be around $1,239,000.

GRATs should only be funded with assets that will grow faster than the current interest rate required by the Internal Revenue Code. If they do not, then the efficiency of using a GRAT is greatly reduced.

There are two drawbacks to using GRATs. The first is that if the maker dies during the GRAT's term, a portion of the GRAT—perhaps even the full value of the GRAT's assets—will be included in the maker's estate. There is no adverse gift tax effect; the transaction is treated as if the gift never occurred. This contingency must be planned for. If not planned correctly, especially if the maker is married, excess estate taxes can be generated.

The second drawback to a GRAT involves its use for generation-skipping. Because of special language in the Internal Revenue Code, the valuation of the assets in a GRAT for generation-skipping transfer tax exemption purposes occurs when the payout term ends, not when the gift is made.

When the payout term does end, the GRAT's assets do not have to pass directly to children. Just as in any other trust, it is possible to retain the assets in trust. If the maker has concerns about making outright gifts, then appropriate provisions can be added to the GRAT.

One technique used to minimize the drawback of the maker dying during the term is to structure the GRAT to last for a short term of years. GRATs can safely be structured for only a two-year term. The shorter the term, the higher the payout needed to minimize the amount of the taxable gift of the remainder interest. Following is an example of a two-year term GRAT used for Margo Maker. Let's assume she is willing to make approximately the same taxable gift as in the example above.

> Margo Maker transfers $1 million in stocks and bonds into a two-year GRAT at a time when the current interest rate for GRATs, as published by the Internal Revenue Service, is still 3.2 percent. She would need to retain an income interest of 37.6 percent ($376,000) a year paid on an annual basis for two years in order to create the same gift of $282,000 to

her children. Assuming the stocks and bonds actually grow at the rate of 10 percent over the two-year term of her GRAT, the amount her children will receive at the end of that term will be around $420,400.

GRATs have been so effective for a number of taxpayers that recently Congress has considered legislation that would require GRATs to have a minimum term of 10 years and limit the amount of the annuity interest retained by the maker. So far this legislation hasn't gotten very far, but it does illustrate that certain members of Congress understand how powerful a tool GRATs can be to transfer wealth to loved ones at a reduced transfer tax cost.

In this chapter we have surveyed two very sophisticated planning techniques. A complete analysis of a family's financial and estate planning objectives must take place before these concepts should be considered. Even then the family's advisors should run the numbers to ensure that these techniques make sense. If they do make sense, the discounting available will allow the transfer of a great deal of wealth at substantially discounted values.

34

Protecting
Your Assets

Safety from Unexpected Liability

One of the common reactions to the concept of asset protection is that an individual, family, or business is trying to avoid paying well-deserved creditors. That is not the purpose of asset protection.

We live in a litigious society. It is common for unhappy people to attempt to solve their problems by resorting to a lawsuit. Creative attorneys and receptive courts have had the effect of broadening the reach of litigation. As a result, huge judgments are awarded in cases that one would not expect to even go to court.

The purpose of asset protection is to title assets in such a manner as to discourage lawsuits that are unreasonable in their scope, as well as avoid the horrendous monetary demands of plaintiffs. Short of discouraging the lawsuit itself, asset protection encourages plaintiffs to settle their claims on a more reasonable basis because of the difficulties they encounter in collecting from the defendant.

There are numerous asset protection techniques. This chapter deals with the best-known methods.

Insurance

A great deal of the liability risks most of us face can be insured against. One of the first steps in asset protection is to meet with your liability insurance carrier to assess your assets and your lifestyle to determine your need for basic liability coverage and amplified umbrella insurance. Find out what the coverage costs and what it covers. You are then better able to determine whether asset protection is necessary and whether the cost of insurance warrants other forms of asset protection.

Holding Property in Tenancy by the Entirety

An inexpensive and relatively effective method of asset protection for married couples is to hold title to marital property in tenancy by the entirety. In Chapter 2, "Title," we discussed this form of title holding.

In the states that allow tenancy by the entirety ownership, generally neither a creditor of only the husband nor of only the wife can get a judgment against tenancy by the entirety property. For example, let's say that John is an executive with a large company and his wife, Terri, is a physician. John's exposure to litigation may be small, but Terri's could be very high. If all of their property was held in tenancy by the entirety, a patient could sue Terri for millions and win a judgment for an amount far greater than her malpractice coverage. But if their property was held in tenancy by the entirety, despite the judgment, the patient could not take John and Terri's assets.

However, if John and Terri were to divorce and split the property, Terri's separate assets would then be subject to the judgment. Also, if John were to die while the judgment was outstanding, all the assets would pass to Terri by law and then be subject to the claims of her creditors.

The more likely outcome is that when the patient's lawyers find out that Terri is judgment-proof because of the way her property is titled, they will want to settle the case. It is also likely that the settlement will be within Terri's malpractice insurance limits. Settling within these limits is a clear victory for Terri and John; it allows them to preserve their assets while paying for the consequences of Dr. Terri's actions.

An exception to the general rule that prohibits the creditor of only one spouse from obtaining a judgment against tenancy by the entirety property is if the creditor is the IRS. In recent years several cases have upheld the validity of IRS liens for taxes owed by only one spouse against tenancy by the entirety property.

Tenancy by the entirety planning is not compatible with basic estate planning, however. If a married couple has all its assets titled in both names, then all of the other disadvantages of jointly held property apply. Thus, this type of planning should be used only if a couple's advisors can provide for other estate planning objectives. This is most often difficult if not impossible to do; we often recommend that other asset protection devices be used.

Community Property and Asset Protection

Community property offers no asset protection. In community property states, a creditor of one spouse has the ability to seize community property. The only property protected from creditors is the separate property of the spouse who does not have a judgment against him or her.

In order to reduce the risk of a creditor of one spouse taking all community property, it is possible to sever a couple's community property. By severing the property, each spouse owns half, usually as a tenant in common, which protects half of those assets from the creditors of one spouse. An alternative is to title all or a majority of the assets in the name of the spouse who appears to have the least amount of exposure to creditors.

There are some disadvantages for each of these techniques. By severing community property, the couple loses the full step-up in cost basis on all of the property when the first spouse dies. While asset protection may be more important than the full step-up in basis, loss of this significant income tax benefit can be quite costly.

Transferring the bulk of a married couple's assets to the spouse who has less exposure is no more than a gamble. For instance, if the spouse who owns all of the property is in a car accident that results in a huge judgment, then all the property may be lost. Unfortunately, it is not always the expected liability that creates exposure. In fact, it is the unexpected that often results in loss of assets.

Other alternatives such as limited partnerships or offshore trust planning should be considered for those couples living in community property states. The other choices do not, in the main, make a great deal of planning sense.

Investing in Exempt Assets

One simple method of asset protection is to invest in assets that are free from the claims of creditors by either state or federal law. While state law provides for more exempt assets than federal law, each can be taken advantage of for purposes of asset protection.

The primary exempt asset under federal law is a qualified retirement plan such as a profit sharing plan or other defined contribution plan; for example, a 401(k) plan or a defined benefit pension plan. Assets in these plans, by law, generally cannot be taken by creditors of the plan participant. However, plans that are not considered to be qualified, such as Individual Retirement Accounts (IRAs), are not fully protected under federal law, though recent law does provide some protection for IRAs when the account owner files for bankruptcy. This bankruptcy protection extends to a maximum of $1 million for all self-funded IRAs and an unlimited amount for all IRAs that have been rolled over from qualified plans. Great care is warranted when planning in this area, and professional assistance is a must to avoid traps for the unwary. For example, combining your self-funded IRA with proceeds rolled over from a qualified plan might prevent you from unlimited federal protection for rollover amounts from qualified plans.

A majority of the states do protect IRAs and other nonqualified retirement plans from creditors. Because this protection is not always available or is only available for a limited amount, it is important that you ask your estate planning professional what the law is in your state.

State law varies as to what assets are exempt from creditors. Most states provide a *homestead exemption*, the objective of which is to protect a person's primary residence from being taken. Most states provide for a certain dollar amount to be exempt from creditors. This means that the house can be seized but the homeowner can retain some of the sales proceeds. A few states, such as Texas and Florida, have an unlimited homestead exemption; the entire value of the homestead, no matter how much it is worth, is protected.

Life insurance proceeds paid to named beneficiaries are generally protected from the claims of creditors of the insured. Sometimes the proceeds are also protected from creditors of the beneficiary. In addition, a number of states protect the cash value of life insurance when the policy is owned by the insured. The value of an annuity and the proceeds from an annuity may also be protected from creditors of the annuitant.

Finally, most states have some minor exemptions for personal property. However, none of these exemptions are very large and they should not be relied upon as any sort of comprehensive asset protection planning.

Using a Corporation to Protect Assets

One of the primary reasons businesses incorporate is for the asset protection of their shareholders. If a corporation is sued or goes bankrupt, the shareholders generally can lose only the value of their stock. Theoretically, they are not personally liable. We say "theoretically" because if a shareholder takes some action that is deemed fraudulent or in violation of the corporate charter, the shareholder could be liable for some or all of the corporate debts. In the case of closely held corporations (those with very few shareholders, who are also involved in the corporation's operations), it is very possible that in any lawsuit against the corporation, the shareholders will also be sued.

Corporations are often used for limited asset protection, to isolate particular assets. For example, let's say that Harvey owns a fireworks company. If the entire operation blows up, Harvey would not like to lose his other assets. He would be wise to incorporate his business. Then, if he has kept his business entity up by paying annual fees, filing annual reports, making sure the public is aware that it is dealing with an entity, not him, and meeting all other state requirements—despite the fact that he could still be sued, odds are that Harvey has protected his other assets.

A corporation can protect an owner's other assets, but only if the business entity is clearly separate and apart from its owners. This does not mean the owners cannot work in the business, but that they must observe all formalities of the business. If Harvey does work in the business and he has negligently packed the fireworks that exploded, then he still can be sued for his personal negligence. A corporation does not protect an owner, officer, or employee from his or her own acts. That is why a corporation may not be the best asset protection for an individual who wants to protect more than his or her investment in a business.

One of the problems of using a corporate structure without other asset protection planning is the application of Murphy's Law: "What can go wrong, will go wrong." If Harvey gets into an automobile accident and is sued for millions of dollars over and above his insurance coverage, then he may lose his corporate stock as well as the remainder of his assets. In asset protection, it is not always the obvious liability that comes back to haunt you. It is just as likely that some unexpected action will cause the need for asset protection.

Limited Partnerships

A *limited partnership* is a business structure that has two types of owners. The *general partner* is in charge of the management of the partnership, and has unlimited liability. The other owners are called *limited partners*. Much like shareholders in a corporation, they do not have any liability other than the value of their limited partnership interests. Limited partners are not allowed to participate in the management of the partnership; if they do, then they lose their liability protection.

Well-structured limited partnership agreements provide that the general partners and the limited partners cannot sell, give, or in any manner dispose of their interests in the limited partnership without the consent of all the other partners. This provision works well in the asset protection arena. If a creditor has a judgment against a partner, then that creditor cannot be a legitimate owner. Therefore, the creditor has no standing to "step in the shoes" of the partner who owes the creditor. This provision makes partnership interests unattractive for creditors.

In most cases the best a creditor can hope for is to go to court and obtain a legal instrument called a *charging order*. This allows the creditor to seize any distributions from the partnership that would otherwise go to the partner who owes the judgment to the creditor.

If the limited partnership is comprised of family members or related parties, as in asset protection limited partnerships, then it is unlikely that a distribution will be forthcoming. Thus, the creditor may have to wait a long time to collect the amount of the judgment. This encourages the creditor to settle rather than wait.

Some state statutes offer stronger charging order protection than others. When seeking maximum charging order protection, it is essential to work with your planning professional to select the state of organization of your limited partnership that works best for your particular planning situation.

A charging order may cause a very serious potential problem for the creditor. The Internal Revenue Service takes the position that a creditor holding a charging order is responsible for the partner's share of taxable income. Let's say that a limited partnership has $100,000 of taxable income but the general partner decides not to distribute any cash. The partners are still responsible for their share of the partnership's taxes. If Limited Partner A owns 25 percent of the partnership, but A's creditor has a charging order, the creditor might be required to include 25 percent of the partnership's taxable income on the creditor's income tax return, even if the creditor has not been paid a dime! This feature discourages some creditors from seeking a charging order; again, it is a method to help settle the debt with the creditor.

One weakness of a limited partnership is that the general partner is liable for all partnership debts and liabilities. Often, a general partner interest is held in a business entity, such as a corporation or a limited liability company, to reduce the exposure of the individual who would otherwise be the general partner.

Another potential weakness of a limited partnership is that a court may find the partnership a sham and thus should be ignored for purposes of a judgment. Courts reach this conclusion if the partnership is not properly formed, funded, operated, or is clearly set up solely for purposes of defrauding creditors. For these reasons it is imperative that an individual or family consult with an attorney who is an expert in asset protection planning before setting up a limited partnership. These complex business organizations call for the attention of a professional.

Limited Liability Companies

A *limited liability company* is a hybrid between a corporation and a limited partnership. Like a corporation, all of a limited liability company's owners are protected from the debts and liabilities of the company. Like a partnership, a limited liability company does not have its own tax liability; income and losses are passed through to the owners, based on their percentage of ownership.

Limited liability companies are popular for several reasons. The primary reason is that all the owners can participate in management. Contrast this participation to that of a limited partnership: in order to maintain limited liability, the limited partners cannot participate in management.

Another reason for the popularity of limited liability companies is that owners can choose how they will be taxed for federal income tax purposes. A multimember limited liability company by default is taxed as a partnership, but may elect to be taxed as a regular corporation or as an S corporation. A single member limited liability company by default is taxed as a sole proprietorship, but may elect to be taxed as a regular corporation or as an S corporation. Limited liability companies by default status do not have a separate tax liability, so all income, deductions, and credits are passed through to the owners based on their ownership percentages. Unlike an S corporation, which is subject to a number of rules concerning who can and cannot be owners, practically any person or entity can own a limited liability company. However, if a limited liability company elects to be treated as an S corporation for federal income tax purposes, it will be subject to all of the same S corporation rules.

A number of states have limited liability company statutes that offer the same charging order creditor protection that applies to limited partnerships, preventing a creditor from taking the ownership interest itself. This general rule may be different in a single member limited liability company. The courts in several states have recently held that the creditor of an individual who was the sole member of a limited liability company was able to reach the assets inside the limited liability company.

Limited liability companies are the newest of the entities we've discussed in this section, and the laws applicable to them are constantly evolving. Be sure to meet with your professional advisor to thoroughly discuss your goals and objectives so he or she can guide you in selecting the best entity for you. If a limited liability company is best suited for you, your professional advisor is essential in its establishment and ongoing operation.

Using Domestic Trusts for Asset Protection

This depends on whether the maker is or is not a beneficiary.

Maker as a Beneficiary

It has long been a basic tenet of law that a person cannot set up a trust, transfer assets to the trust, name himself or herself as the beneficiary, and then prevent creditors from taking the trust assets. This principle applies whether the trust is irrevocable or revocable.

However, recently a number of states have passed trust statutes that offer trust makers the possibility of asset protection in a trust they create under the laws of that state. In 1997, Alaska became the first state to provide a statutory structure for asset protection trusts. That Alaska statute provides that if the trust is drafted and funded correctly, and has an Alaskan trustee, the maker of a trust can be a discretionary beneficiary of the trust. By Alaskan law, creditors of the maker cannot take trust assets even though the maker is a beneficiary. The legal theory behind this law is that because the trust has an independent trustee who can unilaterally make the decision to make income or principal distributions to the maker, the maker has no legal rights to the trust. If the maker has no legal rights, then neither do his or her creditors.

Since Alaska's plunge into asset protection trusts, a number of other states have followed suit, some offering better statutory protections than others. Some of the better state statutes for asset protection trusts include: Alaska, Nevada, South Dakota, and Delaware. The remaining states currently with asset protection trust statutes are: Colorado, Hawaii, Missouri, New Hampshire, Oklahoma, Rhode Island, Tennessee, Utah, and Wyoming.

Much of the law has yet to be written on how effective these state domestic asset protection trust statutes will be in protecting the maker's assets from creditors. For example, the courts have not ruled on whether someone who lives outside the state under whose laws the domestic asset protection trust has been established can create one of these trusts and still avoid creditors. There are some constitutional issues that must be addressed, so for asset protection purposes, these trusts are not necessarily ironclad.

Maker Not a Beneficiary

An irrevocable trust that names someone other than the maker as the beneficiary can be used for asset protection. If the trust contains a spendthrift provision, in most states the assets are protected from the creditors of the beneficiary. A *spendthrift provision* states that neither the trustee nor the beneficiary can use trust assets to pay creditors, and the beneficiary is prohibited from using trust assets as collateral.

Not all states recognize spendthrift provisions, but they should nevertheless be included in all trusts, even revocable trusts. Consider the following:

Suppose you create a revocable living trust that provides, among other things, that upon your death some of your assets will pass to an irrevocable subtrust for the benefit of your children. You allow the trustee to make the decision as to whether or when income and principal will be paid out to your children. You also allow the trustee to pay out trust income and principal on behalf of a child. That means, instead of giving the money directly to the child for rent, for example, the trustee pays the rent directly. The trust also includes a spendthrift provision.

After your death, one of your children has creditor problems. Creditors will seize any money he or she receives directly. However, if the trustee makes payments on behalf of your child, then the creditors cannot seize either the money paid or the trust assets.

Now, let's further assume that when you made the trust you lived in a state that did not recognize a spendthrift provision, but your child lives in a state that does allow spendthrift provisions. It is possible, in a properly drafted trust, to change the location (*situs*) of the trust to the state in which the beneficiary lives. This will likely protect the assets.

As you can see, spendthrift planning is important in trusts for the beneficiaries. You should work with a highly skilled estate planning attorney and other advisors so that these issues can be addressed properly.

Offshore Asset Protection Trusts

The most sophisticated method for asset protection is the offshore asset protection trust (OAPT). These trusts have become quite popular over the last few decades and have proven to be effective in asset protection, despite critical articles to the contrary.

In a nutshell, an OAPT is an irrevocable trust set up in a country outside of the United States. A number of countries can be used, but some of the most popular are the Isle of Man, the Cook Islands, and the Cayman Islands. Even though the trust is irrevocable, it provides provisions that in essence allow the maker to have the benefit of the assets. There are built-in mechanisms that allow the maker to retrieve the assets if he or she needs them.

Unlike a domestic irrevocable trust, OAPTs require that creditors bring their lawsuits in the foreign country rather than the United States. The countries used for the situs of an OAPT generally do not recognize United States judgments. So, for example, if a creditor has a court order to seize the assets of a U.S. citizen who has his or her property in an OAPT, the creditor cannot go to a court in the foreign jurisdiction and ask the courts there to enforce it. The courts in the foreign jurisdiction will require a full trial there in order to determine the validity of the claim.

Even if the claim is valid, the foreign jurisdictions do not allow creditors of the trust maker to take trust assets unless the creditor can prove that the assets were fraudulently conveyed to the trust. Typically, these countries make proving fraudulent conveyances very difficult. In addition, they have relatively short statutes of limitations for bringing a fraudulent conveyance action; it is highly likely that the statute of limitations will expire prior to the time the creditor comes to the foreign country.

Because of the way OAPTs are drafted, the maker of the trust does not lose a great deal of control over his or her assets. Most practitioners who draft these trusts start with a domestic family limited partnership that owns all or substantially all of the maker's assets. The maker then transfers his or her assets to the partnership in exchange for the general and limited partnership interests, which are transferred to the OAPT. The maker controls the assets in the partnership because he or she is the general partner.

The limited partnership allows the maker to invest assets freely, with few restrictions. However, at the first sign of litigation, the maker can liquidate the assets in the partnership and transfer the proceeds into the OAPT. The liquidation and transfer get the assets out of the reach of U.S. courts.

OAPTs are not as effective for real estate as they are for other types of property, such as stocks, bonds, and investment accounts. The latter assets are movable; real estate is not. Because real estate is not movable, a U.S. court can seize it even if the property is technically owned by an OAPT.

One common fear people have about creating an OAPT is that they will get in trouble with a court and a judge might send them to jail if they do not take assets out of their trust. A unique feature of an offshore trust created in a proper jurisdiction is that the foreign jurisdiction's laws will prohibit the trustee from paying the assets to a maker who is under duress. So, if a court orders the maker to force the foreign trustee to give the assets back, the maker can agree to do so. But the trustee cannot comply under the laws of the foreign jurisdiction. The trustee can only pay over assets if the maker requests that the trustee do so, and if the maker is not being forced to make the request.

Do not ever attempt to set up an OAPT by yourself or with someone who does not have absolutely impeccable credentials in offshore asset protection planning. These are complex trusts that require precision in their drafting and implementation. Generally speaking, OAPTs fail because they are not drafted correctly, are incorrectly funded, or are not administered properly. Handled with expertise, they are often very effective in motivating creditors to settle on a reasonable basis.

Fraudulent Conveyances

All states in the United States and most foreign jurisdictions make it unlawful to make a conveyance that is designed to hinder, delay, or defraud an existing creditor or a creditor who is known and could have a basis for a valid claim. That type of transfer is called a *fraudulent conveyance,* and the recipient of the conveyance must return the asset.

Fraudulent conveyance statutes vary from jurisdiction to jurisdiction. Prior to entering into any asset protection planning, consult with an attorney who will give you guidance about these statutes, as well as others that may apply. Asset protection should be accomplished prior to encountering a problem, not afterward. If you have a creditor problem now, or you think that you may, asset protection planning may not be for you. An attorney or other advisor who helps you make such a conveyance can get in a lot of trouble, as you can.

It is in the area of fraudulent conveyances that OAPTs are commonly—and correctly—criticized as being immoral, potentially ineffective, and crooked. However, if they are created innocently before a cause of action arises, none of these labels can be attached.

Asset protection planning, even at its base level, is no area for rookies or do-it-yourselfers. Use a team of professionals if you want it to be a part of your estate planning.

35

Loans to Family Members

It's Hard to Be Your Family's Banker

Loans to family members have the potential to be a good method of freezing the value of an estate and shifting income to family members in lower tax brackets. Unfortunately, the Supreme Court and Congress have done a great deal to discourage the use of loans to family members. However even today loans to family members that require the appropriate rate of interest and are structured and documented correctly offer some major planning opportunities, especially when required minimum interest rates are low.

Historically, two types of intrafamily loans have been used for estate and income tax planning purposes. They are *below-market loans* and *interest-free loans*.

Below-market loans are made by one family member to another for less than the going interest rate. For example, a child could go to a bank and borrow money at 12 percent interest, but a parent could lend the child the money for 6 percent. If this were done, the child would only pay 6 percent interest. The parent would only pay income tax on the 6 percent received, and the child would receive the benefit of paying a much lower interest rate than he or she would receive from a bank in a market-value loan.

Interest-free loans are based on the same principle, except no interest is charged. There is no payment of interest by the child and no income to the parent.

For many years the IRS felt that if a parent made a below-market or interest-free loan to a child, a gift had been made. The amount of the gift, according to the IRS, was the difference between the prevailing market rate of interest and the interest, if any, charged by the parent. In our example, the IRS considered the gift to be 6 percent of the amount loaned if a below-market loan was made, or 12 percent if an interest-free loan was made.

Whether or not a gift was made was generally inconsequential to most Americans. Because every American can give away $13,000 each year in 2012 to as many people as the giver desires, and a husband and wife can team up to give away $26,000, most loans were not big enough to generate a gift tax. For a $100,000 loan, when the going interest rate was 12 percent, the gift on a below-market loan at 6 percent would be $6,000 per year, the difference between $12,000 if full market interest rates were charged and the $6,000 actually charged. On an interest-free loan, the difference would be $12,000 per year.

A $6,000 gift is below the $13,000 annual exclusion, making it gift-tax-free. A $26,000 gift could be made gift-tax-free by having both parents make the gift. Thus, the gift tax, even if the IRS contention was correct, would only come into play on very large interest-free or below-market loans.

For those Americans who made large interest-free or below-market loans, demand loans were used to avoid the gift tax. A *demand loan* can be called or demanded by the lender at any time. This type of loan does not have a fixed due date. Because interest-free or below-market demand loans had no actual due date, the theory was that the amount of a gift could not be computed.

When the IRS contested this theory in the courts, it invariably lost. The courts agreed that the amount of the gift could not be computed, and in addition held that a gift had not really been made. The courts did hold, however, that if a below-market or interest-free loan was made and a demand note was not utilized, a gift did occur. For example, a note for five years at no interest had a gift element. The market interest rate on the note for a five-year term, which was easily computed, was the amount of the gift. The only difference between this transaction and a demand note was that the demand note was not fixed as to time of payment.

The Supreme Court, in an historic 1984 decision, held that interest-free or below-interest loans, whether on a demand basis or for a fixed term, were subject to the gift tax. Worse, the Supreme Court overturned court cases that untold numbers of tax advisors and their clients had relied upon for many years. This decision allowed the IRS to assess gift taxes for loans made prior to the Supreme Court's decision, even though a vast majority of lower courts had come to an opposite conclusion for years.

Congress got into the act too. In the Tax Reform Act of 1984 all interest-free and below-market interest loans were addressed. Massive changes were made in the tax code that severely curtailed interest-free and below-market loans as viable planning devices.

Any interest-free or below-market loan is considered as a whole economic package, encompassing not only gift tax but also income tax.

The amount of interest that is not charged—that is, the difference between the amount charged and the market rate of interest—is considered a gift from the lender to the borrower. The gift is computed on an annual basis, or for the term of the note if less than a year. For term loans of a year or longer in duration, the interest is compounded semiannually. The Treasury Department determines the market rate of interest, and the amounts are announced monthly.

Interest deductions for personal interest are no longer allowed. *Personal interest* is interest that is not related to a trade or business; is not investment interest; is not interest considered in computing income or loss from a passive activity; is not interest on a loan used to acquire a qualified primary or secondary residence; or is not interest on certain estate tax payments. Now, interest-free or below-market loans are even more unattractive, given that it will be more difficult to take a deduction for the interest paid.

The difference between the interest rate charged and the government-imposed rate is considered income to the lender even though it may not be income-tax deductible to the borrower. The effect is to recharacterize the family loan as a business transaction. The assumption is that the lender really did charge interest, the borrower really did pay interest, and a gift was made.

For example, if the prevailing federal rate is 10 percent and an interest-free loan of $100,000 is made from a grandparent to a grandchild for a term of six months, the transaction will be viewed as a gift loan. The grandparent will have income of $5,000, representing the income that the grandparent would have earned on the money in six months at the federal rate. The grandchild may have a tax deduction of $5,000, if the loan is secured by the grandchild's home or second home, or is otherwise not personal interest, and the grandchild can itemize deductions. There also is a gift of $5,000 from the grandparent to the grandchild.

There are two additional rules that may aid taxpayers who are considering a below-market or interest-free loan to a family member. The first is that for all loans of less than $100,000, the amount considered as income to the lender and a deduction by the borrower cannot exceed the investment income of the borrower. If the borrower does not invest the loan proceeds in an income-producing investment or does not have other investment income, generally the income tax provisions will not apply. This leaves the opportunity for below-market interest or interest-free loans for college, buying a house, or other non-income-producing uses. The loan cannot be one that is aimed at tax avoidance, however, and it must be secured by the borrower's primary or secondary residence for the interest to be deductible.

The second rule deals with loans of less than $10,000 per year. As long as the proceeds from these interest-free or below-market loans are not used to buy or carry income-producing property, the loans do not fall under the otherwise complex rules.

Below-market and interest-free family loans are not viable planning tools in most situations. The complex gift tax and income tax rules may make them economically unattractive and difficult to use.

Loans to family members can be good planning when they are structured properly as legitimate loans with adequate interest. However, you need to be careful and work closely with your advisors to make sure intra-family loans are structured properly. The IRS often looks closely at these transactions to be sure they are not gifts disguised as loans.

A key factor the courts and IRS take into account to determine if a "loan" between family members is a legitimate loan or a gift is evidence that the transfer of funds was made with a real expectation of repayment and with the intention to enforce the debt. Facts and circumstances considered to reach this conclusion include:

- Existence of a promissory note or other evidence of the indebtedness.

- Was interest charged?

- Was there any security provided?

- Was there a fixed maturity date?

- Was a demand for repayment made?

- Were any actual payments made?

- Did the borrower have the financial ability to repay?

- Did the lender and the borrower consistently reflect the transaction as a loan?

It's not always necessary to satisfy all of these factors to establish a legitimate loan, but the more factors you can satisfy, the more likely you will be able to avoid the IRS recharacterizing the intended loan as a gift.

Once you've structured the transaction properly as a legitimate loan, it's also necessary to charge at least the minimum required rate of interest to avoid adverse gift tax consequences. Each month the IRS publishes minimum interest rates for short-term loans, three years or less; mid-term loans, more than three years to nine years; and long-term loans, over nine years. The IRS minimum required interest rates also vary based on whether payments on the loans are called for monthly, quarterly, semi-annually, or annually. Finally there are different minimum IRS rates for demand loans. These rates are almost always lower that rates that are being charged by banks and other lending institutions. Used wisely, even loans based on the minimum IRS rates allows family members to use funds at a lower than normal rate, making paying off the loans much easier. This technique is especially effective if the family member who receives the loan can invest the funds in such a way as to receive a rate of return that is greater than the interest rate charged.

Another effective use of these loans are for education. The IRS rates are generally far less than those charged by banks. If parents of students who want to borrow education funds have the cash to lend to a student, it makes much more economic sense for the student to borrow from his or her parents.

While not as wide open as it once was, properly structured loans to family members are still a valuable planning tool for transferring wealth and opportunities to family members. For this strategy to be effective it's very important for you to involve your professional advisors to help you satisfy the many requirements necessary to achieve the desired results. The discussion on below-market rate or interest-free loans to family members can be summarized as follows:

- They create income to the lender.

- They may allow a deduction to the borrower if secured by a residence or not otherwise considered personal interest.

- They are gifts to the extent that they are not legitimate loans and that market interest is not charged.

- They are only free from complex rules if less than $10,000.

When loans to family members are structured as legitimate loans with interest at or above the IRS required minimum rate, they are often an effective planning tool.

36

Sales to Family Members

Caveat Emptor

It is possible to freeze the value of certain assets in an estate by selling them to family members on an installment basis. Just like a loan, an installment sale appears to be easy on its face. Also like a loan, this technique, in order to work, has to be implemented properly.

As a result of inflation, most assets are continually going up in value. As we have discussed, inflation forces taxpayers and their estates into higher tax brackets.

Giving an appreciating asset away may not be feasible because either the annual exclusion is not sufficient to prevent federal gift tax or the applicable exclusion amount is not available. Also, many of us are reluctant to give away assets because we want to make sure we have our assets to provide for our security and comfort as we grow older. Under these circumstances, an installment sale to a family member can be an attractive planning alternative.

A sale to a family member is the same as any other sale. A decision is made by the seller as to what asset or assets will be sold, for what price, and under what terms. The sale is then consummated.

A sale to a family member removes an appreciating asset from the estate of the seller. The asset is replaced by a *promissory note*. A promissory note has a calculated time value. Whatever this calculated value is determined to be at the death of the note owner is the amount included in the estate for federal estate tax purposes. Thus, the value of the promissory note is often less than the value of the asset it replaced in the estate.

By selling an asset on the installment basis, you may convert a non-income-producing asset to an asset that can provide you with income. Many older taxpayers who are asset-rich but cash-poor can use this technique to generate needed income and remove the appreciating value of an asset from their estates.

An installment sale to a family member should be entered into only after careful thought, because of the tax and economic results that can occur.

The profit from an installment sale is subject to income tax. However, the favorable maximum capital gains rate may make a sale income-tax attractive.

The type of property chosen for sale is an important consideration for sales between family members. Depreciable property sold between family members does not qualify for installment sales treatment. The same is true for installment sales of publicly traded securities.

On installment sales the interest payments received by the selling family member are taxable income. On most installment sales the interest paid by the buying family member is not deductible. Interest deductions for loans secured by a primary or secondary residence are deductible subject to certain limitations, but structuring an installment sale to meet this requirement is difficult. The creation of taxable interest income to the seller without the deductibility of the interest paid by the buyer is clearly a tax and economic factor to consider before entering into an installment sale.

IDGT Sales

Another sales technique eliminates the adverse income tax results of typical sales to family members can be used to increase the effectiveness of sales between family members. This technique is called a *sale to an intentionally defective grantor trust*. Professionals refer to this technique as an IDGT sale. For convenience, we will too.

An IDGT is an irrevocable trust drafted in such a way that it is a grantor trust for income tax purposes. This is a special type of grantor trust over which the maker has sufficient control to be considered the owner for income tax purposes but not for estate tax purposes, which is a critical distinction.

In a grantor trust, any income or expenses of the trust are attributed to the maker; he or she must put them on his or her income tax return. However, if the maker has more control than simply as the income owner, the whole trust could be included in the maker's estate. Special language must be added to a grantor trust to achieve the income and estate tax balance. When this language is intentionally included in an irrevocable trust, the trust is an IDGT.

Here is how a typical IDGT sale works:

Alex and Jane, a married couple, own a successful business. It is held in a limited liability company and was just appraised for $1,750,000. They want to sell it to their two children, who work in the business. As a first step Alex and Jane create an IDGT and make a gift of $175,000 to it. Their two children are the trustees and beneficiaries of the IDGT.

The IDGT offers to buy the business from Alex and Jane for $1,750,000. The terms of the sale are 10 percent down, with equal annual payments of principal and interest for nine years. This sale of the company to the IDGT is a formal business transaction and is fully documented as such. There is a purchase and sale agreement, security agreement, and promissory note.

Now, here is the effectiveness of the IDGT. When the sale is made, Alex and Jane are treated for income tax purposes as both the sellers and the buyers. That is, they are the tax owners of the IDGT even though they're not beneficiaries of the IDGT. It has long been established under our tax laws that if you buy something from yourself, you do not owe any income tax. So, when Alex and Jane sell the business, the interest and principal payments come to them tax-free. Over time, they divest themselves of their business, get an income (the interest payments), and get their principal back. The children, as the beneficiaries of the IDGT, in essence own the company, can run it, and will get all of the future appreciation.

To make a sale to an IDGT work, it must have economic substance, at least according to the Internal Revenue Service. That is why at least 10 percent of the value of the asset to be purchased should be put in the trust as a gift to the beneficiaries. Sometimes the beneficiaries also personally guarantee all or a portion of the note payments, adding further economic substance to the transaction.

In addition, the sale must be for fair market value, so an appraisal of the asset being sold is necessary. The interest rate must be at least the minimum rate published by the Treasury Department for the month the sale takes place for the type and term of the promissory note used as consideration for the sale. Finally, the IDGT must be able to generate enough income to pay Alex and Jane the required annual payments for the nine-year term of the note.

An IDGT can be effective in freezing an estate. These trusts are not always appropriate, but given the right circumstances, they can help in effective planning, especially if the business or other assets sold to the IDGT are appreciating at a rate significantly greater than the current interest rate required on the promissory note.

Make sure your advisors run the numbers if you are thinking about using this technique. Expect some Internal Revenue Service scrutiny. This is another technique that works when structured and implemented properly, but upsets the IRS because it has the ability to transfer property very effectively at a reduced tax cost. So once again we strongly advise you to work closely with a team of professional advisors to properly structure and implement all aspects of a sale to an IDGT.

Can the Family Member Make the Payment?

When you sell an asset to a family member, you must be sure the family member has the economic ability to make the payments to you. This important consideration is often overlooked. If, after a sale is made, your loved one is financially unable to meet the payments, what are you going to do? Are you going to foreclose on the note? Probably not. You will probably be inclined to forgive the note. If you do, you will not have the income you need or the asset you sold. Worse yet, you will have made a gift and may have to pay federal gift tax to boot.

If an asset is sold to a family member at a price below its fair market value, the difference between the fair market value of the asset and the actual price paid for it is a gift. Fair market value, remember, is the amount a willing buyer would pay to a willing seller when neither is subject to any compulsion to buy or sell and both are aware of the facts relevant to the sale.

The best way to determine an asset's fair value is to get a professional appraisal. If this is not accomplished, be ready to defend the purchase price used. If there is an IRS audit of the sale, and a professional did not value the asset using a qualified appraisal standard, the price will be subject to even greater scrutiny by the IRS. Under our tax law, the burden of proof as to the asset's value is always on the taxpayer. This means the IRS can disagree with your sales price and make you prove it was the fair market price.

The interest rate you use in your installment note can have tax consequences. If a note has an interest rate lower than the required minimum interest rates, the difference between the value of the property and the time value of the note can be construed as a gift for federal gift tax purposes. In addition, the rules for below-interest loans discussed in Chapter 35, "Loans to Family Members," may apply to the transaction.

The Treasury Department issues minimum interest rates for promissory notes used as consideration for sales between family members. The rates, adjusted every month, vary based on the time period involved; they are issued for short-term periods, mid-term periods, and long-term periods. *Long-term periods* are longer than nine years; *mid-term periods* are from over three to nine years; and *short-term periods* are three years or less. The rates also vary based upon how the note is structured, if it is a term note or a demand note; and on the frequency of scheduled payments—monthly, quarterly, semiannually, or annually.

You can combine a gift and a sale if you choose. If you sell an asset to a family member, you may forgive a future installment payment as it becomes due. For example, if you sell property to your two children for $100,000 at 7 percent interest over 10 years with equal payments of principal plus interest due, the first payment at the end of year one would be $17,000. Of that amount, $10,000 is principal ($100,000 divided by 10 years) and $7,000 is interest ($100,000 multiplied by 7 percent). The annual payment at the end of year two would be $16,300. Of that amount, $10,000 is principal ($90,000 divided by nine years) and $6,300 is interest ($90,000 multiplied by 7 percent).

Assume your children make the required payment at the end of year one but do not make the $16,300 payment at the end of year two. Because you have two children, you have two $13,000 annual exclusions available, a total of $26,000. Thus, the whole $16,300 payment (or any part of it) can be waived. Because the amount waived is less than the combined annual exclusions, there is no taxable gift.

Before you waive an installment payment, be aware of the income tax ramifications. The $6,300 is still income to you, and any income tax you would have paid had the installment actually been paid to you will still be due.

Waiving a note payment may also have adverse gift tax consequences. The IRS and the courts have held that if there was no intent that the note be paid from the beginning because the sale in fact was a plan to make an annual gift of the installment payment, the sale can be defeated and the entire sales price treated as one big gift.

Family members who buy property receive a step-up in basis for income tax purposes. For example:

> Sandy and Rich buy a piece of property from their parents for $100,000. Their parents paid $10,000 for the property. If Sandy and Rich sell it for $110,000, only $10,000 ($110,000 less $100,000) is subject to federal income tax.

Variations of the family installment sale technique have been used so creatively that, in the eyes of Congress, it has been abused. The most common abuse involved a two-sale method.

> In this method, Dad and Mom own a second home worth $100,000. They bought it for $20,000 and now wish to sell it. If they sell it for cash, $80,000 (the difference between the selling price of $100,000 and their cost of $20,000) will be income taxable to them. As a result, if the potential buyer wants to pay cash, Dad and Mom will realize all the gain in the year of the sale. So they sell the house to the kids for $100,000 for 10 years at a fair interest rate, and the kids immediately sell it to the real buyer for cash. The result of the transaction appears to be beneficial for everyone. The kids bought the house for $100,000 and sold it for $100,000. They have no taxable gain. Mom and Dad pay taxes over 10 years as opposed to one year. The kids put the money in the bank and draw interest. They use this same interest and some of the principal each year to pay Mom and Dad. What a great method to save taxes.

Many years ago Congress closed this tax-avoidance door. Now, if the kids were to sell the house within two years of buying it, Mom and Dad cannot pay their taxes over 10 years; they will pay their total tax in the year the kids sell the house. The solution, of course, is for the kids to wait more than two years and then sell the house.

Another loophole that Congress closed was forgiving an installment note on the death of the note owner. At one time a parent could, at death, leave an installment note owed by a child to that child. The result was that the installment note was forgiven with no income tax consequence.

This technique is no longer effective. Income tax will be due if this technique is used. In our experience, many estate plans use this outdated device. If your planning includes this device, you should amend your plan.

Installment Plans

Installment sales are complicated. By way of review, look at the following lists.

Installment sales help sellers because:

- They can get appreciating assets out of sellers' estates.
- Non-income-producing assets can be favorably converted into income-producing assets.

Installment sales help buyers because:

- Buyers get appreciating assets at a fair price on favorable terms.
- Buyers receive a step-up in basis when they buy the asset.

Family installment sales may accomplish some of your estate planning objectives. They have been abused in the past and may not be as attractive as they once were, but they still represent a viable planning tool. Let your professional estate planning advisors guide you in their use.

37

Private Annuities and Self-Canceling Installment Notes

The Ultimate Gamble

The *private annuity* has long been a favored estate planning technique. In recent years self-canceling installment notes, or SCINs, have become an alternative to private annuity. Private annuities and SCINs are discussed by many but, in our experience, understood by few.

A private annuity has three elements. An individual called an *annuitant* (seller) transfers property to a family member called an *obligor* (buyer). The buyer promises to pay the seller certain payments. And finally, these payments are paid to the seller for the duration of the seller's life. Sounds like a sale? It is, but this sale has several unique twists that we will examine.

An installment sale, as we discussed earlier, can eliminate an appreciating asset from your estate; however, the asset removed is replaced by a promissory note. Because of the asset replacement, the installment sale converts an appreciating asset to a nonappreciating asset. The value of the nonappreciating installment note, however, still remains in your estate. The installment note creates income to the seller and may create interest deductions for the buyer. The installments are paid for a definite period of time, no matter what happens to either the buyer or the seller.

A private annuity is designed so the value of your appreciating asset and the value of the promissory obligation are both totally eliminated from your estate.

An *annuity* is a promise by the buyer to pay the seller fixed payments for the life of the seller. When the seller dies, the buyer owns the asset and does not have to make any more payments. If the buyer dies before the seller, the buyer's heirs must continue the payments.

Annuities are governed by the Internal Revenue Code. Its regulations provide a method to value a private annuity and spell out what the payments for the annuity must be. This method must always be used.

The value of the annuity, and the payments resulting from its value, are based on two factors. The first factor is how long the seller is expected to live. The number of years that any seller is expected to live is included in the Internal Revenue Code regulations in the form of actuarial (life expectancy) tables. The second factor is the interest rate that must be charged. It is equal to 120 percent of the federal mid-term rate in effect for the month in which the annuity is valued. Your estate planning advisor can help you find this rate.

If you place a value on the property you sell through an annuity, and that value is less than the fair market value, you also make a gift subject to the federal gift tax. Does this sound familiar?

Using a private annuity is a little bit like gambling. If the seller dies before he or she is statistically supposed to, the buyer wins, because the payments end. In addition, the seller's estate wins, because the annuity is not includable in the estate. On the other hand, if the seller lives longer than predicted, the buyer continues to make the payments for as long as the seller lives. Remember, an annuity is an agreement by the buyer to pay fixed payments to the seller for the seller's life, no matter how long or short that is.

There is no requirement that the seller be in good health. If the seller has a terminal illness, however, a private annuity cannot be used since the IRS only allows use of its life expectancy tables when the seller has a greater than 50 percent likelihood of living more than one year from the date of the sale. An individual who is in poor health but does not have a terminal illness is an excellent candidate for a private annuity.

Care must be taken when an older person contemplates using a private annuity. As age increases, life expectancy decreases. That means that the calculated number of annuity payments decreases and the value of the payments increase. If there are fewer calculated payments to pay for an asset, it necessarily follows that each payment will be higher. These payments may be so high that the buyer cannot afford to make them, particularly if the seller fools everyone and turns into Methuselah.

There may be disadvantageous income tax consequences with a private annuity. The federal income tax treatment of the payments made to a seller is similar to that afforded installment sales. A portion of each payment is a return of the seller's original adjusted cost basis, which is tax-free. Another portion of each payment is the *capital gain* element, which is the difference between the fair market value of the asset transferred under the annuity and the asset's original cost to the seller, as adjusted for depreciation and other factors. The remainder of each payment is the interest factor.

Self-Canceling Installment Notes

A SCIN can be viewed as a combination of an installment sale, discussed in Chapter 36, "Sales to Family Members," and a private annuity. Many of the same rules that apply to installment sales also apply to SCINs. However, unlike installment sales and private annuities, not all of the rules for SCINs are certain.

A SCIN looks very similar to the typical promissory note used in an installment sale except there is language in the SCIN that provides upon the death of the seller all remaining payments otherwise due under the SCIN are canceled. SCINs, like installment sales, can be an estate freezing strategy to the extent of the appreciation that occurs after the assets are sold.

When the seller in an installment sale transaction dies before the promissory note is fully paid, the date of death value of the promissory note is included in the seller's estate for estate tax purposes. When a properly structured SCIN is used instead of a standard promissory note, when the seller dies, any remaining payments under the SCIN are canceled and nothing is included in the seller's estate.

In order to achieve this result and not create a part gift on the date of the sale, it is essential that the installment sale be structured as an arm's-length business transaction. The primary factor in creating an arm's-length transaction is that the consideration received by the seller must equal the fair market value of the assets sold. When using a SCIN, the buyer must pay a risk premium for the cancelation feature in the SCIN so that the overall value of the SCIN is equal to the fair market value of the assets purchased. The risk premium is built into the terms of the SCIN and may be reflected as an interest premium or a principal premium. If it is structured as an interest premium, the interest rate used must be greater than market rate. If the SCIN is structured with a principal premium, it must be reflected by a higher purchase price.

Calculation of the appropriate risk premium can be rather complicated, and you will want to work with professional advisors with expertise in this area to ensure that both the SCIN and the installment sale transaction are structured properly. Also, the IRS has taken the position that the term of years of the SCIN must be less than the seller's life expectancy or the IRS will treat the SCIN as a private annuity. This too must be taken into consideration when structuring the payment terms of a SCIN.

A major disadvantage of using a SCIN rather than a standard promissory note in an installment sale transaction is that the total purchase price paid by the buyer will be much higher if the seller lives to life expectancy or beyond. The ideal candidate for using a SCIN is a seller who has a rather long life expectancy under the actuarial tables but is not likely to live to life expectancy.

A benefit to using a SCIN over a private annuity is that the buyer is allowed to depreciate the assets purchased based upon the purchase price, and is often able to deduct the portion of the payments that are treated as interest expense.

A private annuity and a SCIN are both estate planning techniques that allow a seller to remove an asset completely from the seller's estate, still maintain an income stream from that asset, and assure the buyer that all payments cease on the seller's death.

SCINs, unlike private annuities, do have a fixed term for payments. When the seller of a SCIN is still living at the time SCIN payment obligations end, the buyer will have paid more for the assets than if he or she had used a standard promissory note. However, with a SCIN, the buyer's obligations have a foreseeable ending. Private annuity payments must be made until the seller's death, no matter how long that may be.

Annuities and SCINs, properly drafted and implemented, still represent the ultimate gamble: will the seller live longer—or shorter—than he or she is supposed to?

38

Personal Residence Trusts

Give the House, but Not Your Home

Congress allows a tax-efficient way to give your residence or vacation home to your children. A personal residence trust allows you to reduce the value of your residence or vacation home for gift tax purposes, remove the value of the home from your estate, and enjoy the use of the home for as long as you want. Sound too good to be true? It is all true, but there are a number of rules to be followed and pitfalls to be avoided.

Personal residence trusts are short-term irrevocable trusts in which the trust maker, called the grantor, has the right to retain the use of the residence for a period of years. At the end of that period the home becomes the property of the beneficiaries of the trust. Even then the grantor can continue to use the home, but at that point must pay rent in order to continue to live there. To better understand how a personal residence trust works, an example is in order:

> Let's say that Edwina Edwards, age 58, owns a home that is worth $750,000. It is in a great neighborhood and will continue to increase in value. In fact, it appears that it will appreciate at the rate of about 7 percent per year. Edwina would like to get the value of the house and its future appreciation out of her estate so it will not be taxed, but she wants to live in the house for as long as she wants, at least 10 years. She believes the home will be worth about $1,475,000 at that point.
>
> Edwina can set up a personal residence trust that will allow ownership of the house to pass to her children at the end of 10 years. Let's further assume that the prevailing interest rates are 6 percent (we need to make this assumption in order to compute the value of the gift; more on this later). The amount of the gift to Edwina's children is about $352,000, all

of which can be sheltered by her applicable exemption amount. If she dies after 10 years, the full value of the home will be out of her estate. That means the $1,475,000 will not be subject to federal estate tax.

Types of Personal Residence Trusts

There are two types of personal residence trusts: a *qualified personal residence trust* (QPRT), and a *personal residence trust* (PRT). The difference between the two is that a PRT cannot hold any assets other than a residence, and the residence cannot be sold during the term of the trust. A QPRT is allowed to hold some cash, and the trustee can sell the residence during the trust's term, but the terms of the trust must prohibit a sale of the residence back to the maker or the maker's spouse. Most practitioners prefer to use a QPRT because it is more flexible. For those clients who want to ensure that their residence is not sold, a PRT may be the better choice.

Definition of a Personal Residence

In order to be eligible for a personal residence trust, the home that is transferred must be the maker's primary residence or a vacation home. A person may transfer up to two homes in personal residence trusts, a primary residence and a vacation home. A maker does not have to own the whole residence to use a personal residence trust. For example, if a husband and wife own a residence as joint tenants with right of survivorship, each of them may transfer their respective interest in the residence to one trust, or they may create separate trusts for their interests in the property. From a tax planning perspective, a married couple can further reduce the value of the gift by creating two trusts. This is called *fractionalizing* the ownership of their home. Each spouse transfers his or her fractionalized interest into their respective personal residence trusts.

There is flexibility in the definition of a personal residence. For example, a home rented out for part of the year can qualify as a personal residence trust, but it cannot be a bed and breakfast or a hotel. A personal residence can consist of outbuildings as long as they are part of the residence; there have even been instances in which rental units that are part of a residence have qualified for personal residence trust status. However, a personal residence does not usually consist of a home and a great deal of acreage. Farms or ranches cannot be put into personal residence trusts, but the farm or ranch house, and a reasonable amount of acreage around it, can be.

Income Tax Rules

A personal residence trust, whether a PRT or a QPRT, is a grantor trust, which is treated as if owned by the maker of the trust for income tax purposes. This means that all tax benefits and deductions attributable to a home during the term of the personal residence trust are passed through to the maker. For example, if a QPRT sells the residence, any gain is sheltered, up to $250,000 ($500,000 for married couples). For all income tax purposes, the trust is ignored as a separate taxable entity, and the maker (grantor) is considered the direct owner.

Gift Tax Rules

The amount of the gift a personal residence trust generates depends on several factors. These include the age of the maker, the value of the residence, the term of the trust, and prevailing required interest rates. All these are taken into account in special tables that are part of the Internal Revenue Code and regulations.

The older the maker, the lower the value of the gift. The reason for this is the greater probability that the maker will die during the term of the trust. The death of the maker causes the value of the residence to be included in his or her estate. The probability that the residence will revert to the estate is important in valuation.

Of course, the value of the residence makes a big difference in the value of the gift. The higher the initial value of the residence, the higher the gift. This value can be reduced, however. A long-term trust can reduce the value of the gift. Also, if a husband and wife each create their own personal residence trusts and transfer their undivided one-half interests in the residence to their respective trusts, then the value of each ownership interest can be discounted. Generally, when a person who owns property with another transfers his or her interest, that interest is not valued at one-half of the total value of the property; it's worth less than one-half of the total. The value is discounted to reflect the fact that a third party would pay less for a one-half interest because the third party would not have full control of the property.

Let's assume Don and Cathy own a vacation home in joint tenancy. The home has been appraised at $250,000. Don and Cathy create separate personal residence trusts and transfer their ownership interests into their respective trusts. The appraiser, when valuing the separate interests (the trusts would own the residence as tenants in common), would likely discount the value by around 20 percent, although that figure could be higher or lower. In our example, the value of the partial interest of the residence is being reduced by 20 percent. The value of the partial interest, prior to final valuation of the total gift, is $100,000 rather than $125,000. Obviously, this is an excellent tax result.

The longer the term of the trust, the lower the gift. You want to retain ownership for a long period of time. Of course, if you die during the term, the value of the trust property will be included in your estate, which undoes the benefits of a personal residence trust. A term of 20 years creates a much smaller gift than a term of five years.

It is easy to be confused by what the "term" of the trust really is. A personal residence trust can last past the term of the retained interest. For example, you may have your attorney draft a personal residence trust that in layman's terms states:

> I will retain the right to live in my home for 10 years without paying rent and with all of the benefits of owning a home, including the tax benefits. At the end of 10 years I will relinquish my right to live in the home without paying rent, and I will no longer have the benefits of owning a home. However, I want my home to remain in trust for the remainder of my life, and I wish to have the right to rent my home from the trust at its fair rental value, as determined by appraisal.
>
> Upon my death, the home shall be transferred to my living children in equal shares as tenants in common.

The term of the trust, for purposes of determining the value of the gift to the personal residence, is 10 years. The trust may last for a longer period of time, but this is not relevant to the valuation of the gift.

The final factor taken into account when valuing the gift to a personal residence trust is interest. The Internal Revenue Code requires that an assumed rate of growth be factored into the valuation of a gift to a personal interest trust. The interest rate is 120 percent of the federal mid-term rate in effect at the time of the transfer to the personal residence trust. The Treasury Department publishes this rate on a monthly basis. The higher the rate, the lower the gift. A personal residence trust is more tax-efficient when interest rates are high, the maker is young, and the term of the trust is long.

Estate Tax Rules

After the term of a personal residence trust expires, the value of the residence is not included in the maker's estate. But if the maker dies while the trust term is in effect, the date of death value of the residence is included in the maker's estate. For this reason, personal residence trusts are not used for people who are not likely to live beyond the stated term of the trust.

One of the fundamental considerations in creating a personal residence trust is that its term should not exceed the life expectancy of its maker.

While a person who is 50 years old could consider a personal residence trust that lasts 20 years, an 80-year-old will require a substantially shorter term. Moreover, if a person is ill or there is a family history of early death, a long-term personal residence trust may not be a good choice.

It is important that a personal residence trust be drafted to take into account the early death of the maker. If a maker dies and the trust instrument does not allow the residence to flow back into the maker's estate, federal estate tax may be generated, but the asset is in a separate trust. Bifurcating the two may make it difficult to pay the taxes.

Also, if spouses create separate personal residence trusts and one of them dies, it usually makes sense to have the value of the residence trust qualify for the unlimited marital deduction. To do so, special language must appear in the trust.

Personal Residence Trusts and Generation-Skipping

Personal residence trusts are not used to skip generations. Under the generation-skipping provisions of the Internal Revenue Code, any trust that can be pulled back into the maker's estate precludes an effective allocation of the $5 million generation-skipping exemption amount in effect for 2011 and 2012 at the time the gift is made. The time when the generation-skipping tax exposure is known is when the term of the trust expires.

For example, if the value of the residence were $750,000 at the time the trust was made, one would expect that if the grandchildren were the beneficiaries, $750,000 of the maker's generation-skipping exemption could be applied and have the trust totally exempt from future generation-skipping tax. Not so. Let's say the value of the residence is $2 million when the trust term ends. At that point the residence passes to grandchildren and the maker needs to allocate $2 million of generation-skipping exemption. If the maker does not have enough remaining generation-skipping tax exemption because of prior usage, or changes in the law reducing the amount of the maker's exemption, the difference between the available exemption and the value of the residence is subject to generation-skipping tax. That tax will be in addition to any federal gift tax paid when the trust was established.

In most cases the risk and cost of the generation-skipping transfer tax are too high for a personal residence trust to be used for generation-skipping transfers. That is why personal residence trusts are generally used to make transfers to children, but not to other generations.

Subsequent Sale of a
Residence

In a QPRT, the trustee has the ability to sell the residence. The Internal Revenue Code and regulations set complex rules governing those sales, including rules prohibiting the sale to the maker or the maker's spouse. The rules also apply if the home is destroyed or is taken in a condemnation proceeding.

Generally, the trustee has two years to use the sales proceeds or insurance proceeds to acquire a new residence or to repair a damaged one. If at the end of the two-year period neither of these events have taken place, or all of the proceeds have not been used, then the trust has to state what is to happen. There are basically two alternatives.

The first is that the extra money is returned to the maker. This is not a particularly good result, because the maker ends up with the very assets he or she gave away, back in the maker's estate. In addition, the maker will have used valuable gift tax applicable exclusion, which is irretrievably gone, wasted on a transaction that should have never been entered into.

The second alternative is for the QPRT to require using the proceeds to create a grantor retained annuity trust (GRAT). Under the GRAT rules, the maker receives an annuity for the remaining term of the QPRT. Generally, a GRAT conversion is not as gift-tax-efficient as a QPRT; the maker receives income back, which will be part of his or her estate.

It is not a good idea to create a QPRT with the thought that the residence will be sold. If it is sold, then a new residence of equal value should be purchased. If this is not done, then the alternatives are not attractive from an estate planning perspective.

Personal residence trusts can be very useful in transferring a valuable home to children. They are sophisticated and subject to a number of very exacting rules and regulations. Before embarking on personal residence trust planning, it is extremely important to understand all the ramifications of creating a trust, and to set up a trust that is state-of-the-art and backed by professional advisors.

39

Retirement Planning

Long Life Deserves Good Planning

Since the 1970s there has been an explosion in retirement planning. Congress has passed numerous laws allowing all kinds of innovative retirement plans. Business in general has added and expanded retirement planning opportunities for employees. And, of course, there is a great deal of interest in retirement planning as America ages and the baby boomer generation begins to enter its silver years.

Retirement plans have an enormous impact on estate planning. How they are planned for and structured during one's lifetime and at one's death can have significant income and estate tax consequences. To understand these consequences it is important to have a general understanding of the common types of retirement plans.

Types of Retirement Plans

There are a number of ways to classify retirement plans: employer-sponsored plans and individual plans; qualified plans and nonqualified plans; deferred compensation plans, stock bonus plans, stock option plans, death-benefit-only plans, and hybrid plans.

We have found that the easiest way to understand the many types of plans is to begin with those that are qualified under the Internal Revenue Code. Generally speaking, *qualified plans* are those plans that are sanctioned by the Internal Revenue Code and that provide income tax incentives to employers and employees. These plans are instituted by employers for the benefit of employees.

The most common qualified plans are profit sharing plans—including 401(k) plans—money purchase pension plans, and defined benefit plans. Each of these allows the employer to take an income tax deduction for the amounts paid into the plan in the year the payment is made. However, employees don't have taxable income in the year of the employer contribution. An employee generally does not take the contributions into income until they are distributed out of the plan to the employee.

Within the categories of qualified plans, there are specific types of plans. For example, *employee stock ownership plans* (ESOPs) are allowed to hold the stock of the sponsoring company. There are separate and distinct rules for these types of plans, even though they are qualified plans. Other examples include *savings incentive match plans for employees* (SIMPLE) and *simplified employee pension* (SEP) plans.

Qualified plans are required to cover most of the employees in a business. There are very complicated rules about who must be allowed to participate in these plans. These rules also make sure that employees are vested in the plans over a relatively short period of time. The rules may require that the plan be subject to strict funding rules and insured by an agency of the federal government.

Individual retirement accounts (IRAs) are not qualified plans. They are individual plans, and as such are not generally used by employers as part of compensation plans. In fact, IRAs are covered under separate provisions of the Internal Revenue Code, and are not part of ERISA, the law that governs qualified plans.

Some companies sponsor IRA plans, but IRAs are not designed as compensation plans for business; they are employee savings plans. Contributions to these plans are made directly by the participant, not by the employer. There are rules as to who can contribute to these plans and how much of the contribution is tax deductible. The tax deductible amount that can be contributed to an IRA is far less than the maximum contributions allowed in qualified plans.

Some retirement plans are not qualified. For the most part, a *nonqualified plan* is one for which a company cannot take an immediate income tax deduction. On the employee's side, a nonqualified plan is usually one in which the company promises to make certain payments in the future.

A typical nonqualified plan is a *deferred compensation plan*. Under one of these plans, the company promises to pay compensation to the employee at some time in the future, usually at retirement. There is no assurance that the money will be paid, other than the company's promise. The payments are not deductible to the company until paid. Likewise, the employee does not take the payments as income until they are received.

Nonqualified plans do not have to cover all employees in a company and are almost always reserved for a few employees. Sometimes they are funded by life insurance or by a pool of money set aside for the future payments. The funds that are set aside, including life insurance contracts, must be subject to the claims of the company's creditors. That is why when the funds are set aside for employees, they do not have to be included as income. If a company offered a nonqualified plan that actually set aside money in a way that the company's creditors could not access it, then the employees would have to take the amounts into income immediately.

Because nonqualified plans are mere promises to pay rather than separately funded plans, employees are concerned about the money being available when they retire. Methods have been invented to separate the funds while not making them so separate as to avoid the creditors of the company.

A *Rabbi trust* is such an attempt. A company that sets up a separate irrevocable trust to fund a nonqualified deferred compensation plan is said to have set up a Rabbi trust. Although the trust does hold separate funds for payment of the nonqualified benefits on behalf of the company, those funds must remain subject to the claims of the company's creditors. The trust is merely a holding vehicle so the company itself cannot spend the funds.

The Rabbi trust got its name because this concept of using a trust to set aside funds was first used by a synagogue for the benefit of its rabbi. The Internal Revenue Service attacked the device as being a funded plan, making the rabbi liable for income taxes on the amounts set aside. The courts held that the trust was subject to the claims of the synagogue's creditors and therefore the rabbi did not have to take the amounts in the trust into income.

Another method used to segregate funds is life insurance. Typically, the company purchases a cash value life insurance policy on the life of the employee. The company is the owner and beneficiary of the policy. When the employee retires, the company borrows funds from the policy to pay the deferred compensation owed to the employee.

If the employee dies during the period when he or she is being paid, then the death proceeds are used to pay off the remainder of the payments. If the employee dies before retirement, all or part of the death proceeds are paid to the family, trust, or estate of the employee. In all cases, when the funds are paid as part of compensation, they are deductible to the company and income to the recipient.

A variation of a nonqualified deferred compensation plan is a *death-benefit-only plan*. With a DBO, the company promises to pay a death benefit to a beneficiary named by the employee. Generally, the amount to be paid is funded by a life insurance policy on the employee. When the death benefit is paid, the company takes an income tax deduction and the recipient pays income tax on the proceeds received.

Estate Tax Results of Retirement Plans

With a few exceptions that we will discuss, both qualified and nonqualified retirement plans can have substantial negative estate planning consequences. Anytime retirement funds are paid after the death of the plan participant, at least two taxes apply: the federal estate tax and the federal income tax.

The full value of qualified retirement plans and IRAs are considered part of the participant's estate. The only exception to this rule is for pension plans that terminate on the death of the participant. For many reasons, it is impractical for a person to give a qualified plan to another, so there are very few methods for avoiding federal estate taxation of qualified plans and IRAs.

Nonqualified retirement plans are also included in the estate of the employee, unless at some time the employee gave the rights to the plan to another person or a trust. Because nonqualified plans are not controlled by the same laws as qualified plans, it is possible to remove the proceeds from the estate of the employee with good, forward-thinking planning. However, this planning is not easy and should only be done by an expert in nonqualified plans.

Now let's note what it means to have the value of the plan included in the participant's estate.

First, if the participant's spouse, or a marital trust for the benefit of the participant's spouse, is the beneficiary of the plan, the value of the plan will be subject to the unlimited marital deduction. When the participant dies, no estate tax will be due on the plan proceeds in this situation—regardless of the size of the plan—so long as the participant's spouse is a citizen of the United States. When the spouse dies, the full remaining value of the plan will be included in his or her estate.

When the proceeds are included in an estate, they do not get a step-up in basis. Also, even if the proceeds are paid over a period of time, the estate tax is due nine months after the death of the owner or his or her spouse. This may create a situation in which tax is due but there are no funds to pay the estate tax. Obviously, this result should be avoided or planned for in advance.

Income Tax Results of Retirement Plans

The technical term given to income earned by a decedent before his or her death, but paid after death, is *income in respect of a decedent* (IRD). Special income tax rules are associated with IRD, none of them very positive.

Not only is IRD included in the estate of the decedent, but the proceeds are also subject to income tax when received by the beneficiary. Yes, you read that right. IRD is taxed at least twice, once under the estate tax and once under the income tax. If you live in a state that has its own death tax and an income tax, these taxes may also be assessed.

There is a small tax break that reduces the impact of the taxes: the beneficiary gets an income tax deduction for the estate tax attributable to each payment. At the end of each year, the recipient computes the estate tax associated with the IRD payments made during the year and itemizes the amount as a deduction. If the beneficiary does not itemize or cannot qualify for itemization, then the benefit is lost. This tax deduction is only a partial offset to the estate taxes actually paid; it softens the blow, but it doesn't eliminate the impact.

Depending on the beneficiary's income tax rate and the amount of estate taxes paid, the overall tax rate on IRD may reach as high as 55 to 60 percent.

The income tax results of a *Roth IRA* is different than a standard IRA. The proceeds from a Roth IRA are not subject to income tax, but they are subject to estate tax. For purposes of estate planning and income tax planning, a Roth IRA is generally superior to a standard IRA.

If an IRA owner doesn't want his or her IRA beneficiaries to be subject to income tax on all distributions occurring after the owner's death, the owner can convert some or all of the IRA to a Roth IRA during his or her lifetime. The IRA owner will owe income tax immediately upon the conversion, but after the converted Roth IRA owner's death, their beneficiaries will be allowed to take all distributions from the Roth IRA income tax free. In order for a Roth IRA conversion to make sense, the IRA owner should generally have money outside the IRA to pay the taxes resulting from the conversion. The decision to convert an IRA into a Roth IRA involves many variables and should be done only after careful analysis and consultation with tax advisors.

Retirement Planning Alternatives

Because of the nature of IRD, few retirement plan alternatives will substantially reduce income and estate tax consequences. However, there are alternatives that may work for you.

For those who have large IRAs or qualified plans that will be subject to income and estate tax, the first step is to understand that eventually any funds left in these plans will be subject to taxes. Once that stark fact is assimilated, then a decision has to be made as to what impact it will have on an estate.

A number of people come to the conclusion that it is better to give the proceeds to charity than to see a vast majority of the fund go to taxes. These people, if married, name their spouse (or revocable living trust) as the primary beneficiary of their plan because of the unlimited marital deduction. After the death of the spouse, their plan names a favorite charity or charities as fund beneficiaries.

By naming a charity as the beneficiary, the money passes directly to charity without diminution from taxes. Because much of it could pass to the government otherwise, this allows people to at least control how the proceeds will be used.

A second solution is to create an irrevocable life insurance trust (ILIT) and fund it with enough life insurance to pay the taxes on the retirement plan. The ILIT proceeds are not subject to federal estate tax, so they can be fully used to pay all estate and income taxes on the retirement plan proceeds. ILITs are also used when the proceeds of a plan are paid to charity; the life insurance proceeds are used to replace the retirement plan proceeds.

The retirement plan itself can be the source of the premium payments for the ILIT, even though after-tax dollars are used. As we have seen, a majority of the funds in a retirement plan could be lost to income and estate tax. Plan participants who are not subject to an early distribution penalty (those over age 59½) should consider taking money out of the plan and buying life insurance to protect or replace the retirement plan proceeds when they wish to maximize the funds available to their children and other loved ones. While buying life insurance as protection for heirs is not always the most efficient use of funds, in many cases it can nevertheless be well advised.

ILITs are also used to fund the taxes on nonqualified retirement plans. Because the proceeds from these plans are also IRD and subject to estate and income tax, an ILIT is a source of tax-free cash to pay the taxes generated by the nonqualified deferred compensation amounts.

Finally, some financial planners have taken the view that it is better not to touch retirement plan proceeds for as long as possible. When forced to take the proceeds, they say to take the minimum amount out. The rationale behind this concept is that by growing the retirement funds on a tax-deferred basis (and delaying the payment of taxes for as long as possible), even after taxes, more assets will pass to heirs. Not all planners agree with this point of view, but it should be explored.

Perhaps deferral will create a better tax result; but be careful of the assumptions being made. Many of the favorable computations look good only if the participant lives for a long period of time and receives a fairly decent rate of return. If the deferral route is taken, it is wise to hedge the result by creating an ILIT with at least some life insurance, in case the growth projections are not as accurate as hoped.

Because of the complexity of the rules surrounding retirement planning, the better course for everyone is to read and study as much as possible. Consulting with advisors who rationally and patiently share the available alternatives is also important.

In our view, retirement planning is not sound planning at all unless you have a clear goal in mind. Many times, tax savings are not of the greatest concern to families. Factors such as health, family makeup, and availability of assets outside of the retirement plan all influence the type of planning that is appropriate.

40

Special Use Valuation

Keeping the Farm in the Family

Farmers and ranchers face unique federal estate tax problems. Over the years, farm and ranch income has been declining dramatically as a percentage of land value. Thus, farmers and ranchers are continually forced into higher federal estate tax brackets and unable to generate the income to pay those taxes. This inability to pay can and often does force their families to sell all or part of the family farm or ranch.

A family farm or ranch purchased forty years ago may have cost as little as $10 per acre. During those forty years, a city and its suburbs might have expanded to within a mile of that farm or ranch. Developers might pay $5,000 or more per acre in order to build houses on the land. The farm or ranch may produce only enough income to feed and provide the basics for the agricultural family. If the land is valued in terms of its ability to produce agricultural income, it will not have a very high value. The difference in values of property valued at its agricultural use or its residential use can be staggering. If the federal government used the residential value for federal estate tax purposes, it would force almost every farm and ranch family off their land.

Recognizing this massive problem, Congress, as part of the Tax Reform Act of 1976, passed a relief provision for the special valuation of family farm and ranch property, and for real estate used in other types of family businesses as well. This provision is the *special use valuation*. Congress has tinkered with special use valuation over the years, and it has gotten easier to use. It has been helpful to many farmers, ranchers, and other closely held business owners.

Special use valuation allows farmland and ranchland to be valued at its agricultural value instead of its value as residential property for federal estate tax purposes. This valuation method decreases the value of the farmer's or rancher's estate for federal estate tax purposes and gives those families a better opportunity to continue farm and ranch operations.

The value of farm- and ranchland in an agricultural estate, and land use in a closely held business, can be reduced through special use valuation by as much as $1,040,000 for deaths occurring in 2012. The amount was initially fixed at $750,000. Then, beginning in 1999, it became subject to adjustment for inflation, though this adjustment is not necessarily made every year. Inflation must increase enough so that at least $10,000 is added to the previous year's inflation-adjusted amount. Check with your tax advisors to determine what the current amount is.

To qualify for special use valuation, the value of the farmer's or rancher's assets, including the land and personal property used in the farm or ranch, *less* the debt secured by that land and personal property, must be at least 50 percent of the total value of the estate. In addition, the value of the land itself must be equal to at least 25 percent of the estate. In qualifying under these percentage rules, the agricultural land is valued at its residential value. It must have been used as farm- or ranchland for five of the eight years prior to the owner's death, and actively managed by the owner or other family members. This doesn't means that the owner or family members must actually be out in the field, but they have to materially participate in the decision making. It means they must regularly advise those persons managing the farm and participate in most decisions. Active management can include having the current owner renting the property to a family member. The owner must be a U.S. citizen or resident at the time of death.

The land also must pass upon the death of the owner to an heir who is a close family member. The qualified heir then must operate the farm or ranch for a period of time after the death of the original owner. All these rules must be met to qualify for special use valuation.

Owning agricultural property in joint tenancy or in a community property state may affect the application of the percentage test. If one-half of the estate is considered to be owned by the surviving spouse, a significant portion of the agricultural property will be ignored for purposes of the percentage test.

A family member can actively manage the farm or ranch on behalf of the owner, special use valuation can be retained, and the owner can qualify for Social Security benefits.

Qualification for special use valuation does not end with the closing of the original owner's estate. If the heirs dispose of all or part of the property subject to special use valuation within 10 years of the original owner's death, the tax savings that originally resulted from special use valuation must be paid back to the government.

The Internal Revenue Service monitors the 10-year requirement by placing a tax lien on the property that was subject to special use valuation. Because it has a lien on the property, the IRS will know if the property is sold. The property cannot be sold until the lien is removed. The IRS gets paid.

A federal tax lien on property makes it difficult for its current owners to mortgage the property. As a result, family members actively engaged in farming or ranching may find it difficult to borrow money to keep the farm or ranch going.

With the advent of the unlimited marital deduction, the farm and ranch owner will not owe any estate tax if sufficient property passes to the surviving spouse as long as the surviving spouse is a U.S. citizen, or special planning has been done for a noncitizen. Special use valuation is of no value to the owner under this circumstance because of the marital deduction. However, special use valuation is available for the surviving spouse's estate, provided the surviving spouse actively manages the farm or ranch. This means that he or she must make some management decisions but does not have to be involved in the day-to-day operation.

Special use valuation is a potential life saver for farm or ranch families. Like many provisions of the Internal Revenue Code, it has its traps. Applied wisely, however, it can keep our farms and ranches where they belong—in the family.

Requirements for Special Use Valuation

The discussion on requirements for special use valuation can be summarized as follows:

- The value of the farm or ranch assets (*less* debts on them) must be at least 50 percent of the deceased owner's estate.

- The value of the farmland or ranchland (*less* debts on it) must be at least 25 percent of the deceased owner's estate.

- The property must have been actually managed by the deceased owner for five of the eight years prior to death and used for farming or ranching during the same period.

- A qualified heir must actually manage the property after the owner's death.

- The land must be used as a farm or ranch for 10 years after the owner's death.

- The land is subject to a federal tax lien.

- The land value can be reduced through special use valuation by as much as $1,040,000 in 2012, which is subject to increase for inflation.

- Special use valuation also applies to other types of family businesses.

- Special use valuation may be particularly valuable to the surviving spouse.

41

Using Assets
of a Corporation
to Pay Death Costs

Trading Dollars for Stock

Many of our clients own all or part of the stock of a successful corporation that has cash or assets that can readily be converted to cash. Their estates consist primarily of their corporate stock. This stock may be hard to sell or difficult to borrow against at their deaths. The money needed by their beneficiaries to pay death taxes and expenses is, unfortunately, in the wrong place; it is in the corporation, not the estate.

The federal government has long recognized the difficulty of using corporate assets to pay personal death taxes and, as a result, passed Section 303 of the Internal Revenue Code. Section 303 allows corporations to provide their assets to pay the federal and state death taxes, funeral expenses, and other death expenses of deceased stockholders. Professional estate planners refer to this technique as a *Section 303 redemption.*

A Section 303 redemption is merely the purchase by a corporation of enough of a deceased stockholder's stock of that corporation to pay all or part of the deceased shareholder's state and federal death taxes, funeral expenses, and administrative expenses. Administrative expenses include expenses involved in the operation and maintenance of an estate.

For example, a deceased businessperson owned one million shares in XYZ Corporation worth $1 million, or $1.00 per share. The state and federal death taxes and the funeral and administrative expenses of the estate total $325,000. Assuming the stock meets all of the technical requirements of Section 303, the estate may sell $325,000 worth of stock (325,000 shares) back to XYZ Corporation. The cash received by the estate in exchange for the stock cannot exceed the sum of the total amount of the deceased stockholder's death expenses. As a result, cash or other liquid assets in the corporation have been successfully exchanged for the nonliquid stock.

Section 303 is also a benefit to a corporate owner because of the income tax savings it can generate. Generally, a stockholder who sells only part of his or her stock in a corporation back to that same corporation will be subject to federal income tax on the sale proceeds as if those proceeds were a dividend. A dividend is a terrible way to be taxed: it creates two federal income taxes. When Section 303 applies, the sale proceeds are not treated as a dividend, but are treated as proceeds from a sale or exchange of stock.

Double taxation occurs with a dividend because the money a corporation uses to buy its own stock is usually money that has already been subject to corporate federal income tax. For example, assume that a corporation is in the 34 percent tax bracket. A dollar of profit is made and the corporation pays $0.34 on that $1. This is the first tax. The $0.66 left is then used by the corporation to purchase a portion of the selling stockholder's stock. The selling stockholder receives the $0.66 for his or her stock, and the entire amount is taxed as a dividend. In 2012 qualified dividends are taxed at a maximum rate of 15 percent. (Under current law the qualified dividend preferred tax rate is scheduled to expire at the end of 2012, after which all dividends will be taxed at higher, ordinary income rates.) The result is that the selling stockholder has about $0.56 of the dollar that was originally profit in their corporation when dividend treatment applies. Because of the double tax, this represents a combined income tax rate of 44 percent.

On the death of a stockholder, the stock's cost basis is increased, or stepped-up, to its value as of the day of the stockholder's death. We have discussed step-up in basis rules in other chapters. If the stock is sold back to the corporation, there should be little if any income tax. An example will help you understand:

> The deceased stockholder originally paid $100,000 (cost basis) for 325,000 shares of stock that the estate sold back to the corporation. If the stockholder sold that same stock to a third party before death, the gain would have been $225,000 ($325,000 less $100,000). If the stock was worth $325,000 on death, however, the step-up in basis rule gives the stock a new cost basis of $325,000. As a result, if the stock were sold back to the corporation for $325,000 under Section 303, there would be no gain or federal income tax at all.

Now that we have explained the advantages of Section 303 for the estates of corporate owners, let's discuss some of the requirements that must be met in order to use it (see Figure 41-1).

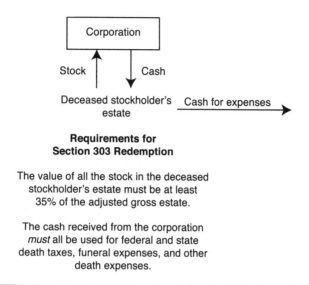

**Requirements for
Section 303 Redemption**

The value of all the stock in the deceased
stockholder's estate must be at least
35% of the adjusted gross estate.

The cash received from the corporation
must all be used for federal and state
death taxes, funeral expenses, and other
death expenses.

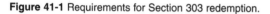

Figure 41-1 Requirements for Section 303 redemption.

The value of the stock owned by the deceased stockholder has to be 35 percent of the value of the adjusted gross estate to qualify for Section 303. Basically, the *adjusted gross estate* is the value of the estate *less* expenses and debts of that estate.

There are other requirements that must be met in order to qualify under Section 303. Some of them deal with the time periods under which the stock must be sold. These are complicated and should be discussed with your professional advisors.

There can be disadvantages related to the use of a Section 303 redemption. If the corporation does not have liquid assets, Section 303 may not be beneficial. The corporation is allowed to distribute property other than money in a Section 303 redemption, but if the property distributed cannot be sold by the estate within the time provided in the section, then the distribution will be taxed as a dividend, a catastrophic result.

Another potential disadvantage of a Section 303 redemption is that the deceased stockholder's family may lose control of the family corporation. For example, if the deceased stockholder owned 51 percent of the corporation before death and enough stock is sold back to the corporation under Section 303, the family may be left with far less than 50 percent ownership; this can occur when there are stockholders other than family members. When a Section 303 redemption is used without proper advice, outsiders can end up controlling a family corporation.

A Section 303 redemption usually takes cash out of a corporation. If that corporation needs its cash to survive after the death of its principal shareholder, the redemption may kill the goose that could lay more golden eggs.

The last disadvantage of Section 303 is that it can create a tax trap for the unwary. This section of the Internal Revenue Code is fairly simple when compared with other code sections; however, the technical requirements of Section 303 are intricate and, if not thoroughly understood, can result in a tax-planning disaster. The following example should prove our point:

> Bob, a stockholder of Bolt Corporation, reads a book on estate planning and is interested in the chapter on Section 303 redemptions. He discovers that 35 percent of the value of his estate must be corporate stock to qualify. He calculates the value of his Bolt stock and finds its value is less than 35 percent of the value of his estate. As a result, our self-taught stockholder figures out that if he gives some property (other than Bolt stock) to his spouse, his estate will qualify. He gives property to his spouse and then dies two years later.
>
> Because of one of the intricacies of Section 303, the amount of the gift Bob made to his spouse is *added back* to his estate for purposes of satisfying the 35 percent requirement. The result is loss of Section 303 treatment.
>
> If Bolt Corporation, following the Section 303 planning, buys its stock back, all the proceeds received by the estate are taxed *as a dividend*.

Section 303 provides an easy way to convert nonliquid stock into liquid dollars on the death of a stockholder. Used wisely, it can be of great benefit to the beneficiaries of a corporate business owner's estate; but it is a technical section of the Internal Revenue Code, and it should never be used without expert professional advice in both its conception and its application.

42
Giving It to Charity
Good Works Deserve Good Benefits

Methods of charitable giving have been the subject of a significant number of technical texts. In a society attuned to charity, it is only logical that myriad methods are available to all of us to make charitable giving attractive. This chapter is aimed at the person who wants to obtain a rudimentary knowledge of the vast income tax, gift tax, and estate tax opportunities afforded by making gifts to charity.

Charitable giving falls into a few general categories. These categories include outright gifts, gifts of a partial interest in property, and gifts in trust. All these methods can be used during one's lifetime or at one's death; each has separate federal income tax, gift tax, and estate tax implications.

Outright gifts of property are the most commonly used form of giving. People making an outright gift can make their gifts in money, personal property, or real property.

To receive all the tax benefits that can result from a charitable gift, the gift must be made to an Internal Revenue Code qualified charity. To qualify, the charity must be a public, semipublic, or private foundation that has received special approval from the IRS. When you make a gift, either during your lifetime or after your death, it is important that you check with the charitable organization to make sure that it is IRS approved. This approval is generally given if the charity is a governmental agency; a religious, charitable, scientific, literary, or educational organization; or a war veterans' or domestic fraternal organization.

A lifetime charitable gift has two distinct tax advantages. The first is that an income tax deduction is generated. The second is that assets, along with their future appreciation, are removed from the value of an estate.

Normally, the income tax deduction that can be taken by the giver is limited to a maximum of 50 percent of *adjusted gross income.* (AGI), which is not taxable income; it is all income *less* certain deductions. The maximum income tax deduction is limited, however, to 30 percent of AGI when the gift is made to semipublic or private charities. These include certain veterans' and fraternal organizations and private foundations. When checking to see whether an organization is IRS-approved, you should also check its status as a public, semipublic, or private charity.

There is another income tax deduction limitation that can apply when giving property to charity. It applies generally to property which if sold would be taxed at the capital gain rate. The deduction that applies to this type of property is limited to either 50 or 30 percent of AGI when it is given to a public charity, and 20 percent of AGI when given to a semipublic or private charity.

When giving capital gain property to a public charity, normally the amount of the deduction is limited to 30 percent of the donor's AGI. If the capital gain property qualifies for long-term capital gain treatment (held for more than one year) the full fair market value of the property can be deducted from AGI for the year of the gift, as long as the deduction does not exceed 30 percent of AGI. If it does, the excess amount can be used in one or more of the next five years until the full amount has been deducted.

You must make a special election on your income tax return if you wish to use the 50 percent AGI limitation for a gift of long-term capital gain property to a public charity. If you make this special election, then the total amount of the deduction is limited to the basis or cost of the property, rather than its fair market value. The basis amount is then subject to the 50 percent limitation. Any excess amount cannot be carried forward to future years.

These rules can be illustrated as follows:

> If your AGI is $100,000 and you give $60,000 in cash to a public charity, then only $50,000 can be deducted in the current year. The remaining $10,000 can be used in the future for up to five years. But if the $60,000 is given to a semipublic or private charity, only $30,000 can be deducted in the current year (30 percent of $100,000). The remainder can be carried forward to the next five years.

> Let us assume that your gift is of stock you bought three years ago for $45,000 and that it is currently valued at $55,000. A sale of the stock would create a $10,000 taxable gain.

> A gift of the stock to a public charity using the 30 percent rule would result in a $30,000 deduction from your AGI in that current year. The remaining $25,000 could be deducted in a future year, as long as it is deducted within the next five years.

> If you choose the 50 percent limitation, then your cost basis, $45,000, is deducted in the current year.

> A gift of this stock to a semipublic or private charity will result in a deduction that will be limited to 20 percent of your AGI, or $20,000. The remaining $35,000 can be carried over for the next five years.

There are further limitations on the amount you can deduct when making a gift of appreciated property to a public charity. One example is that if you give a work of art to a hospital, your deduction is limited. Because the hospital cannot generally use artwork to further its exempt purpose, you can only deduct the original cost of the work of art.

These income tax rules, believe it or not, are not exhaustive. A lot of other income tax rules can come into play, depending on the nature of the property and the type of charity to which you are giving it. You can see how important it is for you to consult a tax advisor before making a charitable gift other than a gift of cash.

While charitable giving almost always has income tax ramifications, direct charitable giving—providing it follows the rules—never results in gift taxes. A charitable gift made within three years of your death generally cannot be brought back into your estate for federal estate tax purposes. An exception to this rule is a gift of life insurance as well as other minor types of gifts.

An outright gift upon death has no income tax advantages or disadvantages. But for federal estate tax purposes, the value of a gift made to a qualified charity does result in a deduction equal to the fair market value of the gift.

Unlike the income tax deduction rules for charitable gifts, there is *no* percentage limitation for gifts made at death.

If a charitably minded individual is in ill health and may not live very long, a lifetime charitable gift should be considered instead of a charitable gift on death. A lifetime gift has the potential advantage of reducing income taxes as well as reducing the giver's estate for federal estate tax purposes, as shown in Figure 42-1.

Many people want to give property to charity at their deaths but want to retain the property for their use during their lifetimes. They would also like, if possible, to receive a current income tax deduction. The Internal Revenue Code allows both of these benefits through the gift of a remainder interest to charity.

A gift of a remainder interest that is not in trust is restricted to gifts of a farm, ranch, or a personal residence. This type of gift allows the giver to

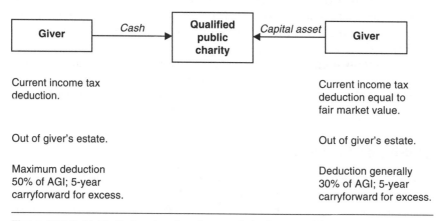

Current income tax deduction.

Out of giver's estate.

Maximum deduction 50% of AGI; 5-year carryforward for excess.

Current income tax deduction equal to fair market value.

Out of giver's estate.

Deduction generally 30% of AGI; 5-year carryforward for excess.

Figure 42-1 Outright gift of cash or long-term capital gain asset while giver is alive.

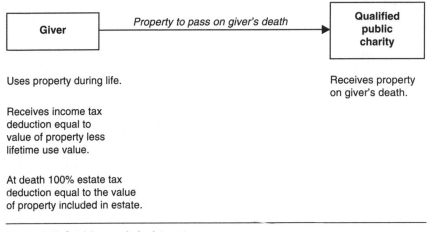

Figure 42-2 Outright remainder interest.

retain a life estate in the property. Thus, the giver can use the property, receive income from the property, and live on the property during life. At the death of the giver, the property automatically passes to the charity. This gift is accomplished with a real estate deed in which the owner executes a new deed retaining a life estate in the farm or residence and naming a charity as the owner of the remainder interest.

The value of the remainder interest is determined under Internal Revenue Code guidelines. Valuation is based on the life expectancy of the giver of the property; if a husband and wife are joint givers, their joint life expectancy can also be calculated. The value of the remainder interest is taken as a charitable income tax deduction in the year of the gift. In addition to this income tax advantage, the property passing to charity at death entitles the estate to a charitable estate tax deduction equal to the value of the property included in the giver's estate. Remember, the charitable gift of a remainder interest that is not in trust is restricted to a farm, ranch, or personal residence (see Figure 42-2).

Gifts to charity from a trust can take many forms. In our experience, the most commonly used charitable trusts are the remainder trust and the lead trust. These vehicles are extremely complex in terms of the rules that govern them. Our discussion is directed toward an understanding of their basic principles.

Charitable Remainder Trust

A *charitable remainder trust* is a trust to which the maker of the trust typically transfers appreciated property irrevocably and then retains an income interest in the trust property for the maker or the maker's family (see Figure 42-3).

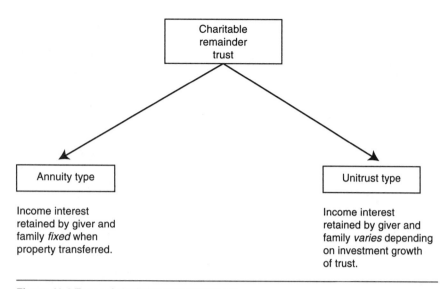

Figure 42-3 Types of charitable remainder trusts.

A properly created and operated charitable remainder trust is a tax exempt entity. Following the contribution of appreciated property to this trust, the trustee may sell the property and reinvest all the proceeds from the sale without any income taxes because of the tax exempt status of the trust.

When the income interest retained by the giver or the giver's family is a fixed amount of the value of the property at the time it is transferred to the trust, it is called a *charitable remainder annuity trust*. When the income interest that is retained by the giver or the giver's family is a fixed percentage of the value of the trust assets as determined annually, the trust is called a *charitable remainder unitrust*. Regardless of which trust is used, the income interest must be at least 5 percent of the value of the property in the trust and cannot exceed 50 percent. In addition, at the creation of the trust the present value of the remainder interest passing to charity must equal at least 10 percent of the value of the contributed property.

A charitable remainder annuity trust is not a good hedge against inflation because its annual payment amount is fixed and does not increase as the trust assets increase in value. For example, assume a maker contributes assets valued at $500,000 to a 6 percent charitable remainder annuity trust and the maker retains the right to the annual payment for her lifetime. The maker will receive $30,000 from the trust each year no matter what happens to the ongoing value of the trust assets. A charitable remainder annuity trust tends to benefit the charity more than the giver or the giver's family when inflation increases the value of the trust assets over time because the annuity payments never increase.

A charitable remainder unitrust, however, favors the income beneficiary when the value of the trust assets increase because the income distributions increase as the trust assets increase. For example, assume a maker contributes assets valued at $500,000 to a 6 percent charitable remainder unitrust and retains the right to the unitrust interest for the maker's lifetime. The year one payment to the maker is $30,000. If at the beginning of year two the value of the charitable remainder unitrust assets are $550,000, the year two unitrust payment to the maker is $33,000.

In both these remainder trusts the beneficiaries of the trusts have a lifetime interest in a percentage value of the assets. At death the remaining trust assets pass automatically to the named charity or charities (see Figure 42-4).

All charitable remainder trusts are similar to remainder interests in property. The annual annuity or unitrust payments belong to the income

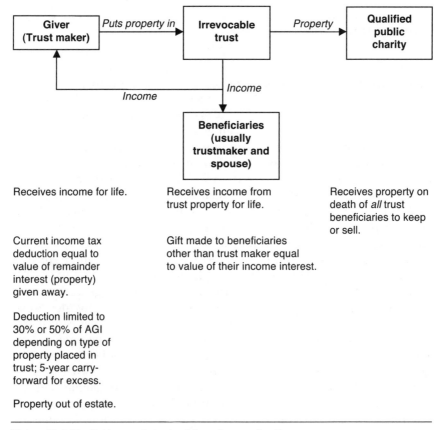

Figure 42-4 Charitable remainder trust (annuity or unitrust).

beneficiaries, and whatever is left belongs to charity. There is an income tax deduction available to the giver at the time the property is put into the trust in the amount of the present value of the remainder interest. This amount is calculated by using Internal Revenue Code guidelines, as we discussed earlier. Here is an example:

> Sarah Jackson, age 65, contributes $1 million worth of Google stock she has owned for 10 years with a basis of $100,000 to a 7 percent charitable remainder unitrust that will pay her the unitrust payment annually for the remainder of her life. The Internal Revenue Service required rate for calculating the amount of the charitable income tax deduction for the month of the contribution is 5 percent. (This rate is published monthly and may change every month.) Shortly after the contribution, the trustee sells the Google stock and reinvests the $1 million proceeds in a diversified portfolio. Based upon all these facts, Sarah receives a income tax charitable deduction of $340,000 in addition to the annual 6 percent unitrust payment for her life. Upon her death, the full value of the charitable remainder trust is included in her estate for estate tax purposes because she retained the unitrust interest for life. However, Sarah's estate will receive an offsetting charitable estate tax deduction for this amount being included in her estate.

Benefits of a charitable remainder trust include:

- Tax-free sale of appreciated assets transferred to the trust
- Charitable income tax deduction to the maker when created during lifetime equal to the present value of the remainder interest passing to charity
- Tax-free diversification of the assets transferred to the trust
- Increased cash flow to the maker when appreciated nonincome or low income assets are transferred to the trust and sold by the trust
- Maker can create a charitable legacy with the remainder amount left to the maker's charity of choice.

Charitable Lead Trust

A *charitable lead trust* is often described as the reverse of a charitable remainder trust. Instead of providing income to the noncharitable beneficiaries and giving the property to charity at the end of the income term, a lead trust gives income to charity for a period of time and passes the remainder of the property to the giver's beneficiaries at the end of the income term, at a reduced transfer tax cost based on the present value of the remainder interest (see Figure 42-5).

Charitable lead trusts come in two basic types: *charitable lead annuity trusts* and *charitable lead unitrusts*. Charitable lead trusts must pay out an income

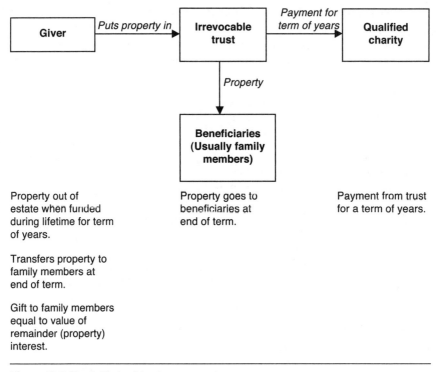

Figure 42-5 Charitable lead trust.

interest at least annually to a charity approved by the IRS. Charitable lead trusts may be created during lifetime or at the maker's death under the terms of the maker's will or revocable living trust.

When created either during lifetime or at death, the maker, or his or her estate, is making two transfers for tax purposes. One transfer is the income interest to charity and the other is the remainder interest to an individual or individuals who are usually family members. The value of the income interest to charity is eligible for the charitable gift tax deduction when the charitable lead trust is created during lifetime, and a charitable estate tax deduction when it's created at death. The present value of the remainder interest is a taxable gift when the charitable lead trust is created during lifetime, or a transfer subject to estate tax when it's created at the death of the maker. If the lead trust is structured carefully by a professional estate planner, the amount of the taxable transfer to the remainder beneficiaries can be very low compared to the value of the property initially transferred to the trust.

It is possible to structure a lifetime charitable lead trust so that the present value of the annual income interest is a charitable income tax deduction to the giver in the year the property is placed in the lead trust. The income tax deduction that the giver can take is limited to 30 percent of AGI for gifts of cash and 20 percent for capital assets. This AGI limitation applies regardless of whether the charity is public, semipublic, or private. The big limitation is, however, that the giver only gets an income tax deduction in the year the property is given to the trust with no carry forward. Worse yet, in all future years of the charitable lead trust, all the trust income is taxed to the giver. Because of this income tax disadvantage, many people decide not to create the type of charitable lead trust that will give them an income tax deduction.

Individuals with very large taxable estates can incorporate a charitable lead annuity trust into their revocable living trust to significantly minimize, and sometimes eliminate, federal estate taxes. Here is an example of the incredible leverage that is obtainable with a testamentary charitable lead annuity trust:

> Mary Megabucks has an estate of $25 million. Her living trust provides that upon her death $20 million of her estate goes into a testamentary charitable lead annuity trust paying 7 percent annually to the local college for 20 years. The remainder of her estate, including the assets in the charitable lead trust after 20 years, goes to her children in trust. Let's say the IRS required interest rate for valuing the remainder interest in the charitable lead annuity trust on Mary's death is 4.2 percent. The estate tax consequences of funding the charitable lead trust are a charitable deduction of $19,718,580 and $281,420 that is subject to estate tax, along with the other $5 million of assets included in Mary's estate. Mary has saved millions of dollars in federal estate tax, while benefiting charity and her children.

Unlike a charitable remainder trust, a charitable lead trust is a taxable entity. We often refer to it as a *tax preferred entity* because the lead trust is entitled to a charitable income tax deduction for the full amount of the annual payment made to charity and there is no AGI limitation.

A lead trust can be beneficial for several reasons:

- Avoids or minimizes gift or estate tax on the value of the assets transferred to the trust as well as the appreciation on those assets.
- Maker's children or other beneficiaries receive the assets remaining in the trust, often at a greatly reduced gift or estate tax cost.
- Maker's chosen charity or charities receive an annual payment from the trust for the term of the trust.

As shown in Table 42-1, charitable giving is a broad area, encompassing not only federal estate and gift tax planning, but also federal income tax planning. The array of charitable giving techniques is limited only by one's imagination and, as always, certain provisions of the Internal Revenue Code. If you are genuinely interested in charitable giving, seek expert assistance.

Table 42-1
Gifts to Public Charities

Gift Method	Description	Benefits to Maker or Family	Limitation	Income Tax Consequences	Gift Tax Consequences	Estate Tax Consequences	Charity Receives
1. Cash	Outright while giver alive	Tax	50% of AGI; 5-year carry forward for excess	Current deduction	None	Out of	Cash
2. Cash	On death from estate	Tax	None	None	None	Deduction	Cash
3. Capital assets	Outright while giver alive	Tax	30% or 50% of AGI; 5-year carry forward for 30% limit	Current deduction	None	Out of	Capital assets to keep or sell
4. Capital assets	On death from estate	Tax	None	None	None	Deduction equal to fair market value	Capital assets to keep or sell
5. Outright remainder interest	Giver keeps income and use of property for life	Tax and use of property for life	Personal residence or farm *only*	Deduction equal to value of remainder interest	None	Included with 100% deduction	Property on death of giver

Table 42-1 *(Continued)*
Gifts to Public Charities

Gift Method	Description	Benefits to Maker or Family	Limitation	Income Tax Consequences	Gift Tax Consequences	Estate Tax Consequences	Charity Receives
6. Remainder trust	Giver puts property in trust	Tax and family retains income for their lives	50% or 30% of AGI, depending on type of property put in trust; 5-year carry forward for excess	Current deduction equal to value of remainder interest	Gift to family members equal to value of their income interest	Included with deduction equal to present value of remainder interest	Property on deaths of all trust beneficiaries, to keep or sell
7. Lead trust	Giver puts property in trust	Tax and property goes to family beneficiaries when trust terminates	30% of AGI; 5-year carry forward for excess	Deduction limited to first year, if taken at all	Gift to family members equal to value of remainder interest they will receive	Included with deduction equal to present value of charitable interest	Income from trust for giver's life or term of years

43

An Estate Planning Summary

Protecting and Enhancing Your Estate

We know of no average or representative estate planning situation that could be used as an example or illustration to summarize all the estate planning principles and techniques we have discussed. People have individual estates requiring individual planning techniques. That is why using forms or software is dangerous and mostly ineffective.

There are, however, certain basics or universals common to the estate planning process. To summarize them:

- Inventory the assets you own.

- Know where all your title papers are located, and understand how you have taken title.

- If title is in your name alone, you own the property in fee simple and can give it away, sell it, or leave it to whomever you please. If you own it in tenancy in common, you only own part of it and can only give, sell, or leave your part. If you own property in joint tenancy, you own all of it with someone else. You may give your interest away or even sell it, but you cannot dispose of it on death.

- The laws of the state of your domicile will provide an estate plan for you if you do not provide your own.

- If you choose to accomplish your planning by using a will, you should remember that wills are only effective on death and require a public probate process. In addition, your will may not control the passage of all your property. If you move to another state, you should have your will reviewed—each state's laws are different, and your will may have to be rewritten.

- Your will does not help you if you become so disabled that you can no longer handle your financial affairs. Absent disability planning, you may have to face a living probate.

- Probate, whether for disability or death, involves unnecessary red tape and expense; it puts the real control in the judge's chambers. Probate can and should be avoided.

- Federal estate taxes are imposed on your right to transfer almost all your property interests on death. Estate tax is levied on the fair market value of your property and is generally paid within nine months of death; it is paid before your beneficiaries receive their inheritance.

- The federal estate tax rules are in flux. For 2011 and 2012, the federal estate tax applies only to estates greater than $5 million for an individual and $10 million for a married couple. The 2012 amount was indexed for inflation and that amount is $5,120,000. After 2012, absent congressional action and presidential approval, the federal estate tax will apply to individual estates greater than $1 million and married couple's estates greater than $2 million. The maximum tax bracket for 2011 and 2012 is 35 percent. In 2013 and beyond, absent congressional action, the maximum amount will be 55 percent.

- Spouses in all states can give or leave an unlimited amount of property to their U.S. citizen spouses tax-free. The major requirement associated with the unlimited marital deduction is that surviving spouses receive all of the income from the property during their lifetimes.

- Federal estate tax can be deferred in estates that lack liquidity or in those in which 35 percent of the value consists of closely held business interests. If a family business is incorporated and certain technical tax requirements are met, the surviving family may trade corporate dollars to the estate in return for stock with no adverse tax consequences. Congress has also provided special relief for businesses and farm and ranch families who wish to retain ownership of their farms or ranches following the deaths of the farm or ranch owners.

- The federal estate and gift tax systems have now been unified as they were under prior law. The applicable exclusion amount and the unlimited marital deduction apply to gifts made during life as well as on death for U.S citizen spouses.

- The law allows you to make annual exclusion gifts to anyone of up to $13,000 (adjusted for inflation) without the requirement of filing a federal gift tax return. If your spouse chooses to split the gift with you, the amount doubles. You should exercise care to avoid inadvertent gifts. How you give may be as important as the amount and nature of your gifts.

- If you make a gift to your noncitizen spouse, the annual exclusion is $139,000 as of 2012, because the unlimited marital deduction only applies to U.S. citizen spouses. This amount is also adjusted for inflation. Most states have their own death and gift taxes. Always consider your state's laws when planning.

- Most of your property interests receive a step-up in basis at your death. This fact should be taken into consideration when structuring your plan.

- Trusts are truly the estate planner's golf clubs because they can accomplish just about any of your objectives. Any number of separate trusts can be created in a single trust document. A death trust is called a testamentary trust and can only be created in your will. A living trust is always created during your lifetime. A living trust that allows you the right to change your mind and thereby change the trust is called a revocable living trust; one that cannot be changed is called an irrevocable living trust. A revocable living trust does not involve a gift; an irrevocable trust does.

- An irrevocable living trust commonly used to give property to minors is the 2503(c) trust.

- A revocable living trust can provide for the control, coordination, and distribution of your property while you are alive, during any period of disability, as well as on your death. It can also provide for your care and needs as well as those of your beneficiaries. Revocable living trusts are not public and are good in all states. They are extremely difficult for disgruntled heirs to attack.

- Your revocable living trust can be unfunded, partially funded, or totally funded during your lifetime. It can also be funded subsequent to your death. Your trust can be funded directly, through the use of a nominee partnership, or, in some states, through other techniques such as unrecorded deeds, POD and TOD designations, and postmortem assignments. A properly funded revocable living trust avoids the probate process.

- Your trust planning will only be as good as the performance of your trustees. Trustees are totally responsible for expert performance and judgment while following the written instructions provided in your trust document. Trustees have awesome power, accountability, and liability, all wrapped together in their roles as superagents.

- Both individual and institutional trustees have their strengths and weaknesses. You should select the types of trustees that best serve your planning purposes. Trustees are compensated. Institutional trustees publish fee schedules that are pretty much the same. Individual trustees usually negotiate their fees within parameters set by local state statutes or court rules.

- Giving property to a minor can be difficult. Under the laws of most states, in order to make a gift to a minor, you must set up a Uniform Gifts to Minors Act or Uniform Transfers to Minors Act account, establish a Totten trust, or fund a living trust created for the minor's benefit.

- Property left directly to a minor will be waylaid in a court-imposed custodianship until the minor reaches legal age. Leaving property directly to a minor involves a great deal of red tape; it depersonalizes the planning process and can create confusion and insecurity for your loved ones while generating substantial expense and delay.

- When planning for children, you should provide for a succession of guardians and discuss your situation with the guardians you choose; it is always a good idea to share your planning objectives with them.

- How you divide and distribute your property among your loved ones is your business. However, some general rules of thumb are: Do not divide your property among your children until the youngest of your children is an adult. Once your property is divided, you can provide for different distribution dates for each child to allow for specific thoughts you may have with regard to each. It is important for you to recognize that you *can* control how you wish your property to pass to your children and grandchildren. If you wish to bypass your children in favor of your grandchildren, you must take into account the generation-skipping transfer tax rules.

- When planning for your spouse, you must consider your own state's law and the rights it gives your spouse to your property regardless of your planning attempts to the contrary. You may, however, avail yourself of two planning techniques: premarriage and after-marriage contracts. Given a choice between the two, always opt for the former; they are valid and binding if fair and fairly made and have always been favored under the laws of most states.

- The number of planning possibilities available when planning for a spouse is staggering. There is no hypothetical best or optimum planning approach that can be used when planning for a spouse today. Great care must be taken to analyze all the spousal planning possibilities before you select that best personal tax choice.

- Your life insurance program is absolutely critical to the success of your planning. It is the fuel that makes the estate planning car reach its goal. Life insurance that you own on your life will be federal estate taxable on your death and may be taxed by your state as well. It is important for you to properly record both primary and contingent beneficiary designations with your agent. Never make your estate or minors the direct beneficiaries of your insurance proceeds.

- Reexamine your life insurance portfolio. You may be able to do much better in terms of coverage and price. Consider insuring the younger spouse or purchasing second-to-die insurance, depending on your needs.

- Life insurance can be purchased and structured to totally avoid federal estate tax. In general this is best accomplished through the use of an irrevocable life insurance trust. ILITs can be structured by estate planning specialists to accommodate almost any type of insurance you may own.

- Some estate planning techniques are often not appropriate and do not always work. These include cross-ownership of life insurance policies, joint tenancy, Uniform Transfers to Minors Act accounts, Uniform Gifts to Minor Act accounts, and unlimited general powers of attorney. There are also some estate planning gimmicks that never seem to work. These include form books, commercially available will and trust software, hiding property in a safe-deposit box, and attempting total tax avoidance through the use of a so-called constitutional or pure equity trust.

- Protecting your assets from creditors is always an estate planning consideration. There are a number of ways you can protect your assets, including insurance, investing in exempt assets, and creating entities such as limited partnerships and offshore asset protection trusts.

- Often, retirement benefits represent the largest assets in an estate and are subject to the most tax. Knowing how to treat retirement benefits as part of your estate planning is critical in creating an effective estate plan.

- While Congress has curtailed many of the traditional estate freezing techniques, many opportunities remain. Family limited partnerships, limited liability companies, and grantor retained income trusts can be very effective in freezing an estate. In addition, these devices can be used to substantially discount the value of gifts, allowing a much greater amount to be given away.

- Installment sales are complicated and have been substantially curtailed. Under some circumstances, especially when used with an intentionally defective grantor trust, they can help you as a seller because they can allow you to get appreciating assets out of your estate, and at the same time create tax-free cash flow. If you are a buyer, an installment sale will allow you to purchase an appreciating asset under favorable terms. If you like the installment sales law but desire potentially greater benefits, you may wish to consider a private annuity or a SCIN. A private annuity can be designed so that the value of your appreciating assets and the value of the promissory obligation are *both* totally removed from your estate; the danger is in the gamble between your real and anticipated life expectancy.

- A personal residence trust is an excellent method for reducing the value of your estate by giving your primary residence or a vacation home to your children. The value of the home is discounted; you may treat it as your own for the duration of the trust, and after the trust term ends, you may rent your home back from your children. Substantial tax benefits can be derived from such an arrangement.

- If you desire to make contributions of cash or assets other than cash to qualified charities, either currently or on death, you may receive tax benefits for your good works. The rules surrounding the income tax, estate tax, and gift tax deductibility of your munificence are extremely complex. Always seek out expert assistance in planning for your charitable objectives.

- Estate planning is no place for loners. Professional advisors should be selected for the knowledge they possess within their particular disciplines. All your advisors should participate in your estate planning process and should work well not only with you, but also with each other.

- It may be worthwhile for you to seek the advice and counsel of a collaborative group of professionals who work together on a regular basis. These professionals should be from the law, accounting, insurance, and financial planning professions. This type of collaborative group will be able to help you far more than the traditional team of unrelated advisors.

If you properly approach the estate planning process, you can be assured that you will be successful in protecting and enhancing your estate.

Appendix A

Getting Organized

If you do not have enough space, please attach supplemental information.

FAMILY INFORMATION

Name_____ Nickname _____

Home address_____ City _____

State_____ Zip_____ Home telephone_____ Home fax _____

Birthdate_____ Social Security number_____ Personal e-mail _____

Employer_____ Position _____

Business address_____ City _____

State _____ Zip _____ Business telephone _____

Business e-mail _____

Spouse's name_____ Nickname _____

Birthdate_____ Social Security number _____

Personal e-mail _____

Employer_____ Position _____

Business address _____ City _____

State _____ Zip _____ Business telephone _____

Business e-mail _____

Your Children (*use full names*)   BIRTHDATE

_____ _____

_____ _____

_____ _____

_____ _____

Spouse's Children (*if different from above*)   BIRTHDATE

_____ _____

_____ _____

_____ _____

_____ _____

Advisors   TELEPHONE   E-MAIL

Accountant_____ _____ _____

Attorney_____ _____ _____

Primary personal bank_____ _____ _____

Stockbroker_____ _____ _____

Insurance Advisor_____ _____ _____

FINANCIAL INFORMATION
CASH

All certificates of deposit, checking, savings, and money market accounts should be included here.

Name of Institution   TYPE*   A/C NUMBER   OWNER[†]   AMOUNT   ONLINE

*Checking Account (CA), Savings Account (SA), Certificate of Deposit (CD).
[†]Husband (H), Wife (W), Joint (JT), Tenants in Common (TC), Community Property (CP).
If the account is a POD or TOD, please furnish a copy of the designation.

NOTE: If account is in your name for benefit of a minor, please specify and give minor's name.

NOTES RECEIVABLE

Name of Debtor   DATE OF NOTE   DATE NOTE DUE   OWED TO*   CURRENT BALANCE OWED

*Husband (H), Wife (W), Joint (JT), Tenants in Common (TC), Community Property (CP).

BONDS

Description (*U.S. Savings Bonds, corporate, municipal, etc.*)   OWNER[†]   FACE VALUE

[†]Husband (H), Wife (W), Joint (JT), Tenants in Common (TC), Community Property (CP).
If bond is owned either JT or TC with someone other than spouse, please furnish name and relationship.

NOTE: Please put a check mark next to bearer bonds.

REAL ESTATE

For which you have either a deeded or land contract interest *(land or buildings that you own in partnership with someone else should be listed in the Partnership/LLC Interests section)*:

General description and/or address	OWNER*	FAIR MARKET VALUE	MORTGAGE
_____	_____	_____	_____
_____	_____	_____	_____
_____	_____	_____	_____
_____	_____	_____	_____

*Husband (H), Wife (W), Joint (JT), Tenants in Common (TC), Community Property (CP).
If property is owned either JT or TC with someone other than spouse, please furnish name and relationship.

NOTE: If two or more names are on deed or contract without stating type of ownership, please use ? to designate ownership.

CORPORATE BUSINESS INTERESTS

Privately owned (*not publicly traded*)

Company	NUMBER OF SHARES	BUY/SELL AGREEMENT*	PERCENTAGE OWNERSHIP	OWNER†	VALUE
_____	_____	_____	_____	____	___
_____	_____	_____	_____	____	___
_____	_____	_____	_____	____	___
_____	_____	_____	_____	____	___

*Please check (✓) if a buy/sell agreement exists.
†Husband (H), Wife (W), Joint (JT), Tenants in Common (TC), Community Property (CP).
If stock is owned either JT or TC with someone other than spouse, please furnish name and relationship.

STOCKS

Please list all stock ownership in publicly owned corporations (*stock traded on an exchange or over the counter*). Stock owned in a family or nonpublic company should be listed in the Corporate Business Interests section.

Name of Institution	OWNER*	NUMBER OF SHARES	FAIR MARKET VALUE
_____	_____	_____	_____
_____	_____	_____	_____
_____	_____	_____	_____
_____	_____	_____	_____
_____	_____	_____	_____
_____	_____	_____	_____
Total	_____	_____	_____

*Husband (H), Wife (W), Joint (JT), Tenants in Common (TC), Community Property (CP).
If stock is owned either JT or TC with someone other than spouse, please furnish name and relationship.

If any of your shares are held in a street name account with your broker, please furnish:

Brokerage firm _____

Broker _____

Exact name and number of account _____

If you access your account online, please add Web site information _____

Please also furnish a copy of your latest statement(s).

PARTNERSHIP OR LIMITED LIABILITY COMPANY (LLC) INTERESTS

Partnership Name	PERCENTAGE OF PARTNERSHIP/LLC INTEREST GENERAL PARTNER/ MANAGER	LIMITED PARTNER	OWNER*	VALUE
____	____	____	____	____
____	____	____	____	____
____	____	____	____	____
____	____	____	____	____
____	____	____	____	____
____	____	____	____	____

*Husband (H), Wife (W), Joint (JT), Tenants in Common (TC), Community Property (CP).

SOLE PROPRIETORSHIP BUSINESS INTERESTS

Name of Business	DESCRIPTION OF BUSINESS	OWNER*	VALUE
____	____	____	____
____	____	____	____
____	____	____	____
____	____	____	____
____	____	____	____

*Husband (H), Wife (W), Joint (JT), Tenants in Common (TC), Community Property (CP).

FARM AND RANCH INTERESTS

Description (*livestock, machinery, leases, etc.*)	OWNER*	VALUE
____	____	____
____	____	____
____	____	____
____	____	____
____	____	____
____	____	____

*Husband (H), Wife (W), Joint (JT), Tenants in Common (TC), Community Property (CP).

OIL AND GAS INTERESTS

Description *(lease, overriding royalty, fee mineral estate,*
working interest, pooling agreement, etc.)   OWNER*   FACE VALUE

_____   _____   _____

_____   _____   _____

_____   _____   _____

_____   _____   _____

*Husband (H), Wife (W), Joint (JT), Tenants in Common (TC), Community Property (CP).

ANTICIPATED INHERITANCE, GIFT, OR LAWSUIT JUDGMENT

Description _____

_____

_____

_____

                                    Total estimated value _____

RETIREMENT PLANS

| | | BENEFICIARY ON | PERCENT | |
Type of Plan*	COMPANY	YOUR DEATH	VESTED	VALUE
_____	_____	_____	_____	_____
_____	_____	_____	_____	_____
_____	_____	_____	_____	_____
_____	_____	_____	_____	_____

*Pension (P), Profit Sharing (PS), H.R.10, IRA. Please attach copies of beneficiary designations and online account information.

PERSONAL EFFECTS AND OTHER ASSETS

Furniture, automobiles, jewelry, collectibles, and other personal assets of more than nominal value.

_____

_____

_____

_____

_____

_____

_____

_____

                            Total estimated fair market value _____

LIFE INSURANCE POLICIES/ANNUITIES

Please furnish a copy of each policy.
Policy Number and Company _____

Type* _____ Insured/Annuitant _____

Owner _____

Primary beneficiary _____ Secondary _____

Who pays premium?† _____ Cash value _____

Amount of loans on policy _____ Face amount _____

*Term, whole life, split dollar, group life, annuity.
†Husband (H), Wife (W), Corporation (C).

Policy Number and Company _____

Type* _____ Insured/Annuitant _____

Owner _____

Primary beneficiary _____ Secondary _____

Who pays premium?† _____ Cash value _____

Amount of loans on policy _____ Face amount _____

*Term, whole life, split dollar, group life, annuity.
†Husband (H), Wife (W), Corporation (C).

Policy Number and Company _____

Type* _____ Insured/Annuitant _____

Owner _____

Primary beneficiary _____ Secondary _____

Who pays premium?† _____ Cash value _____

Amount of loans on policy _____ Face amount _____

*Term, whole life, split dollar, group life, annuity.
†Husband (H), Wife (W), Corporation (C).

SUMMARY OF VALUES

ASSETS

AMOUNTS†

	HUSBAND	WIFE	JOINT
Cash	$ _____	_____	_____
Notes receivable	_____	_____	_____
Bonds	_____	_____	_____
Real estate	_____	_____	_____
Corporate business interests	_____	_____	_____
Stocks	_____	_____	_____
Partnership/LLC interests	_____	_____	_____
Sole proprietorship interests	_____	_____	_____
Farm and ranch interests	_____	_____	_____
Oil and gas interests	_____	_____	_____
Anticipated inheritance, gifts, or judgments	_____	_____	_____
Retirement plans	_____	_____	_____
Personal effects/other assets	_____	_____	_____
Life insurance, annuity face amounts	_____	_____	_____*
Total assets	$ _____	_____	_____

LIABILITIES

AMOUNTS†

	HUSBAND	WIFE	JOINT
Loans payable	$ _____	_____	_____
Accounts payable	_____	_____	_____
Real estate mortgages	_____	_____	_____
Contingent liabilities	_____	_____	_____
Loans against life insurance	_____	_____	_____*
Unpaid taxes	_____	_____	_____
Other obligations	_____	_____	_____
_____	_____	_____	_____
_____	_____	_____	_____
Total liabilities	$ _____	_____	_____
Net Estate	$ _____	_____	_____

*Second-to-die policies should be entered here.

†Joint tenancy (JT), Tenancy in Common (TC), and Community Property (CP) values should be entered half in husband's column and half in wife's column.

Appendix B

Federal Estate and Gift Tax Tables

Table B-1
Federal Estate and Gift Tax Rates 2011 and 2012

Column A Taxable Amount ($) over	Column B Taxable Amount ($) not over	Column C Tax on amount ($) in column A	Column D Rate (%) of tax on excess over amount in column A
0	10,000	0	18
$10,000	20,000	$ 1,800	20
20,000	40,000	3,800	22
40,000	60,000	8,200	24
60,000	80,000	13,000	26
80,000	100,000	18,200	28
100,000	150,000	23,800	30
150,000	250,000	38,800	32
250,000	500,000	70,800	34
500,000	and over	155,800	35

Table B-2
Federal Estate and Gift Tax Rates 2013 and Beyond If Congress Does
Not Change the Law*

Column A Taxable Amount ($) over	Column B Taxable Amount ($) not over	Column C Tax on amount ($) in column A	Column D Rate (%) of tax on excess over amount in column A
0	$10,000	0	18
$10,000	20,000	$1,800	20
20,000	40,000	3,800	22
40,000	60,000	8,200	24
60,000	80,000	13,000	26
80,000	100,000	18,200	28
100,000	150,000	23,800	30
150,000	250,000	38,800	32
250,000	500,000	70,800	34
500,000	750,000	155,800	37
750,000	1,000,000	248,300	39

Table B-2 *(Continued)*
Federal Estate and Gift Tax Rates 2013 and Beyond If Congress Does Not Change the Law*

Column A Taxable Amount ($) over	Column B Taxable Amount ($) not over	Column C Tax on amount ($) in column A	Column D Rate (%) of tax on excess over amount in column A
$1,000,000	$1,250,000	$345,800	41
1,250,000	1,500,000	448,300	43
1,500,000	2,000,000	555,800	45
2,000,000	2,500,000	780,800	49
2,500,000	3,000,000	1,025,800	53
3,000,000	———	1,290,800	55

*There is a 5 percent surcharge for estates between $10 million and $17,184,000.

Table B-3
Miscellaneous Notes

In the case of estates of decedents dying during:	The applicable exclusion amount is:	The unified credit is:
2011 and 2012	$5 million†	$1,730,800*
2013 or thereafter	$1 million	$ 345,800

†Indexed for inflation beginning in 2012.

Appendix C

Spouses Have Rights Too

Throughout the United States the law has evolved to protect the interests of a surviving husband or wife. Depending upon the state involved, these spousal rights are called a *right to elect against the will*, a *dissent from the will*, or by other terms. Their purpose remains the same, regardless of terminology. As a matter of public policy and based on an historical context, society has decided that it serves the public good to prevent husbands and wives from completely disinheriting their spouses.

This appendix includes a brief explanation of the terms used in state laws, and a state-by-state synopsis of spousal rights and obligations on death. Remember that state legislatures meet at least every other year, often much more frequently; therefore, it is imperative that you contact your estate planning professional to determine the current law in your state.

Terminology

The concept that husbands and wives should receive at least a minimum amount of their spouses' property on death is based on English common law. The *English common law* is the body of principles and customs developed in England and brought to this country at the time of its settlement.

Historically, the first terms used to describe spousal rights were dower and curtesy. *Dower* is the wife's right to participate in the husband's estate; *curtesy* is the entitlement of the husband to share in his wife's estate. Usually these represented limited rights, most commonly life estates. To have a *life estate in property* means that you are entitled to all income from that property for your life.

A life estate cannot be transferred by will. After the death of the surviving spouse, the property usually reverts, or goes back, to the descendants of the deceased person (decedent). Frequently life estates are expressed in terms of a fraction of the estate; for example, a wife could receive a life estate in one-half of her husband's property. If personal property is involved, it might be placed in a trust by law with income going to the surviving spouse. When real estate is involved, a deed for the life of the survivor is usually prepared.

In the past there was frequently a distinction made between the rights of the husband and the rights of the wife. These differences were based on the way society viewed the roles of men and women at that time. For the most part those distinctions have been removed, but some states still retain vestiges of this type of sex discrimination.

As the law changed, more and more states decided that the dower and curtesy rights were either outdated or insufficient to protect the interests of the surviving spouse. The right of spouses to elect against the will or to dissent from the will of their spouses was then created by state legislatures.

In some states these new laws did not replace dower and curtesy, but merely supplemented them.

To *elect against* or *dissent from the will* (synonymous terms) means that the surviving spouse chooses to take what the law provides in lieu of what the deceased spouse's will provides. It is not possible to take under the will and also dissent from it; you cannot have both.

The amount a spouse receives through a will election varies depending upon the state involved. There are two terms with which you should become familiar. The first term, *augmented estate*, is used in the states that have adopted the Uniform Probate Code (UPC). The augmented estate generally includes all property in which the deceased spouse retained any ownership as well as certain types of gifts. In UPC states the electing spouse receives a fraction of the augmented estate, usually one-half or one-third.

Another term used when the surviving spouse elects against the will is the *intestate share*. This is derived from the word *intestacy*, which means to die without a will. If intestacy occurs, the law provides the specific share of the estate that the wife or husband receives. This varies depending upon the number of children involved and a host of other factors. In some states, if a spouse dissents against the will, it is as if the decedent left no will. The dissenting spouse receives an intestate share of the estate as prescribed by state law.

Other states use neither the augmented estate nor the intestate share. They may rely solely upon forms of dower or curtesy, or they provide what essentially are the same rights by their law.

If a spouse elects against the will, the election is against probate assets. A *probate asset* is property the passage of which must be proved in court. In fact, the word *probate* has its roots in the Latin term for proof or truth. Whether the election will reach nonprobate assets is frequently an open question. Examples of nonprobate assets are life insurance policies, pension plans, funded living trusts, and jointly held property.

One type of living trust is a revocable living trust. The person who creates this trust (the settlor or maker) can cancel, alter, or revoke its terms. The trust is called "living" because it exists while the settlor is alive and is funded with assets, directly or indirectly. This is in contrast to a testamentary trust, which does not exist until after death. The latter type is virtually always included in the elective share. Whether a revocable living trust is included in the elective share depends upon the state involved. In almost all UPC states this type of trust is part of the elective share because the maker retains the right to revoke it, as well as other powers.

In addition to the right to take against the will, most states also provide allowances for the surviving spouse. These are generally in addition to the right to elect against the will. The allowances are taken off the top before computing the elective share. In some states the allowances are substantial, and they are frequently exempt from other claims against the estate.

The *homestead allowance* or *exemption* is based on a legislative desire to pre-serve the family home. In many states homestead allowances are inadequate and have been outpaced by inflation. For example, a state might permit $10,000 for a homestead exemption. If creditors demand it, there could be a forced sale of the family home; the first $10,000 would go to the spouse and/or children of the decedent. The balance of the proceeds would be subject to the claims of creditors.

The surviving spouse may be entitled to an allowance intended to sup-port him or her as well as surviving minor children during the administra-tion of the estate. These allowances are usually restricted to one year but can be extended by court order. The amount and frequency of payment dif-fers from state to state. Sometimes the allowance is intended solely for the spouse. Occasionally it is a lump-sum payment. This is called a *maintenance, family,* or *support allowance.*

Many states provide an *exempt personal property allowance* that can cover everything from sentimental objects and the decedent's clothing to house-hold furniture and even the family car. This allowance is a fixed amount, and it is usually in the $5,000 to $15,000 range.

It is not necessary to elect against the will in order to be entitled to allowances; they are in addition to either the elective share or the share under the will. Proper procedure must be followed to file claims for allowances.

In most states it is required that the decedent be domiciled in the state in order for the allowance provisions to apply. *Domicile* is a legal term having a different meaning than *residence*, but one that does not lend itself to a particular definition. If there are any doubts, always consult an attorney to verify the question of domicile.

Frequently a person will have already made a will prior to marriage. If there is no provision in the will for a spouse, the spouse may receive a share of the estate anyway. This is known as the *omitted spouse provision*; how-ever, in almost all states, if the person making the will specifically states that the omission is intentional, this law will not apply.

The rules in community property states are different. Most property owned by spouses in these states is marital property; however, community property spouses may have separate property. This is usually property acquired before the marriage. If a community property spouse attempts to dispose of more than his or her community property interest, the other spouse can usually elect against the will.

In reading the material in this appendix, you will frequently note that the word "descendant" is used. Generally, a *descendant* is a child, grandchild, or great-grandchild of the *decedent*. People in previous generations are referred to as "ancestors." People in subsequent generations are referred to as descendants.

Locate your state in this appendix to determine what your spousal rights and obligations are. Remember, however, to always seek the advice of a knowledgeable professional before utilizing any of these concepts in your estate plan.

State Synopses

Alabama. In the state of Alabama a surviving spouse has a right to the *lesser* of (1) all of the estate of the deceased spouse, reduced by the value of the surviving spouse's separate property, or (2) one-third of the estate of the deceased spouse. The surviving spouse's separate property includes all lifetime transfers from the deceased spouse to the surviving spouse, as well as property the surviving spouse may have received from other sources.

The surviving spouse and minor children whom the deceased spouse was obligated to support, or children who were in fact being supported by the deceased spouse, are entitled to a reasonable allowance in money from the estate during the period of administration. This allowance applies whether or not the spouse has elected against the estate.

The surviving spouse has a homestead allowance of $6,000, a personal property allowance of $3,500, and rights to miscellaneous other personal property. A spouse may waive the right to the elective share, the homestead allowance, and the family allowance before or after marriage. The surviving spouse may also retain possession of the dwelling house, under what is known as the *widow's quarantine*, where the surviving spouse lived with the decedent before his or her death. The decedent's estate must pay any rent due.

Alaska. The Alaskan augmented estate statute provides for the surviving spouse to take one-third of the augmented estate. If the amount of the elective share is less than $50,000, the surviving spouse is generally entitled to a supplemental elective share equal to $50,000, minus the amount of the elective share. The Alaskan code generally incorporates the UPC definition of augmented estate, so this would seem to include trust property as well as property owned outright. This is true because the UPC refers to all assets that are transferred gratuitously, and in which the transferring spouse retained an interest, as part of the augmented estate.

There are also various types of family allowances in Alaska. A homestead allowance of $27,000 is available to protect the family home. A personal property allowance is available of up to $10,000. Finally, a family allowance, defined as a reasonable sum for the family, not to exceed $18,000, is available for a period of up to one year. The probate court can, in its discretion, modify the family allowance.

In 1998, Alaska adopted an opt-in community property law. Under the Alaska Community Property Act, married couples who are Alaska residents may elect to treat some or all of their property as community property by contract or by establishing an Alaska Community Property Trust. In addition, couples who are residents of separate property states may utilize Alaska law to transmute ("convert") some or all of their separate property to community property by establishing an Alaska Community Property Trust.

Arizona is a community property state, so one-half of the property acquired during marriage belongs to the surviving spouse.

Arizona has general allowance provisions. The homestead allowance is $18,000. A personal property allowance of $7,000 is intended to protect such items as furniture. A standard family allowance of up to $12,000 lump sum or $1,000 per month permits a reasonable amount for care of the family for up to one year. There is no distinction between the sexes under Arizona law as concerns these rights. As in most community property states, the right of the decedent to dispose of his or her property is limited to one-half.

Arkansas. The laws of Arkansas that protect the surviving spouse are generally based on dower and curtesy rights. For a surviving wife it's a dower interest; for a surviving husband it's a curtesy interest. Under current law there is no distinction in the property based on the sex of the surviving spouse.

The dower right and curtesy right each consists of a one-third life estate in the part of the land the deceased spouse owned, and one-third full ownership in the personal property if there are surviving children. Again, terminology that includes property owned "for his use" would seem to include living trust property. One-third of the personal property is also given to the surviving spouse if a child or children survive.

If there are no surviving children, the surviving spouse can receive up to one-half of the real and personal property as against the other heirs, but only one-third as against creditors.

A somewhat unique provision in Arkansas is that the surviving spouse also receives one-third of any mineral rights.

The homestead provision in Arkansas extends up to $5,000 and can be taken from the sale of a qualifying home. Check with your professional advisors for details.

Another allowance provides that in addition to homestead and dower rights, the surviving spouse is entitled to $4,000 against other distributees (that is, people who would take under the will) and $1,000 against creditors. There is a living allowance for the two-month period following the death of the decedent, not to exceed $1,000.

One final nuance under Arkansas law is that in order to elect against the will—that is, to receive dower or curtesy—the surviving spouse must have been married to the decedent for more than one year.

California is a community property state so one-half of the property acquired during the marriage belongs to the surviving spouse. The other half is subject to the will of the decedent; if he or she leaves no will, the surviving spouse will receive the property subject to the general intestacy provisions.

California uses the concept of *quasicommunity property* as well. This is property acquired elsewhere, while the person was not domiciled in California, but that would have been considered community property if the person had been domiciled in California at the time of acquisition. The effect this has on the estate can be complicated; therefore, it should be investigated early.

California has a homestead provision that apparently has no dollar limitation. It offers protection for the family home and, at the court's discretion, other assets. The protection is only available for a limited period and in no case beyond the lifetime of the surviving spouse. There is also a standard family allowance intended to provide reasonable support for up to one year.

Colorado is a UPC state. Either the husband or the wife can elect against the will; the election includes trust property. The share received is one-half of the augmented estate, which is the net estate with certain prescribed additions. This is the share regardless of whether there are children. A supplementary elective share of up to $50,000 may also apply.

There is a $60,000 homestead exemption. The decedent's homestead exemption inures to the surviving spouse or the children if they held the house as joint tenants of the decedent. The exempt property allowance is $30,000 in 2012 to cover personal property. There is also a reasonable family allowance, which is limited to one year but can be longer if the court deems it necessary. Under Colorado law these allowances are in addition to the elective share.

Connecticut. Under Connecticut law the surviving spouse is entitled to the use for his or her life of one-third of the value of all property, whether it be real or personal, owned by the decedent. It is important to know that the statute refers to property owned legally or equitably, and thus appears to include living trust assets. The share is the same whether or not there are children.

A support allowance is provided for the surviving spouse or the family as deemed necessary by the court. The amount is intended to cover living expenses during administration.

Delaware. Under Delaware law the surviving spouse can receive one-third of the elective estate less the amount of certain transfers of property that are made to the surviving spouse by the deceased spouse by virtue of his or her death (including beneficial interests in a trust created during the decedent's lifetime). *Elective estate* means the adjusted gross estate, as that term is used on the federal estate tax return, after subtracting all transfers included on that tax return and that were made with the consent of the surviving spouse. The elective estate in Delaware is highly technical; consult your estate planning professional for the details. The share is the same whether or not there are children.

Also under Delaware law the surviving spouse is given an allowance of $2,000; this is a onetime fixed amount given to the spouse. The allowance has priority over other debts.

District of Columbia. The surviving spouse is entitled to a homestead allowance of $15,000 and an exempt property allowance of $10,000. A family allowance is provided; the amounts and times of distribution are decided by the court.

The surviving spouse, husband or wife, has a right to elect to take the intestate share against the will. The intestate share is one-third if there are children or descendants. If there are no children, but the deceased had parents, brothers, sisters, nieces, or nephews, the spouse receives one-half of the estate. The spouse could receive all of the estate if there are no descendants, parents, brothers, sisters, nieces, or nephews. He or she may take dower rights in the real estate of the decedent, if desired, in lieu of the intestate provisions affecting real estate. This means that the surviving spouse, if taking dower rights, receives one-half of the personal property outright and a dower interest in the real estate.

Florida. The surviving spouse in the state of Florida may elect against the will and receive 30 percent of the fair market value of the assets in the estate. This does not include real estate located outside the state of Florida. This share is the same whether or not there are children.

The homestead provision in Florida consists of a life estate if survived by a surviving spouse and children and the homestead was not held as tenants by the entirety, which is a special type of legal title to real estate that exists only between husbands and wives. A surviving spouse is entitled to household items up to a value of $20,000, as well as all automobiles in the decedent's name and regularly used by the decedent or the decedent's immediate family. Finally, there is a standard family allowance not to exceed $18,000. That amount is for living expenses during administration.

Georgia. Until January 1, 1998, Georgia was the only state that did not have any provision for an election against the will. As of January 1, 1998, the court can make separate awards to the surviving spouse and minor children. If there are no separate awards, the surviving spouse is given the equivalent of a life estate with power to include corpus for support, with the remainder going to the children. The surviving spouse takes equally with the children, except that the surviving spouse's share shall not be less than one-third of the estate. There are also provisions to give up to one year's support and maintenance to the surviving spouse and minor children, for which a minimum figure of $1,600 is set. Georgia has a homestead exemption of $5,000, which may be reduced by the value of the support awarded for living expenses.

Hawaii. Under Hawaiian law the surviving spouse, husband or wife, is entitled to an elective share of the decedent's augmented estate. The percentage of the elective share is based upon the number of years the surviving spouse was married to the decedent on the date of death. For a marriage of more than one year but less than two years, the elective share is 3 percent of the augmented estate. This percentage increases for each additional year of marriage until 15 years or more, when the elective share is 50 percent of the augmented estate. If the elective share is less than $50,000, the surviving spouse is entitled to an additional supplemental elective share amount, which is $50,000 less the amount of the elective share. The surviving spouse takes the entire estate if there are no surviving children or parents of the deceased.

A homestead allowance provides up to $15,000 for the protection of the family home, and an exempt property allowance provides $10,000 for personal property items. A family allowance is provided for support of the surviving spouse and any children whom the deceased was obligated to and in fact did support.

Idaho is a community property state so one-half of the property acquired during the marriage belongs to the surviving spouse. However, if a transfer is made of quasicommunity property without adequate consideration, it can be included under the augmented estate provisions of the Idaho law. *It should not be assumed that quasicommunity property means the same in each community property state, as there are variations.* Always consult an attorney before making a decision in this regard. If the election is made, it covers one-half of the property that was transferred and in which the decedent has retained certain types of interests. The share is the same whether or not there are children.

The homestead exemption is $50,000. The spouse's elective share is taken subject to the homestead exemption. A family allowance provides for living expenses of the family for up to one year. There is also a $10,000 exempt property allowance to cover personal property items and other protected assets. The decedent may limit the homestead and exempt property allowance by specific provisions in his or her will.

Illinois law provides a spousal support allowance for up to nine months. This amount is not less than $20,000, together with an additional sum of not less than $10,000 for each dependent child. There is also a $15,000 homestead exemption for the surviving spouse and minor children.

The surviving spouse may elect against the will. If he or she does so, one-half of the entire estate is given to the spouse if there are descendants; the surviving spouse receives the entire estate if there are no descendants. Descendants include children and their children.

Indiana. The electing surviving spouse receives one-half of the net personal property and real estate, but if there are children from a prior marriage surviving, and the surviving spouse has no children from the marriage with the deceased spouse, the following provisions apply: the surviving spouse receives one-third of the net personal property and 25 percent of the remainder of the fair market value of the real property at the deceased spouse's date of death, minus liens and encumbrances.

The statute says that the net estate shall consider only property that would have passed under the laws of descent and distribution, which appears to exclude living trust property.

There is a special personal property allowance of $25,000 under Indiana law. If the value of all the personal property is less than $25,000, the remainder can be taken from the proceeds of any sales of real property.

Iowa. If the surviving spouse elects against the will, he or she is entitled to one-third of all real estate, all personal property that was in the hands of the decedent head of household exempt from execution, and one-third of all remaining personal property of the decedent not necessary for payment of debts.

The surviving spouse is entitled to the decedent's personal property that is exempt from execution. A standard family allowance of up to one year is provided for the living expenses of the family. The amount involved may vary depending on needs.

Kansas. The surviving spouse may elect against the will and receive an elective share. The percentage of the elective share is based upon the number of years the surviving spouse was married to the decedent on the date of death. For a marriage of more than one year but less than two years, the elective share is 3 percent of the augmented estate. This percentage increases for each additional year of marriage until 15 years or more, when the elective share is 50 percent of the augmented estate. If the elective share is less than $50,000, the surviving spouse is entitled to an additional supplemental elective share amount, which is $50,000 less the amount of the elective share.

Kansas has a homestead allowance of up to 160 acres if the property is outside the city limits and one acre if it is within city limits. This helps to protect the family home, regardless of value. There is a reasonable personal property allowance to be determined by the court that cannot exceed $50,000. Consult your professional advisor for the details.

Kentucky. In Kentucky, when a husband or a wife dies intestate (without a will), the surviving spouse has a dower right, which is a one-half interest in all surplus real estate, and a life estate in one-third of any real estate owned by the decedent during marriage, but not at death. The surviving spouse also receives a one-half interest in all surplus personal property. A surviving spouse who elects against a will can take a modified dower share, which is identical to the intestate dower share except that the one-half interest in surplus real estate is reduced to one-third.

The surviving spouse has the right to the use of the homestead for as long as he or she continues to occupy the homestead. A $15,000 personal property or money exemption to cover household effects and so on is available when the deceased spouse dies without a will or when the surviving spouse renounces the will.

Louisiana is a community property state, so one-half of the property acquired during the marriage belongs to the surviving spouse.

Louisiana's civil code is extremely intricate and quite different from any other state's law. *Generally speaking, there is no right to elect against the will.*

A $15,000 homestead exemption applies. If the decedent dies rich compared to the surviving spouse, a marital portion in varying amounts may be available up to $1 million. When it appears during administration there will be a marital portion, the surviving spouse has the right to receive a periodic allowance from the personal representative. The periodic allowance will be offset against the marital portion when it is awarded. Be sure to check with a local estate planning attorney, for this is a complex matter.

Maine. Under Maine law the surviving spouse is entitled to one-third of the augmented estate, which is the net estate with certain additions. The share is the same whether or not there are children.

Maine law includes a homestead allowance in the amount of $10,000; an exempt property allowance in the amount of $7,000 for household furniture and so on; and a family allowance to provide for the reasonable living expenses of the family, which is limited in duration to one year.

Maryland. The elective intestate share in Maryland is as follows: the surviving spouse, husband or wife, may take one-third of the net estate if there is surviving issue from the marriage. If there was no surviving issue, the surviving spouse takes one-half of the net estate.

Net estate is defined to mean property of the decedent exclusive of allowances and claims. It is therefore uncertain whether Maryland would include a revocable inter vivos trust as part of the elective share.

There is also a family allowance in the amount of $5,000 to provide for living expenses, plus $2,500 for each unmarried child under the age of 18.

Massachusetts. The elective share in Massachusetts is as follows: If there are issues surviving the decedent, the surviving spouse is entitled to elect one-third of the personal property and one-third of the real estate. If there are no surviving issue but there are kindred, the surviving spouse receives $25,000 plus one-half of the estate. It should be noted that in the two above categories, if either amount exceeds $25,000, the surviving spouse receives only a life estate and a share of the excess.

Finally, if there are no issue and no kindred, the surviving spouse receives $25,000 plus one-half of the real estate and personal property absolutely, and not as a life estate.

Kindred are generally defined in Massachusetts as those members of the family computed according to the rules of civil law; it apparently includes most close family members.

The surviving spouse receives a personal property allowance of up to $10,000 to cover such items as furniture, automobiles, appliances, and personal effects. He or she may live in the house for a period of six months without being charged rent. The surviving spouse and minor children are entitled to a reasonable allowance from the estate during the period of administration.

Michigan. The elective share is one-half of the amount the surviving spouse would have received in an intestate estate, reduced by one-half the value of all property derived from the deceased spouse upon his or her death by any means other than testate or intestate succession. The intestate share for a surviving spouse is normally the entire estate, or if there are parents or issue who are also issue of the surviving spouse, the first $60,000 plus one-half of the balance. If one or more of the issue are not the issue of the survivor, the normal share is one-half. Remember that these amounts are halved under an election against the will.

Because Michigan law speaks in terms of an intestate share, the inclusion of living trusts is questionable.

The homestead allowance in Michigan is $20,000. This serves to protect the family home. The personal property allowance is $14,000 for assets such as furniture. Finally, a family allowance is provided that is intended to give a reasonable amount of support to the family for living expenses for up to one year, not to exceed $24,000 in 2011. The homestead, personal property, and family allowances are automatically increased each year by a cost-of-living adjustment.

As an alternative to the elective share, a widow is entitled to power of a life estate in one-third of the property acquired during the marriage that is part of estate.

Minnesota has adopted the Uniform Probate Code, with several modifications. The surviving spouse has the right to a percentage of the augmented estate. The percentage of the elective share is based upon the number of years the surviving spouse was married to the decedent on the date of death. For a marriage of more than one year but less than two years, the elective share is 3 percent of the augmented estate. This percentage increases for each additional year of marriage until 15 years or more, when the elective share is 50 percent of the augmented estate. If the elective share is less than $50,000, the surviving spouse is entitled to an additional supplemental elective share amount, which is $50,000 less the amount of the elective share.

The following allowances are available to the spouse: a $10,000 furniture and household goods allowance; personal property; one automobile; and a family allowance for a period varying from 12 to 18 months, or longer, at the court's discretion, of not more than $1,500 per month. The surviving spouse is entitled to a life estate in the homestead if the decedent has issue, or the entire homestead if the decedent has no issue. The homestead and allowances are separate from the elective share.

Mississippi. In Mississippi the elective share is the intestate share, not to exceed one-half of the estate. It can be less than one-half if there are children of the decedent. Because the statute speaks in terms of an intestate share, one might conclude that living trust property is not included, but there is no definitive answer to this question.

There is also a separate estate provision in Mississippi law. If the spouse has a separate estate equal to the elective share, he or she will receive nothing. If there is a difference, the elective share will be made up accordingly.

The homestead provision in Mississippi is $75,000; this is intended to protect the family home, up to 160 acres. The spouse is allowed personal property of the deceased spouse up to $10,000.

There is also a support provision for the surviving spouse of one year; it gives him or her a living allowance for reasonable needs.

Missouri. The surviving spouse in Missouri is entitled to elect against the will and receive the following assets: one-half of the estate goes to him or her if there are no lineal descendants; one-third of the estate goes to the surviving spouse if there are lineal descendants. In determining the surviving spouse's share, all property is considered, even if it is not subject to probate. This includes trust property, proceeds of life insurance policies, and other nonprobate assets.

The homestead allowance is $15,000, but is offset against the elective share of the surviving spouse. There is an exempt personal property allowance and a reasonable family allowance for one year, as determined by the court. The personal property allowance includes one car, without regard to value.

Montana is a UPC state, and the surviving spouse has the right to a percentage of the augmented estate. The percentage of the elective share is based upon the number of years the surviving spouse was married to the decedent on the date of death. For a marriage of more than one year but less than two years, the elective share is 3 percent of the augmented estate. This percentage increases for each additional year of marriage until 15 years or more, when the elective share is 50 percent of the augmented estate. If the elective share is less than $50,000, the surviving spouse is entitled to an additional supplemental elective share amount, which is $50,000 less the amount of the elective share.

The homestead allowance is $20,000 to protect the family home; the exempt property allowance is $10,000 for personal property; and a family allowance is also provided. The family allowance is for reasonable living expenses for one year. The homestead and other allowances are separate from the elective share in Montana.

Nebraska. In Nebraska the elective share is one-third of the augmented estate. Again, the augmented estate is defined as including those assets subject to the codes, which probably includes living trust assets. The share is the same whether or not there are children.

The homestead provision in Nebraska is $20,000; the exempt personal property allowance is $20,500; and a family allowance is also provided for under law. That allowance gives a reasonable amount to the family for living expenses.

The general comments to the Nebraska law imply that the views of New York and Pennsylvania law toward will substitutes (that is, that they should be included in the augmented estates) are viewed favorably under the Nebraska law.

Nevada is a community property state, so one-half of the property acquired during the marriage belongs to the surviving spouse.

Nevada has no elective share provision. There is a homestead exemption of $500,000 that extends to the surviving spouse and minor children and allows the surviving spouse to reside in the homestead for the remainder of his or her life. There is also a certain amount of personal property reserved to the surviving spouse. A family allowance is provided at the discretion of the court.

New Hampshire. The elective share for the surviving husband or wife in New Hampshire varies widely, depending upon the other survivors. It ranges from one-third of the estate to a one-half interest. If there are children, the surviving spouse receives one-third. There is no mention of living trust assets as includable or excludable from the elective share; however, case law indicates that transfers to a living trust will defeat the statutory rights of a surviving spouse unless it can be shown that the transfers were made for that purpose.

There is a reasonable allowance provision for present support that the court may, in its discretion, count as part of the elective share. This contrasts with most other states' handling of the support allowance.

The surviving spouse is entitled to reside in the residence of the decedent rent-free for 40 days. However, the surviving spouse must waive the homestead exemption when electing against the will.

New Jersey. Under New Jersey law the surviving spouse has a right of election to take one-third of the augmented estate, which is patterned after the Uniform Probate Code's definition of augmented estate. The surviving spouse has the right up to $5,000 worth of the decedent's personal property.

New Mexico is a community property state, so one-half of the property acquired during the marriage belongs to the surviving spouse.

New Mexico has no elective share at the present time. There is a family allowance of $30,000 to provide for living expenses. A personal property allowance of $15,000 is also available.

New York. Under New York law the surviving spouse has an elective share provision as follows: he or she may receive one-third of the net estate if issue survive, one-half of the net estate if there are no issue.

New York has specifically addressed the issue of the living trust as it relates to the election against the will. Treatment of the matter is divided depending upon when the will was executed. If the will was signed after August 31, 1930 (the beginning of the elective share period), but before September 1, 1966, the statute does not apparently reach living trust assets. The law was amended for wills executed after August 31, 1966, to include living trust assets. The same fractions are involved, that is, one-third or one-half of the net estate, regardless of the date of the will. If the decedent died after August 31, 1992, the surviving spouse may elect for the greater of $50,000 or one-third of the decedent's net estate, taking into consideration amounts passing absolutely by will or trust.

The surviving spouse has the right to certain items of personal and household property of the deceased spouse, limited by various dollar amounts, and may remain in the family home rent-free for 40 days.

North Carolina. In North Carolina a surviving spouse has an elective share of one-half of the net assets if there are no surviving children or descendants or only one surviving child or descendant; the elective share is one-third of the net assets if there are two or more surviving children and or descendants. If the surviving spouse is a second or successive spouse and the decedent has one or more surviving lineal descendants who are not the lineal descendants of the decedent's marriage to the surviving spouse, then the surviving spouse's elective share is reduced by one-half.

The homestead in North Carolina is exempt from debts of the homesteader during widowhood of the surviving spouse. The surviving spouse can get an allowance of up to $20,000 for support for a period of one year after the death of the deceased spouse and $2,000 per child up to age 18, or age 22 if a full-time student.

North Dakota. In this state the surviving spouse has the right to an elective share in the amount of one-half of the augmented estate. The share is the same whether or not there are children.

There is a homestead allowance of $100,000 in North Dakota to the surviving spouse for life estate or until remarriage. There is also a family allowance of a reasonable amount, generally for up to one year, to provide for the family's living expenses. The exempt property allowance is $15,000 for personal property.

Ohio. In Ohio the surviving spouse can elect to receive a share of the balance of the estate, depending upon the number of children or descendants who survive the decedent. The spouse receives one-half of the net estate unless there are two or more descendants surviving, in which case the spouse receives one-third. The surviving spouse may elect to receive the decedent's interest in the homestead as part of the elective share amount.

A living trust can probably be used to defeat rights of the surviving spouse in Ohio. State law provides that the surviving spouse has no dower in the corpus of a living trust and cannot reach the living trust as part of the spouse's distributive share or election to take against the will.

The support allowance in Ohio is $40,000 for the living expenses of the family, and is deducted before computing the elective share.

Oklahoma. In Oklahoma a surviving spouse can elect to take an interest in one-half of the property acquired by the joint industry of the husband and wife during marriage, a concept somewhat akin to community property.

The surviving spouse has a life estate in the entire homestead, subject to various conditions. The surviving spouse also has a right to certain personal property. In addition, if the homestead and personal property amounts are not sufficient for the care of the surviving spouse, the court can award a reasonable family allowance for maintenance during estate settlement. A reasonable amount for a family allowance is at the discretion of the court.

Oregon. The surviving husband or wife may elect against the will and receive up to one-third of the augmented estate if married 15 years or longer. The elective share is reduced for shorter marriages on a sliding scale. The share is the same whether or not there are children. The calculation of the one-third elective share is complex, and you should work with your estate planning advisor for precise details.

The allowances for the spouse permit him or her to occupy the dwelling for one year after the death for no rent, and to receive reasonable support.

Pennsylvania. The surviving spouse in Pennsylvania may elect against the will and receive one-third of the decedent's estate, which includes property the decedent transferred to a living trust.

There is a family exemption of $3,500 in real or personal property; this amount is exempt from creditors' claims. There is no homestead exemption in Pennsylvania.

Rhode Island. The surviving husband or wife may elect a life estate in all real estate instead of receiving property under the will. The share is the same whether or not there are children. When a will fails to indicate an intention that it has made provisions for the surviving spouse in lieu of the statutory life estate in real estate, then the surviving spouse gets the life estate in real estate in addition to the provisions in the will.

There are also family allowances of varying amounts; they cover support for the family and wearing apparel. Also included is a generous provision that permits real estate to go to the spouse as necessary and deemed suitable by the court if there are no issue.

South Carolina has adopted its own version of the Uniform Probate Code. A surviving spouse has the right to one-third of the decedent's estate. This right includes one-third of the assets in a revocable inter vivos trust established by the decedent.

There is a personal property allowance of $5,000 and a provision for personal property, both of which can also be waived by agreement of the spouses. There are no provisions for support of the surviving spouse and family pending administration.

South Dakota has adopted the Uniform Probate Code, with several modifications. The surviving spouse has the right to a percentage of the augmented estate. The percentage of the elective share is based upon the number of years the surviving spouse was married to the decedent on the date of death. For a marriage of more than one year but less than two years, the elective share is 3 percent of the augmented estate. This percentage increases for each additional year of marriage until 15 years or more, when the elective share is 50 percent of the augmented estate. If the elective share is less than $50,000, the surviving spouse is entitled to an additional supplemental elective share amount, which is $50,000 less the amount of the elective share.

South Dakota provides for a homestead allowance. There is a family allowance in an amount to be determined by the personal representative not exceeding $18,000, unless a larger amount is approved by the court.

Tennessee. The surviving spouse may decide to take an elective share of the estate in lieu of what is left to him or her under the will. The elective share is a percentage of the net estate. The amount of the percentage is determined based on the length of the marriage. For marriages less than three years it's 10 percent; three years but less than six years, 20 percent; six years but less than nine years, 30 percent; and nine years or more, 40 percent. The net estate does not seem to include property in a living trust.

Personal property of the decedent up to $50,000 and a one-year family support allowance for living expenses are provided.

The surviving spouse takes a life estate in the homestead property.

Texas is a community property state, so one-half of the property acquired during the marriage belongs to the surviving spouse.

In Texas if the deceased spouse attempts to dispose of more than his or her interest in the community property, the surviving spouse may elect his or her interest in the community property. The share is the same whether or not there are children.

A homestead exemption gives the surviving spouse a life estate in the family home, up to one acre in the city and up to 200 acres in rural areas. A personal property allowance not to exceed $60,000 covers such things as furniture, clothing, and so on. A cash allowance in lieu of exempt property may be claimed, not to exceed $5,000; and a cash allowance in lieu of homestead may be claimed, not to exceed $15,000. The cash allowance is a onetime allotment. The court may award a family allowance for one year's reasonable maintenance if the surviving spouse and children have insufficient property of their own.

Utah uses a somewhat complicated mathematical formula for computing the elective share. The surviving spouse can take one-third of the augmented estate multiplied by a certain fraction that is determined under that formula. The share is the same whether or not there are children.

The homestead allowance in Utah is $22,500 for the surviving spouse. The law provides a personal property allowance of $15,000 and family allowance during the period of administration, which may extend beyond one year if the estate has sufficient funds. The family allowance is limited to $27,000.

The matter of living trust property is not specifically addressed.

Vermont. Under Vermont law the surviving spouse can elect against the will and receive one-half of the probate estate. Generally this would not include assets transferred into a living trust, but it may if the transfers to the living trust were done with the intent to defeat the spouse's elective share.

A personal property allowance and a provision for support during the administration of the estate are provided, including living expenses for the spouse and children. There is also a homestead allowance of $125,000 to protect the family home.

Virginia. The surviving spouse has the right to an elective share of one-third of the augmented estate if there are surviving children or their descendants. Otherwise, the surviving spouse has the right to an elective share of one-half of the augmented estate.

There is a $15,000 homestead allowance, which reduces any other amounts received by the surviving spouse. In addition there is a personal property allowance of up to $15,000. A reasonable family allowance can be awarded by the court at its discretion, but is not to exceed the amount of $18,000.

Washington is a community property state, so one-half of the property acquired during the marriage belongs to the surviving spouse.

Washington permits the surviving spouse to elect his or her interest in the community property if the deceased spouse attempts to dispose of it.

There is a personal property exemption allowance of up to $15,000.

West Virginia. The surviving spouse may elect a percentage of the augmented estate based upon the length of the marriage. The percentage of the elective share is based upon the number of years the surviving spouse was married to the decedent on the date of death. For a marriage of more than one year but less than two years, the elective share is 3 percent of the augmented estate. This percentage increases for each additional year of marriage until 15 years or more, when the elective share is 50 percent of the augmented estate. If the elective share is less than $25,000, the surviving spouse is entitled to an additional supplemental elective share amount which is $25,000 less the amount of the elective share. The augmented estate consists of the couple's combined assets.

Wisconsin has adopted the Marital Property Act, which is somewhat similar to the community property concept. A surviving spouse may elect to take a one-half interest in all deferred marital property, including property not subject to probate. *Deferred marital property* is defined in a relatively complex manner, but generally includes all property acquired during a marriage, excluding individual property. Certain effective dates apply, so consult your advisor for details.

There is a generous personal property allowance that includes clothing, jewelry, an automobile, and certain other property. It will be limited to $10,000 only if claims cannot be paid in full. The court has the discretion to provide allowances for support during administration or for a longer period of time, depending on circumstances, including providing for educational expenses of minor children. The surviving spouse may also petition the court for a fee or life estate in the family home.

Wyoming. The Wyoming surviving spouse may elect against the estate and receive from an elective share amount based upon the surviving issue of the decedent. The elective share is one-half of the decedent's property, if there are no surviving issue of the decedent, or if the surviving spouse is the parent of at least one of the surviving issue of the decedent. The elective share is one-fourth of the decedent's property if the surviving spouse is not the parent of any surviving issue of the decedent.

There is a family right to continue to live in the homestead and to a maintenance allowance. The maintenance allowance provides for the reasonable living expenses of the family unit.

Puerto Rico uses a version of community property. A surviving spouse has a legal share in community property and a life estate in a portion of the remaining estate, which varies depending on the number of children.

There is limited homestead protection for the surviving spouse, children, and other relatives. Certain personal property is exempt. The surviving spouse may petition the court for a reasonable family support allowance.

Virgin Islands. The surviving spouse has the right to an elective share of one-half of the marital portion of the augmented estate. If the amount of the elective share is less than $75,000, the surviving spouse has the right to a supplemental elective share equal to $75,000 minus the amount of the elective share.

There is a $22,500 homestead allowance for the surviving spouse or for the surviving children if there is no surviving spouse. There is a $15,000 personal property allowance and a family support allowance generally for not more than one year for the surviving spouse and children.

Appendix D

Estate Planning History

Primitive people did not recognize that land could be owned; the land belonged to all people. It was unthinkable that land could be transferred at all, much less on death.

Only personal property was possessed and owned by primitive people, and on death, our early ancestors either destroyed or buried such property with its owner.

When people began to recognize the value in their possessions, they were concerned with passing those possessions on death. Perhaps the earliest written evidence of the penchant for passing property on can be found in the hieroglyphics of the early Egyptians. Although our knowledge of these early wills is limited, we do know they passed property to select heirs.

In Babylonia, as a result of the Code of Hammurabi, property, with only a very few exceptions, had to pass to heirs on death. This was true under the laws of Solon in Greece also. Roman law, especially under Caesar Augustus, followed this practice as well. As a matter of fact, it would appear that Augustus was the inventor of the estate tax; he levied a tax of 5 percent on the value of all estates to help support his army.

Emperor Justin of the Byzantine Empire, long recognized as one of the greatest lawmakers of all time, created the Justinian Code. It was this code that prescribed the first formal requirements that attached to wills. The code also allowed a certain form of contract that is remarkably similar to modern-day trusts.

Many of our current will and estate laws can be traced to both Rome and the Justinian Code. Rome extended its rule to most of the known world; its rule included creating a system of law for each territory it conquered, and Great Britain was no exception. Even though the Romans were pushed out of Great Britain by the Anglo-Saxons, much Roman law remained.

Up until the Norman conquest in A.D. 1066, the Anglo-Saxon law allowed people to pass title to most of their property through the use of wills on their deaths. Their laws even provided that in the absence of a will, certain property would pass to heirs. All of this changed, however, after the Norman invasion of England and the advent of feudalism.

The foundation of the English feudal system was that the king owned all the land under his domain. Land was to be disposed of only by the king. Even though he distributed land among his nobles, he still retained an interest called a *military tenure*. In fact, the nobles took the property given them by the king subject to their making continuing financial contributions toward the king's war efforts.

The king needed large armies that could only be raised by nobles owning large estates. To prevent the dilution of land into smaller parcels by inheritance, the English law prohibited land from being left by will. Such property passed automatically to the eldest living male heir, called *primogeniture*, which allowed wealth to accumulate in a very few hands. It also created a large caste of property-poor nobles and knights.

English feudal wills could, in the main, pass only personal property. There was a constant battle between the church and the king about who had the authority to administer these feudal wills. At first the king took on this task and charged for his services. This charge, or "herriot," covered his expenses of administering the will and created tax revenue for the king's coffers.

When the church began to administer these estates, it also charged a fee. It also inherited substantial property through deathbed persuasion and the bequests that resulted from that persuasion. The king feared the power the church was accumulating by its increased wealth, and the saga of their power struggle began.

Over the years, property was vested in fewer and fewer hands because of primogeniture. Events, however, were to change this. Nobles wanted to control the passing of their lands. Primogeniture was too restrictive; it took the fun out of being rich.

Under the English feudal system, two courts and systems of law developed. The first was the system of the common-law courts. These courts applied the king's laws strictly and without compassion. Participants began to appeal to the king for mercy and equitable relief. The second system came into being when the king appointed a chancellor to take charge of his royal courts of mercy or equity. Two court systems were emerging in tandem: common courts of law and royal courts of equity. Often these courts would conflict, but over time their functions became separated. Basically, the common-law courts would say what the law was, and the courts of equity gave relief to litigants under their rules. The law of trusts, as we shall see, grew out of the conflict and confusion between the two systems.

As we mentioned earlier, it was impossible, under feudal law, to dispose of land by will. The common-law courts had jurisdiction in this area.

During this time a new concept was developing that allowed a noble to sell property to a third person; not leave it, but sell it while alive. Legal title would be in the name of that third party; however, the property was to be used for the benefit of another person named in the seller's will. This great legal scam to get around primogeniture, with all its restrictions, landed in the lap of the courts of equity. These courts developed a body of law that allowed the transfer of property to one person subject to somebody *else's* use or benefit. This was called *beneficial ownership*, the beginning of the law of trusts.

Land began to have two title holders: (1) the legal title holder, the person whose name appeared on the deed, and (2) the beneficial title holder, the person for whom the property was held. Can you see the law of trusts emerging?

By the early 1500s it is estimated that over two-thirds of all land in England was held in the form of a "use" (trust). Uses were handy devices. They could *deter* creditors, particularly spouses with claims, and they could also avoid the herriot (transfer fees) of the king.

Now the plot thickens. The king was not happy. Parliament, at the king's bidding, passed the Statute of Uses in 1535. This law attacked and attempted to prohibit these early trust devices. There were too many loopholes in the Statute of Uses, and Parliament acknowledged the public sentiment and passed the Statute of Wills in 1540.

The Statute of Wills, for the first time, allowed a person to pass title to real estate (real property) through a will. By the mid–1660s all property was allowed to pass by will; and in the latter part of the seventeenth century, the last great statute in this area was passed: the Statute of Frauds.

The Statute of Frauds required that all transfers of land be in writing, signed by the transferor, and witnessed by a plurality of witnesses.

Most of the rules created through this historic process have been adopted in the United States and are referred to as our English common-law heritage. In most states, courts of law and equity have been merged into the courts we have today.

Out of this heritage came the idea and ability for government to tax property at the owner's death. In the late 1700s England passed the Stamp Act, which required people to write their wills on paper printed by the government. The paper had stamps on it. Different paper and stamps were used depending upon the size of the estate. When the paper was needed because it was will-drafting time, it had to be paid for. When the decedent's estate was administered, the court would check the size of the estate against the stamps on the will paper to make sure the proper tax was paid. They would also check to see whether any gifts were made in contemplation of death. These gifts were assumed to be death devices and would also be taxed. Thus the first gift tax law came into existence.

The first American attempt at a federal estate tax was the Revolutionary War Tax passed in 1797. The purpose of this tax was to pay the war debt. This was adopted from the English Stamp Act, and the person who inherited the estate paid a stamp duty. The act was repealed in 1802 when the revenue was no longer needed. In 1826 the state of Pennsylvania adopted the first inheritance tax. It was based on the Revolutionary War Tax. Instead of taxing the estate of the decedent, it taxed the recipient of the inheritance. By the late 1800s nine states had adopted an inheritance tax.

The second federal estate tax was passed in 1862. This also was a stamp tax, to raise revenue for the Civil War; it was repealed in 1870. In 1898 the Spanish War Tax was enacted, which was a tax on personal property passing by will or otherwise; it was repealed in 1902.

The forerunner of our current federal estate tax was the German War Tax passed in 1916. This tax, like the others, was to raise revenue for the war. However, unlike the others, it did not go away.

The federal estate tax was held constitutional by the Supreme Court of the United States. Article 1, Section 8, Clause 1, of the U.S. Constitution states as follows:

> The Congress shall have Power to lay and collect Taxes, Duties, Imposts and Excises, to pay Debts and provide for the common Defense and general Welfare of the United States; but all Duties, Imposts, and Excises shall be uniform throughout the United States.

In addition, Article 1, Section 9, Clause 4, of the U.S. Constitution states as follows: "No capitation, or other direct, Tax shall be laid, unless in Proportion to the Census or Enumeration herein before directed to be taken."

This new federal estate tax was not a direct tax on property. As a matter of fact, the federal estate tax as it was then and is now is merely a tax on the transfers of assets from deceased persons to their heirs. Technically, it is not a tax against property. Thus, unlike the income tax, which had to be added as a constitutional amendment to become legal, the federal estate tax did fit within the strict original confines of the U.S. Constitution.

The gift tax was a natural extension of the federal estate tax. When the federal estate tax began in 1916, it was constantly amended. There was an amendment in 1917, one in 1918, and a major amendment in 1926. In 1926, the gift tax was formally recognized. Before then, a gift in contemplation of death was not taxed at the same rate as the federal estate tax. It was found that much revenue was being lost because people were making gifts during their lifetimes and these gifts were free from tax. Thus, in 1926, the first gift tax was passed so that there would be a tax on all property transferred from the owner to another person without charging a fair market value.

It seems clear to us that most laws historically restricted ownership based on social policy, not revenue policy. In feudal times wealth was held in a few hands for purposes of control and transfer. With the modern concept of centralized government, the "holding together" of estates in the hands of a few was considered antidemocratic and was politically unpopular.

Redistribution of wealth came into vogue for a variety of reasons; it seemed appropriate to have more people own a share of the available wealth.

The United States enacted estate taxes to fund specific military escapades. In 1935 President Franklin D. Roosevelt stated that the federal estate tax was based on "the very sound policy of encouraging a wider distribution of wealth," or, in other words, redistribution of wealth. He made this statement during the introduction of another rise in the estate tax rates in 1935.

President Roosevelt's words have stood for a very long time, but due to ERTA, TRA 1986, EGTRRA, and TRA 2010, the pendulum swung back in the opposite direction. For 2013 and beyond, we do not know what the pendulum will do. We do know that no matter where the pendulum falls, planning to enhance and protect your estate is the only way to reduce how the pendulum affects you and your family.

Index

New York Stock Transfer Association, 112
Nominee partnerships, 108–111
Noncitizen spouses:
  gift exclusions for, 63, 68
  and gift taxes, 15
  and income taxes after death, 17
  marital deduction for, 53
  planning for, 174–175
Nonspouses, joint ownership with, 16
North Carolina, 77, 335
North Dakota, 41, 47, 76, 335
Nuncupative wills, 34

Obligor (annuities), 267
Offshore asset protection trusts (OAPTs), 251–253
Ohio, 78, 335–336
Oklahoma, 76, 250, 336
Omitted spouse provision, 324
100 percent marital deduction, 68
Online accounts, accessing, 113–114
Oral wills, 33, 34
Oregon, 77, 336
Outright gifts, 291, 293
Ownership of property:
  fractionalizing, 272
  joint (see Joint tenancy (joint ownership, joint property))
  policies for, 345
  (See also Titles)

Partition, 10
Partnership freezes, 229–231
Pass-through entities, 238
Passwords (online accounts), 113–114
Payable-on-death (POD), 47, 112, 113
Pennsylvania, 41, 78, 336
Pensions, 39 (See also Retirement plans)
Per capita distribution, 141–145
Per stirpes distribution, 141–145
Permanent life insurance, 194–200
Perpetuities, Rule against, 151
Personal guardians, 19, 20, 32
Personal interest, 257
Personal representative (probate agent), 42
Personal residence (term), 272
Personal residence trusts, 91, 271–276
  estate tax rules, 274–275
  and generation-skipping, 275
  gift tax rules, 273–274
  income tax rules, 273

PRTs, 272, 273
QPRTs, 272, 273, 276
  and subsequent sale of residence, 276
Personal residence trusts (PRTs), 272, 273
Personal trustees (see Individual trustees)
Pickup tax states, 75, 77
POD (see Payable-on-death)
Postmortem assignments, 112
Postnuptial contracts, 154
Pour-over wills, 96, 106, 133
Power of appointment, 34
Powers of attorney:
  durable, 21–24
  general, 21, 221
  health care, 24–25
Predeceased ancestor exception, 149
Preferred stock, 226–227
Premarital contracts, 154
Premarriage contracts, 154, 155
Primary beneficiaries, 87
Primogeniture, 342–343
Principal (general power of attorney), 21
Private annuities, 267–269
Probate, 2, 35, 41–48
  avoiding, 45–48, 100, 222
  creditors in, 44, 45
  defined, 35
  living, 19–20
  process of, 43–45
  as term, 323
  Uniform Probate Code, 41–42
Probate agents, 42, 44, 45
Probate assets, 323
Probate attorneys, 43–45
Probate judges, 42, 45
Professional advisors, 2, 3, 123
Profit sharing proceeds, 39
Profit sharing retirement plans, 277–278
Promissory notes, 261, 264
Property, finding and valuing (in probate), 43–44
PRTs (personal residence trusts), 272, 273
Prudent Investor Rule, 116
Puerto Rico, 68, 71, 78, 339
Pure equity trusts, 223–224

QPRTs (see Qualified personal residence trusts)
QTIP (qualified terminable interest property), 69